Inner Knowing

A NEW
CONSCIOUSNESS
READER

This *New Consciousness Reader* is part of a new series of original and classic writing by renowned experts on leading-edge concepts in personal development, psychology, spiritual growth, and healing. Other books in this series include:

The Art of Staying Together
EDITED BY MARK ROBERT WALDMAN

The Awakened Warrior
EDITED BY RICK FIELDS

Creators on Creating
EDITED BY FRANK BARRON, ALFONSO MONTUORI, AND ANTHEA BARRON

Dreamtime and Dreamwork
EDITED BY STANLEY KRIPPNER, PH.D.

The Erotic Impulse
EDITED BY DAVID STEINBERG

Fathers, Sons, and Daughters
EDITED BY CHARLES SCULL, PH.D.

Gay Men at the Millennium
EDITED BY MICHAEL LOWENTHAL

Healers on Healing
EDITED BY RICHARD CARLSON, PH.D., AND BENJAMIN SHIELD

In the Company of Others
EDITED BY CLAUDE WHITMYER

Meeting the Shadow
EDITED BY CONNIE ZWEIG AND JEREMIAH ABRAMS

Mirrors of the Self
EDITED BY CHRISTINE DOWNING

The New Paradigm in Business
EDITED BY MICHAEL RAY AND ALAN RINZLER
FOR THE WORLD BUSINESS ACADEMY

Paths Beyond Ego
EDITED BY ROGER WALSH, M.D., PH.D., AND FRANCES VAUGHAN, PH.D.

Reclaiming the Inner Child
EDITED BY JEREMIAH ABRAMS

Sacred Sorrows
EDITED BY JOHN E. NELSON, M.D., AND ANDREA NELSON, PSY.D.

The Soul Unearthed
EDITED BY CASS ADAMS

Spiritual Emergency
EDITED BY STANISLAV GROF, M.D., AND CHRISTINA GROF

The Truth about the Truth
EDITED BY WALTER TRUETT ANDERSON

To Be a Man
EDITED BY KEITH THOMPSON

To Be a Woman
EDITED BY CONNIE ZWEIG

What Survives?
EDITED BY GARY DOORE

Who Am I?
EDITED BY ROBERT FRAGER, PH.D.

Founding Series Editor: CONNIE ZWEIG, PH.D.

Inner Knowing

Consciousness, Creativity, Insight, and Intuition

Edited by Helen Palmer

JEREMY P. TARCHER/PUTNAM

a member of Penguin Putnam Inc. • *New York*

Most Tarcher/Putnam books are available at special quantity discounts for bulk purchases
for sales promotions, premiums, fund-raising, and educational needs. Special books or
book excerpts also can be created to fit specific needs. For details, write
Putnam Special Markets, 375 Hudson Street, New York, NY 10014.

Jeremy P. Tarcher/Putnam
a member of
Penguin Putnam Inc.
375 Hudson Street
New York, NY 10014
www.penguinputnam.com

Library of Congress Cataloging-in-Publication Data

Inner knowing : consciousness, creativity, insight, and intuition /
edited by Helen Palmer.
p.   cm.—(A new consciousness reader)
Includes bibliographical references.
ISBN 0-87477-936-7 (alk. paper)
1. Consciousness.   2. Intuition (Psychology)   3. Insight.
I. Palmer, Helen.   II. Series.
BF311.I54 1998   98-24871 CIP
153—dc21

Printed in the United States of America

1   3   5   7   9   10   8   6   4   2

This book is printed on acid-free paper. ∞

Book design by Debbie Glasserman

To the memory of Willis Harman,
who gave us an example of what it
means to be a human being

Contents

Foreword   CHARLES H. SIMPKINSON, PH.D.   xiii

Introduction to Inner Knowing   HELEN PALMER   xv

Part One:
Knowing for the Twenty-first Century: Nonduality

1. Doors in the Wall   ALDOUS HUXLEY   5

2. The Archaeology of
   Consciousness: An Interview
   with Owen Barfield   GARY LACHMAN   8

3. The Passion of the
   Western Mind   RICHARD TARNAS   14

4. Hidden Wisdom   ROGER WALSH   21

5. Technology of Transcendence   FRANCES VAUGHAN AND
   ROGER WALSH   24

Part Two:
Ancient Avenues of Wisdom

6. The Tradition of Oracles
   and Channels   ARTHUR HASTINGS   35

7. Synchronistic Knowing:
   Understanding Meaningful
   Coincidence   JEAN SHINODA BOLEN   43

8. Foreword to the
   I Ching or Book of Changes   CARL JUNG   51

9. Shamanism   ROGER WALSH   60

10. Aboriginal Men of High Degree   A. P. ELKIN   68

Part Three:
From Imagination to Inner Knowing

11. Experiential Knowing   ABRAHAM H. MASLOW   81

12. On Fairy Tales   BRUNO BETTELHEIM   85

13. Dreaming Consciousness   MONTAGUE ULLMAN, M.D.   91

14. Psychoanalysis and the
    Art of Knowing   ERICH FROMM   98

15. Active Imagination in Practice   JANET DALLETT   103

Part Four:
Personal Accounts of Inner Knowing

16. Indigenous Teaching   HYEMEYOHSTS STORM   114

17. Conversation with
    Isabel Allende   JANET LYNN ROSEMAN   120

18. Lightning Bolts
    and Illuminations   RICHARD HEINBERG, WITH
    ADAPTATIONS FROM
    WILLIS HARMAN AND
    HOWARD RHEINGOLD   124

Part Five:
Developing Your Awareness

19. Listening to the Silence   J. KRISHNAMURTI   136

20. The Mechanics of Attention   DANIEL GOLEMAN   139

21. The Practice of Attention   PHILIP NOVAK   144

22. The Flow Experience   MIHALY CSIKSZENTMIHALYI   150

23. The Focusing Technique   ANN WEISER CORNELL   159

24. Creative Knowing   BETTY EDWARDS   165

Part Six:
Highways to Higher Consciousness:
The Sacred Wisdom of Mind, Body, and Heart

The Intuitive Faculty

25. Intuition   ARTHUR DEIKMAN   177

26. Mental, Emotional, and Body-
    Based Intuition   FRANCES VAUGHAN   185

27. The Intuitive Edge   PHILIP GOLDBERG   195

Path of the Mind

28. Mindfulness Training   JACK KORNFIELD   202

29. Sitting and Walking Meditation   JACK KORNFIELD   206

30. Mindfulness Practice for
    the Whole Spectrum of Life   CHARLES T. TART   209

31. The Hindrances   JOSEPH GOLDSTEIN   215

Wisdom of the Body

32. Hara—The Belly Center   KARLFRIED GRAF VON DÜRCKHEIM   218

33. The Intuitive Body   WENDY PALMER   224

Knowing of the Heart

34. Perceptions of the Heart   SYLVIA BOORSTEIN   229

35. A Practice of Compassion   PEMA CHÖDRÖN   233

36. The Cloud of Unknowing   WILLIAM JOHNSTON   239

37. The Heart: Threshold
    Between Two Worlds   KABIR HELMINSKI   245

38. Epilogue: The Old Man
    and the Tree   MARK ROBERT WALDMAN   256

Notes   259

Permissions   269

Contributors   273

Acknowledgments

First off, this book would never have happened without the intelligence, perseverance, and just plain good will on the part of Katie Jones and Debra Olsen. I have never met a more patient team, certainly compensating for my own bouts of creative frustration. Just in the nick of time, the editorial skills of Mark Waldman made what needed to happen, happen, and to boot, he also really understands the field.

Years ago, it seems, an old friend in the work, Peter Beren, suggested a small compendium of materials suitable for my students. Now, this anthology points the way to the literature of the three centers of subtle perception, an approach that Peter has always supported.

My gratitude forever to Larry Spiro, an extraordinarily gifted teacher of the inner ways. What breadth of comprehension! In the same vein, I appreciate Jeremy Tarcher, who exemplifies and carries a vision of the great work, of which we are a part. Finally, I must also acknowledge how grateful I feel for the work of Rick Tarnas, a contemporary spokesman for both intellect and intuition.

Foreword

Socrates said that the unexamined life is not worth living. Helen Palmer agrees and takes this dictum one step further by adding that it's also *how* we examine our life that determines its worth. Her addition is no small matter. Since the days of Socrates, our source for obtaining meaning and value has shifted from a unified societal consciousness to an individual consciousness. Today people can no longer depend on the society they live in to confer an identity or role that validates their existence. While people still enact social roles, and offer recognizable social personas, these roles and identities no longer provide sufficient meaning and value.

This shift has taken place because of the almost universal breakdown of a sense of shared communal meanings. To compensate for the loss of our major connecting links, people have developed a private set of values based on their own subjective experiences. This trend means that we now have to examine our life in a different way to discover the meanings and values that make life worth living.

Helen Palmer's well-reasoned anthology brings together an extraordinary group of writers who are pioneering the exploration of inner space and the acquisition of knowledge through our internal senses. For example, each from their own discipline imply how important it is to pay attention to *how* we pay attention. This is because *what* we notice is determined by *how* our attention is organized. In growing up, we develop habits for placing our attention, and this in turn determines what we know.

For example, a man who is inwardly angry may well notice the many irritating conditions of his life. Yet some of those annoyances simply do not attract his attention, when he can relax his focus and begin to enjoy himself.

This sequence, however, is the reverse of what many people assume. It is erroneously believed that attention is attracted out of interest, but actually our interests are more often determined by our own inner state, and we stay interested because of the way we have learned to place our attention.

This is a crucial point since our customary placement of attention prevents us from noticing the very aspects of life that could make it more meaningful and worth living, and we simply do not notice the extent of our own impoverishment. For example, a detached analytic mode allows us to notice certain things, while eliminating others. If a physician becomes preoccupied with detached analysis during an examination, this way of placing attention is going to elicit different information from the patient than that evoked when attention is focused in a warm, intimate manner. Likewise, when either you or your physician places attention on internal body signals, previously fuzzy, preverbal hunches that may affect the treatment can be brought into fuller awareness.

However, when we separate ourselves from our internal experience by objectifying things in order to categorize and intellectualize them, we override the informative signals of body, heart, and mental imagery, all of which creates doubt regarding our own internal experience. Clearly, we need different kinds of information, but our cultural way of placing attention is too heavily stacked in favor of the outer senses of seeing and hearing and the tendency toward rational analysis.

Yet there are many technologies that have been employed throughout the ages to support different methods of paying attention. Many of those ways, such as attending to body signals, dreamwork, empathy, intuitive hunches, imagination, meditation, and trance, are very important and for this reason they have been presented at the *Common Boundary* conferences, which I have the pleasure of organizing.

In my years as conference organizer, I have personally met with many of the contributors whose works appear in this book. Each describes a door of perception, and Helen does an excellent job of unifying their diverse points of view within the framework of inner knowing.

Bethesda, Maryland —Charles H. Simpkinson, Ph.D.
Publisher, *Common Boundary* magazine

Introduction to Inner Knowing
by Helen Palmer

Within the context of a modern society, it might easily appear that inner ways of knowing are a recent discovery. Out of necessity, our attention is directed to the exterior world of objects and the people around us, as if we are separate from them—and of course we are, but only from the perspective of the outer senses. The possibility of more subtle senses, or so-called organs of perception, for inner knowing are not commonly considered, not because they are new to the human condition, but because the sacred technologies that awaken subtle perceptions have fallen out of favor.

The rediscovery of Aristotle's logical and naturalistic works, in the late twelfth century, initiated a path to acquiring knowledge that eventually eclipsed inner wisdom. According to the conditions laid down by Aristotle, there were only two ways to acquire valid and useful knowledge: through sense experience and through logical deduction or induction. Eventually, the entire edifice of modern science was built upon these two axioms, sending a clear message to the world that other forms of knowledge are invalid and untrustworthy.

Granted, our contemporary definition of sense experience has been stretched to include whatever today's technology can measure or calibrate, and our definition of logic has also stretched to include methods of inference such as probability theory and factor analysis, but still, Aristotle's two axioms for acquiring knowledge undergird almost all acceptable science taught during the twentieth century.

Yet throughout the modern era there have been submerged currents of total protest and rebellion against rationalism, until today, when, despite all arguments against them, the ancient ways of knowing are surfacing with renewed vitality. Public attention is magnetized by accounts of empathy, intuition, and spiritual experience, simply because that hidden wisdom makes life worth living.

Some are fortunate enough to be so gradually and gracefully introduced to the ways of inner knowing that they assume everyone operates from the same level of consciousness. Others, like myself, were knocked off their perceptual moorings by an apparently out-of-the-blue series of events that defy logic yet seem far more fundamental than sensory reality. A direct jolt of inner knowing is especially startling to people like myself, whose confidence previously lay in intellectualism, because it urges us toward a way of life that we might never have rationally chosen.

CROSSROADS OF CONSCIOUSNESS — A PERSONAL ACCOUNT

In 1967, the East Coast movement of resistance to the Vietnam War was in crisis. The Manhattan pacifist organizers had rapidly polarized into a faction favoring acts of disruption versus those who were determined to maintain a nonviolent position. In a series of horrifying incidents I witnessed several friends get badly hurt in demonstrations, and as I saw the movement splinter, my imagination went wild. I was deeply involved but very frightened—a perfect condition for precipitous intuitive openings.

I remember sitting up nights unable to sleep, frantic about what might happen to my friends, and imagining the worst to be prepared. Images of the events about to take place became increasingly animated, until one night— with an incremental extension of focus—my imagination became as believable and solid as the furniture in my room. Oddly, none of this seemed unusual. For weeks I had lived with the heightened concentration that danger produces, and turning attention inward shifted that single-pointed focus to my imagination. I was still aware of sitting in a chair imagining the next day's events, but the inner impressions intensified until I was fully absorbed.

Spontaneously, I found myself inhabiting the images of my own mind. I watched, and I also participated in the sequence of events like a character in a dream. It was utterly real. I was sitting in my chair imagining tomorrow, and simultaneously playing my part in what would be happening tomorrow. This double perception, being in two places at once and firmly anchored in each, lasted just until I recognized that my awareness was split. That startled me, and my concentration broke, snapping the connection. Looking back, I see that I was not frightened by the vision itself, but the realization of dual perception was shocking, and I couldn't maintain the connection.

Suspended anxiety flooded back as I regained awareness of myself sitting in the chair. The inner perception had collapsed, but the vision's message was unmistakable. Without hesitation, I made a call, relating the guidance I had received to my friend Tom, without disclosing its source. He was to drive across the Canadian border using a different route from what had been planned. Without questioning me, Tom agreed to change his approach. That day another car was stopped at the original checkpoint, and the resisters were arrested.

Several similar incidents of inner knowing took place within a very short time. Without mentioning the source of my information, I saw and warned others about an impending police action. And while pinned to my living room chair, I also witnessed the unfortunate outcome of a vote that finalized the Manhattan pacifist split, days before it happened.

My absorption into inner sight felt consistently tranquil, even pleasurable, but the realization that I was entering another zone of existence continued to be alarming and disruptive to my career path. At the time, I was a university student, planning to be an experimental psychologist, a field that emphasized reason and intellect as the comprehensive source of knowledge. But now I had more pressing questions: Can visions produce real information? Where does that information originate? How could I tell the difference between a projection and the real thing? If inner sight is real, then what are its mechanisms? Its organs of perception? What are the parameters and limits of knowing, and how could I test for accuracy? In a confused and fractured way I was living out the key questions of epistemology, but my anchor in intellectualism made it difficult to accept even profoundly convincing intuition as being meaningful and real.

With the marvelous clarity of hindsight, I now see how psychological training, with its emphasis on experimental distance and neutral objectivity, not only excluded intuitive understanding, but also aroused suspicions about it. Like the scientific community surrounding me, I simply didn't think about altered states of awareness. At the time, even words like "empathy" were frowned upon as nonobjective, and the concept of a higher consciousness was categorized as magical thinking. My intuitions were accurate, but without a guide I couldn't trust what I was getting into. Altering my mental state was too frightening, and so I threw myself into other activities, hoping that it wouldn't happen again.

Shortly after graduation I moved to California. The shift from pressured New York academia to the loosely knit San Francisco political scene was dramatic. It was so slowed down, I used to think I could read a book between the sentences of a conversation. But the new context served me well, and I quickly found others who had experiences similar to my own. Within months I was doing a regular meditation practice, and was beginning to observe the difference between my thoughts and the flow of inner images that had caused so much anguish and concern in New York.

I soon discovered that certain concentration practices were designed to produce intuitive imagery and began to consciously replicate the shifts of attention that spontaneously occurred when I had focused inward under pressure. I also found ways of placing my attention that had a calming effect, and my meditation group was a marvelous source of emotional support.

In the years following my initial experiences, I've collected many personal accounts of extraordinary events happening to ordinary people when the conditions were right. Some described a gradually developing capacity for inner knowing in the context of a meditation practice. Other experiences were spontaneous and out of context, making them difficult to retrieve. These stories illustrate the vast scope of inner knowing, ranging from simple *déjà vu*—I know I've been here, but how could I know?—to far more elaborate impressions of events happening at a distance, in the past, or at future points in time. In most accounts, it was abundantly clear that the literal "message" received was far less important to the perceiver than the sense of stepping into another reality behind surface appearances.

Some recollections that people have shared with me could easily appear in the pages of a sacred text, illuminating the fruits of contemplative practice. There are accounts of inner openings to nature, when thoughts vanish and emotions drop away, and people merge inseparably with the environment. A recent example came from a skier making a downhill run in bad weather, who suddenly felt his presence expand to encompass the entire mountainside. Although the snowfall made it difficult to see, his ecstatic sense of physical extension included every boulder in the dangerous descent, allowing him to navigate safely. Such moments are living proof of what we all secretly believe, however alienated or religiously disaffected we may be. Even years later, the mystery remains written on the rapturous faces of people recalling these events: "This can't have happened, but it did! And it happened to *me*."

IN CONTRAST TO SCIENTIFIC OPINION

Current national opinion polls find most Americans believing in intuition, precognition, and the validity of dreams as a source of information. Indeed, the fact of nonconceptual knowing is so embedded in the popular mind, so entirely accepted, that we take it for granted. Yet we have no educational context for developing these abilities.

Even those who report unusually refined qualities of knowing do not typically speak of returning to their inner world. For most, the great moment passes as a peak event quickly becoming a treasured memory, rather than initiating a new cycle of personal development. For example: I recently spoke with a computer scientist who was busily working his way up the ladder at Microsoft in Seattle. He was also a semiprofessional opera singer, and liked to vocalize in the mornings in front of an upper-story window. He had a practice of casting his voice full-out, toward a distant grove of trees, expanding his voice to engage his natural audience.

One day the scope of his practice deepened. Without intention he spontaneously threw the balcony window open and began singing full-out, his last thought being, "This is like a Pavarotti movie!" Seeming to be everywhere at once, his voice was one of many, until he came awake to hear the world singing back. Years later, the memory of being sung to still moved him to tears. He said he would remember it when he died, yet even so, our conversation quickly moved elsewhere.

Most altered states of consciousness slip away like a dream, as attention returns to ordinary thinking. The peak moment is inadvertently rationalized or forgotten, but occasionally the question persists—"How did I know?"—accompanied by a natural coda: "How can I return?"

Outstanding moments of empathy appear in many stories, but the quality of feeling described is different from close understanding or sympathetic listening. Empathetic connection bridges the gap from imagining what another feels to "being them" as they go through it. It's described in metaphors like "feeling so touched that I lost myself, and was swept into their world," or "It was like merging with a rainstorm, and I couldn't tell whose face was crying."

What makes these stories similar is the nonordinary state of mind in which the events took place. These people were deeply engaged with the task at hand, and something suddenly switched. Fully concentrated on the object of their knowing—a song, a downhill ski run, talking with a friend—they felt a shift of consciousness occur and lost their sense of separation: the very same shift that I underwent in New York when I moved from watching images in my mind to directly interacting with the people and places I imagined.

Qualities of knowing that cannot be grasped by intellect or analysis involve being at one with the object of your attention. When the knower and the known unite, the student becomes at one with the scene she imagines. Far from being unusual, nondual states of mind occur in small ways throughout the day, but we do not often recognize them.

We've all had, for example, the pleasure of a walk when the sense of separation between ourselves and the environment disappears. Suddenly we're suffused with the empty-headed clarity of our connection to nature that is so definite, so indelibly known to our being, that thought simply recedes. The same experience commonly happens at the movies. When the story heats up, we forget that we're sitting in a theater watching the screen—we forget time, place, and our own thoughts while we join with the action on screen.

NONDUAL CONSCIOUSNESS

Experiences of nonduality are typically communicated to others through metaphor and vividly impressionistic language: "It was like merging with a rainstorm" or "My body suddenly expanded" or "I was everywhere at once." But subjective descriptions of unified consciousness are often difficult to grasp, unless you've shared a similar experience. The gap between experience and explanation is further widened by the fact that self-descriptions change their meaning when the psychological context changes. Commonly used words like "mind," "self," or "my unconscious" have specific meanings to each of us, but the same descriptors heard in a different context convey a radically altered message.

Consider the statement: "I stood with the elm tree in our backyard, feeling its love within my heart." However convincing to the perceiver, this statement is likely to be heard as a classic example of magical thinking, anthropomorphism, projection, or simple emotionality tinged with New Age beliefs. In the modern world, being loved by trees is unlikely to be heard as data transmitted through nondual consciousness.

"Being in my heart" is a universal experience that we've all shared, but each of us describes that knowing in highly personal language. A psychologist, for example, might listen carefully to the woman who was loved by trees but totally miss the fact that she was in a nondual state of mind. The moment in which tree and woman shared a single consciousness passed quickly. Unless that moment is highlighted and recognized as a door to inner knowing, she returns to ordinary consciousness, and cannot find a way back.

Our psychologist might also interpret the incident within the context of diagnostic theory, which tends to dismiss nondual experiences as projection, and ascribes inner knowing to childhood patterning. Now it may be quite true that the woman imagined the whole incident or was indeed caught in an unconscious projection. It may also be true that she craves love as a result of childhood abandonment or feelings of low self-esteem. But it is true beyond doubt, that to label her experience simply as either projection or a result of childhood patterning does not take into account the option of authentic intuition. Rather than seeing an opportunity to regain the nondual consciousness where knowing of the heart occurs, the woman who was loved by trees is encouraged to misinterpret her own signals.

Now consider similar events in a different context. A Kalahari Bushman receives an inner impression of water located at a considerable distance. Based on what he knows, he and his family undertake a grueling desert trek, undeterred by questions of projection. His inner impression is taken as valid information by his people, for it is precisely the intelligence of being at one with natural forces that helps the Bushman's tribe survive.

Consider another comparison between intellectual and intuitive knowing. An Aboriginal doctor receives an inner impression of a patient's prognosis and acts on that understanding, in the same way that Western physicians analyze test results and follow diagnostic procedures. Both Aboriginal and Westerner are focused on the same healing goal, but they utilize different states of mind. Yet Aboriginals are quite capable of complex conceptual thinking. The tribal doctor could, for example, have traveled to study medicine at a Western university. Likewise, the Western physician may be equally capable of discovering nondual states of mind as people are trained to do in Aboriginal communities.

In this generation, we are fortunate to have rediscovered the value of nondual perceptions, in which perceiver and perceived participate in a single reality. Not a moment too soon! The effects of treating the planet in ways that ignore our inherent inseparability were never more evident. And from the perspective of a consciousness shared by all beings, the peoples of the Earth are not isolated individuals. We seem to have come full circle in retrieving the hidden wisdom of previous generations, and honoring the state of mind in which that wisdom originates.

This book concerns knowledge that cannot be grasped by intellect or analysis. It is structured for those who, like myself, discovered what is traditionally called hidden wisdom, without the background to either understand or develop the experiences that came upon them. Because of my own precipitous intuitive awakening, I have chosen to include readings that spurred me along the way, knowing that they will be helpful to others.

Westerners who have moments of direct inner knowing often suppress its memory, or rationalize it away, or remember what happened as a once-in-a-lifetime peak experience. There is however, another choice for those who feel themselves blessed by glimpsing even a crack in the door leading to nondual perception. In this generation, the technologies of sacred tradition are freely available to anyone who is drawn to explore a greater consciousness.

Part One

Knowing for the Twenty-first Century

Nonduality

*I*t was stunning when I first realized that whole epochs of human history depended on modes of consciousness that are radically different from my own. For example, I had assumed that builders of monumental works such as Stonehenge and the Avebury circle functioned in the same way that I do. I thought their driven need to find their place in an orderly cosmos was a spiritual quest, and supposed they had taken astronomical measurements, analyzed the situation, and carried out some form of geometric discovery.

And perhaps they did.

But what if our ancestors also carried out their work within a consciousness where builder and materials are experienced as a single being? Of course that idea crossed my mind. But here again, I presumed that the builders consciously made connection with their environment as I would do in meditation practice—where I temporarily alter my consciousness, and then come right back to the familiar subject-object intellectual framework. The idea that people might have lived in a consciousness permanently unified with the environment—without benefit of an objectifying intellect—escaped me entirely.

Robert McDermott, a leading theorist on the evolution of consciousness, suggests that the intelligence guiding achievements like the stone circles did indeed flow from a nondual state of mind and that the builders literally didn't see the same world that we do.

> We find it natural and interesting to think abstractly about ourselves and the meaning of our lives, but that form of thought was apparently inconceivable for archaic humanity. Their way of knowing emerged from their interaction with nature and the environment. . . . It may have been closer to imaginal consciousness than the abstract intellectual faculty that we call "thinking. . . ." Experiences which modern Western thinking typically regards as profoundly transformative and revelatory, or too remarkable to be believable, might take on a different meaning when considered within the context of the consciousness in and by which they occurred.*

We are so used to analyzing our own lives, and observing what we think and feel from a detached point of view, that we don't realize how a dualistic

* Public lecture, June 1992.

state of mind determines what we know. For example, every time we open our mouths to speak, the structure of language itself reinforces duality. In English, nouns make everything separate things. Every sentence we utter requires us to separate subject from object. Verbs demand that we categorize every event as past, present, or future. Our grammar forces us to separate "I" from "you" and "you" from "them." Our external reality — persons, places, and things — becomes not only objects separate from ourselves but objects to be analyzed, dissected, dismembered, captured. All by itself, the structure of our language serves to ward off unitive experience.

Clearly, the Western mode of consciousness produces certain ideas and not others. When the qualities of information conveyed through empathy, intuition, and the consciousness that created Stonehenge cannot even be properly communicated, they simply cease to exist. And not surprisingly, powers of imagination once so active in childhood fall into disuse.

The modern era, dedicated to repeatable experimental data, buried something valuable that cannot be resurrected by scientific language: namely, the qualities of knowing that rely on unification between an observer and the object observed. Yet people keep right on having unitive experiences, despite the fact that it's illogical. And they are inexplicably drawn to the states of mind where inner knowing occurs. Rather than being exotic, or distant, or dependent upon an alien culture, inner knowing is a source of information that we use on a daily basis. We regularly demonstrate intuition and loving kindness, and a host of other promptings, often without realizing the state of mind from which we act.

Against the background of a technological age, the wisdoms of nondual realities seem like freshly emerging human potentials. But the truth is, we are moved to retrieve dimensions of knowing that we wouldn't ordinarily consider, simply because the limitations of intellectualism have become so apparent. Without rejecting its scientific orientation, Western culture is beginning to explore the royal road to hidden wisdom, mapped in the technologies of sacred tradition. The quest is spurred on by discoveries that our own ancestors, as well as people from other cultures, simply didn't and don't think like contemporary Eurocentric rationalists.

The authors in Part I explore different aspects of nonduality, helping us to recognize that many different facets of consciousness exist in addition to the mode called rational. These excerpts represent a wonderful convergence of thinking from philosophical, psychological, and spiritual perspectives, all of which demonstrate that our state of mind determines what we know.

1.   *Doors in the Wall by Aldous Huxley*

Writing in the 1950s, Aldous Huxley was far ahead of his time in articulating the limitations of the intellectualism that surrounded him. He was a superb and impassioned exemplar for those of us who were barely on the edge of recognizing our own potentials for an inner life. Just by being who he was, Huxley gave off the message that a direct, personal experience of higher consciousness was possible for ordinary people, precisely at a time when American education was focused on behaviorism. The Doors of Perception, which contains this selection, was written by a man struck with awe at finding his own place in a transcendent order of consciousness. It is an anthem of its time, not only because Huxley dared to speak of altered states of consciousness, but because he had the gift of communicating his inner worlds to others.

THAT HUMANITY AT large will ever be able to dispense with Artificial Paradise seems very unlikely. Most men and women lead lives at the worst so painful, at the best so monotonous, poor, and limited, that the urge to escape, the longing to transcend themselves if only for a few moments, is and has always been one of the principal appetites of the soul. Art and religion, carnivals and saturnalia, dancing and listening to oratory—all these have served, in H.G. Wells' phrase, as Doors in the Wall.

In a world where education is predominantly verbal, highly educated people find it all but impossible to pay serious attention to anything but words and notions. There is always money for, there are always doctorates in, the learned foolery of research into what, for scholars, is the all-important problem: Who influenced whom to say what when? Even in this age of technology, the verbal humanities are honored. The non-verbal humanities, the arts of being directly aware of the given facts of our existence, are almost completely ignored. A catalogue, a bibliography, a definitive edition of a third-rate versifier's *ipsissima verba,* a stupendous index to end all indexes—any genuinely Alexandrian project is sure of approval and financial support. But when it comes to finding out how you and I, our children and grandchildren, may become more perceptive, more intensely aware of inward and outward reality, more open to the Spirit, less apt, by psychological malpractices, to make ourselves physically ill, and more capable of controlling our own autonomic nervous system—when it comes to any form of non-verbal education more fundamental (and more likely to be of some practical use) than Swedish drill, no really respectable person in any really respectable university or church will do anything about it. Verbalists are suspicious of the non-verbal; rationalists fear the given, non-rational fact; intellectuals feel that "what we perceive by the eye (or in any other way) is foreign to us as such and need not impress us deeply." Besides, this matter of education in the non-verbal humanities will not fit into any of the established pigeonholes. It is not religion, not neurology, not gymnastics, not morality or civics, not even experimental psychology. This being so the subject is, for academic and ecclesiastical purposes, non-existent and may safely be ignored altogether or left, with a patronizing smile, to those whom the Pharisees of verbal orthodoxy call cranks, quacks, charlatans and unqualified amateurs.

"I have always found," Blake wrote rather bitterly, "that Angels have the vanity to speak of themselves as the only wise. This they do with a confident insolence sprouting from systematic reasoning."

Systematic reasoning is something we could not, as a species or as individuals, possibly do without. But neither, if we are to remain sane, can we possibly do without direct perception, the more unsystematic the better, of the inner and outer worlds into which we have been born. This given reality is an infinite which passes all understanding and yet admits of being directly and in some sort totally apprehended. It is a transcendence belonging to another order than the human, and yet it may be present to us as a felt immanence, an experienced participation. To be enlightened is to be aware, always, of total reality in its immanent otherness—to be aware of it and yet to remain in a condition to survive as an animal, to think and feel as a human being, to resort whenever expedient to systematic reasoning. Our goal is to discover that we have always been where we ought to be. Unhappily, we make the task exceedingly difficult for ourselves. Meanwhile, however, there are gratuitous graces in the form of partial and fleeting realizations. Under a more realistic, a less exclusively verbal system of education than ours, every Angel (in Blake's sense of that word) would be permitted as a sabbatical treat, would be urged and even, if necessary, compelled to take an occasional trip through some Door in the Wall into the world of transcendental experience. If it terrified him, it would be unfortunate but probably salutary. If it brought him a brief but timeless illumination, so much the better. In either case the Angel might lose a little of the confident insolence sprouting from systematic reasoning and the consciousness of having read all the books.

———

Near the end of his life Aquinas experienced Infused Contemplation. Thereafter he refused to go back to work on his unfinished book. Compared with *this,* everything he had read and argued about and written—Aristotle and the Sentences, the questions, the Propositions, the majestic Summas— was no better than chaff or straw. For most intellectuals such a sit-down strike would be inadvisable, even morally wrong. But the Angelic Doctor had done more systematic reasoning than any twelve ordinary Angels, and was already ripe for death. He had earned the right, in those last months of his mortality, to turn away from merely symbolic straw and chaff to the bread of actual and substantial Fact. For Angels of a lower order and with better prospects of longevity, there must be a return to the straw. But the man who comes back through the Door in the Wall will never be quite the same as the man who went out. He will be wiser but less cocksure, happier but less self-satisfied, humbler in acknowledging his ignorance yet better equipped to understand the relationship of words to things, of systematic reasoning to the unfathomable Mystery which it tries, forever vainly, to comprehend.

2. The Archaeology of Consciousness: An Interview with Owen Barfield by Gary Lachman

Here is a lovely glimpse of the Western philosophical tradition in the flesh. Barfield, now in his nineties, is a seminal thinker in the related fields of language and the evolution of consciousness. To the few who recognize his name, he is identified with the emerging term "participatory epistemology," the knowing that occurs when perceiver and perceived are united as a single consciousness.

In this excellent summary, Lachman consolidates key points from Barfield's work: that consciousness is perpetually evolving; that the history of language itself reveals an "original participation" with nature and the environment; and that imagination is the vehicle for participatory consciousness, a fact that is self-evident to anyone who has ever received a significant dream. This was certainly true for me when I had accurate waking visions of supposedly unknowable future events.

But rather than stay with the passive knowing that occurs in dreams and reveries, Barfield sees the next evolutionary step for humanity as an ability to actively recognize the inner meaning of our surroundings through heightened powers of imagination.

OWEN BARFIELD IS not a name on everyone's lips. Even in the relatively small community of scholars who should know him, mention of Barfield usually brings looks of ignorance or, at best, dim recognition. "Oh yes. He's that fellow who was friends with C. S. Lewis, wasn't he?" Given some familiarity with Barfield's work, you might receive a more in-depth but not necessarily more enlightened remark, as I did when mentioning him to a university academic in a London pub. "Barfield?" he said. "You mean that Coleridge loony?"

With perceptions like this, is it surprising that a writer of books about the origin of language and the evolution of consciousness should be unknown to the general public? Hardly. But when that writer is one of the most interesting thinkers of the twentieth century, one can only comment, "More's the pity."

Owen Barfield—scholar, philosopher, poet, novelist, friend of C. S. Lewis, and interpreter of Rudolf Steiner—is, at 97, one of the most remarkable men alive today. Born in North London in 1898, Barfield fought in the First World War, lived through the Blitz, [and] endured the tensions of the Cold War. . . .

In terms of intellectual and cultural history, his career has been a chronology of twentieth century thought. Early books, like *History in English Words* (1926) and *Poetic Diction* (1927), were written in the suffocating atmosphere of logical positivism, when philosophy as a "love of wisdom" was abandoned for a sterile hair-splitting of syntax. Barfield's belief in language as an archaeological record of "the evolution of consciousness," was as at odds with the reigning Zeitgeist as you could get. . . .

THE ARCHAEOLOGY OF CONSCIOUSNESS

The basic idea behind the evolution of consciousness is, as Barfield briefly put it in *Romanticism Comes of Age,* "the concept of man's self-consciousness as a process in time." Compare this with the notion of the "history of ideas." In the standard history of ideas, an ancient Greek and a postmodern American have very different ideas about the world, but both perceive the world the same way—with the understanding that our ideas, informed by modern science, are closer to the truth. There's no difference between the consciousness of the ancient Greek and ours, only between the concepts "inside" it. When we open our eyes, we see the same world. It's just that we have better ideas about it.

For Barfield this is totally wrong. Not only do their ideas about the world differ, but the world the ancient Greek saw and the one we see are not the same. The kind of consciousness we enjoy—if that's the right word for it—is very different from that of the ancient Greek—or the Greek of late antiquity, or a person from the Middle Ages, or even one of the early Modern Age. Not only our ideas about things, Barfield tells us, but our consciousness itself has evolved over time. And if we are to take seriously the contention of philosophers like Immanuel Kant—that the world we perceive is a product of our perceptual apparatus—then a world produced by different consciousnesses at different times will be, well, different.

One of the most fascinating conclusions Barfield draws from this is that all ideas about the pre-historic world, from paleontological textbooks to popular depictions like *Jurassic Park* are, at the least, questionable. "They project a picture of that world as it would be seen by a consciousness alive today. We have no way of knowing what that world looked like to a different consciousness because we have no record from a consciousness of that time. We can only speculate." To the contention that we have the palaeontological record Barfield replies, "It's nevertheless our consciousness that discovers fossils and organizes them into the schemata of ancient life."

But if we can only speculate about the nature of reality before the rise of consciousness, there is another record, one we find not by digging through ancient earth, but by scrutinizing ancient texts. This is language, the study of which, according to Barfield, is "a kind of archaeology of consciousness." As he writes in *History in English Words:*

> . . . in language . . . the past history of mankind is spread out in an imperishable map, just as the history of the mineral earth lies embedded in the layers of its outer crust. But there is this difference: whereas the former can only give us a knowledge of outward, dead things . . . language has preserved for us the inner, living history of man's soul. It reveals the evolution of consciousness.

And whereas the orthodox view of evolution has a pre-existing, external world much like our own, made up of distinct, independent, impermeable objects, the record left us by language, Barfield argues, suggests something different.

FROM POETRY TO PROSE

"The standard understanding of the evolution of language," Barfield told me, "is that all words referring to something spiritual or abstract have their origin in literal meaning. So when we refer to a 'spirit' enlivening the physical body, what we are talking about is something like breath. We find this in the Hebrew *ruach* and the Greek *pneuma.*" Or, as he wrote in *Poetic Diction:*

> . . . it is a commonplace . . . that, whatever word we hit on, if we trace its meaning far enough back, we find it apparently expressive of some tangible, or at all events, perceptible object or some physical activity . . . Throughout the recorded history of language the movement of meaning has been from the concrete to the abstract.

The result of this is the insight, voiced by thinkers like Emerson and Nietzsche, that modern language, with its abstract terms and nuances of meaning, is, as Barfield writes, "apparently nothing . . . but an unconscionable tissue of dead, or petrified, metaphors." The further we dig into language, the more metaphors we find.

But there's something wrong with this, Barfield says. Etymologists, like the famous Oriental scholar Max Mueller, believed that early humans began with very simple, literal words and phrases for tangible, perceptible things. Then, with the "dawn of reason" (itself a metaphor), our ancestors began to use these phrases "metaphorically," to describe inner and outer experience. If we take this theory to its logical conclusion, Barfield argues, "the result should be that today, after millenia of metaphor building, we should all be spouting poetry whenever we speak." And likewise, we should, being so much more sophisticated, find poetry from earlier times rather less poetic. Neither of which, of course, is true. Homer still thrills like nothing else. Mueller and his followers erred, Barfield believes, by adopting an unquestioned Darwinian approach to the history of language. Just as simple organisms became more complex over time, so too language evolved, from simple "root" words denoting tangible "things," into our highly abstract and metaphorical speech. "The only problem with this, is the evidence from language itself," Barfield argues.

What the history of language tells us, Barfield says, is that "our ancestors didn't use language as Mueller believed, because they didn't see the same world as Mueller did. Mueller projected the world as perceived by late-nineteenth century European man into the past. That's why the only account of the history of language he could give was one that followed Darwinian ideas of progress." The kind of world ancient man saw—and our ancestors continued to see until fairly recent times—Barfield believes, was one in which human consciousness "participated." At that stage of the evolution of consciousness, the distinction between "self" and "the world" was not as rigid as it is today. What Mueller misunderstood as metaphoric was early man's ability to see the "inside" of things, just as we now are aware of our own "inside"—our minds. Accounts of nature spirits; folk tales and myths about fairies, nymphs, and sylphs; legends of gods walking the earth, are all rooted in this "participatory consciousness." This was the kind of world (and consciousness) that poets like Blake, Coleridge, and Goethe believed in and at times felt. It was also the kind of consciousness described by Rudolf Steiner. Barfield calls it "original participation."

ORIGINAL AND FINAL PARTICIPATION

"Original participation," according to Barfield, is a "primal unity of mind and nature, with no separation between inner and outer worlds." At that point, nature, he believes, was as subjective, as inward, as we are. But what happened is that gradually "unconscious nature" became localized in human consciousness. If we think of "unconscious nature" as a vast ocean, and the initial separation of human consciousness as wavelets lifting themselves up from the surface, we'll have an idea of what Barfield means. Gradually this process continues, with an increasingly tenuous link between our new "self" consciousness and its "unconscious" source, until we arrive at our present state: a completely other "outside world" with separate islands of inwardness housed within our individual skulls. At this point we are as far away from "original participation" as we can get.

But although some bemoan our exodus from the garden, this estrangement from our source was absolutely necessary, Barfield tells us. The path of evolution, he says, isn't a straight line; it is much more like a U. The left hand of the U traces the path from "original participation" to our current estrangement from nature. By the nineteenth century and the rise of a completely materialist "explanation" of the world, including the most "immaterial" thing we know, consciousness, we had reached the bottom of the U. Now we are just beginning to make our ascent back up, this time on the right hand of the U. This is the essential difference. Because now we can begin to "participate" in "the world" not passively—as we had as "primitive" humans and as animals do today—but actively, by becoming conscious of the power of our imagination in creating "the world." (And if we need an example of the difference between active and passive participation, we need merely recognize the difference between our dreams, in which we passively encounter a series of strange symbolic experiences, over which we have no, or extremely little, control, and the consciousness of an artist or poet focused intently on his work.) We had to leave the security of "original participation" in order for consciousness to take the next step in its evolution. Having hit bottom on the evolutionary curve, we are beginning our ascent to what he calls "final participation," a conscious participation in the cosmos.

POLARITY AND CREATIVE IMAGINATION

The idea of an evolution of consciousness, though unorthodox, is not as strange today as it may have seemed when Barfield first presented it. Since then it's been argued by several thinkers, notably the philosopher Jean Gebser in *The Ever-present Origin,* and the Jungian theorist Erich Neumann in *The Origin and History of Consciousness.* But Barfield's take on it is peculiar, and perhaps his most startling idea is a reversal of the standard materialist account of mind's emergence from matter. Rather than a fluke product of material evolution, Barfield argues that consciousness itself is responsible for "the world." That's why there's no answer to questions about the "origin of language" when asked from the orthodox position. Asking about the origin of language, Barfield says, is like asking about "the origin of origin." Language didn't come about as a way to imitate, master, or explain nature, as it is usually assumed, because "nature" as we understand it didn't exist until language did. According to Barfield, the polarities mind/world and language/nature are the result of splitting up "original participation." To understand language, Barfield tells us, we must imagine ourselves back to a stage at which human consciousness hadn't yet separated from its unconscious background. At that point there was no "nature" and no "consciousness"—at least not as we understand it. "Nature," Barfield tells us, didn't exist until human consciousness came into its own. The "world" we see is the result of thousands of years of work by the human mind.

3. *The Passion of the Western Mind by Richard Tarnas*

Before we can fully understand the emergence of the postmodern mind, we should first understand the modern consciousness that came before it. In the evolution of that modern mentality, which has shaped the thinking of Western civilization for almost five hundred years, there are three pivotal players: Copernicus, Descartes, and Kant.

Here philosopher Richard Tarnas explores the key positions of these three thinkers, from the perspective of epistemology, or the study of how knowledge is acquired. He shows how their ideas, at once brilliant and problematic, eventually led us to our dualistic twentieth century consciousness—estranged from nature, our own deepest selves, and the ways of inner knowing.

To me, the Tarnas magic is about his superb mastery of his material but also the fact that over and over again he encourages us to integrate the power of intellectual analysis with the full spectrum of human consciousness. His works do not reflect the temptation to trash intellectualism or to despise the personal self as merely an annoying handicap on the road to higher consciousness. Instead he demonstrates the rise of intellectual understanding as an evolutionary step toward unifying the knowledge of inner and outer realities.

THE POSTMODERN MIND for obvious reasons has been confronting fundamental questions of epistemology with more than the usual sense of urgency, and I believe that certain recent developments in the field of depth psychology have immense relevance for resolving some of these questions. I'll begin here with a brief overview of the background to our present intellectual situation, starting with a look at the Copernican revolution, understood in its broadest sense.

In a narrow sense the Copernican revolution can be understood as simply a specific paradigm shift in modern astronomy and cosmology, initiated by Copernicus, established by Kepler and Galileo, and completed by Newton. Yet the Copernican revolution can also be understood in a much wider and more significant sense. For when Copernicus recognized that the Earth was not the absolute fixed center of the universe, and equally important, when he recognized that the movement of the heavens could be explained in terms of the movement of the observer, he established what was perhaps the pivotal insight of the modern mind. The Copernican shift of perspective can be seen as a fundamental metaphor for the entire modern world view: the massive deconstruction of the naive understanding, the critical recognition that the apparent condition of the objective world was unconsciously determined by the condition of the subject, the consequent liberation from the ancient and medieval cosmic womb, the radical displacement of the human being to a relative and peripheral position in a vast and impersonal universe, the ensuing disenchantment of the natural world. In this broadest sense—as an event which took place not only in astronomy and the sciences but in philosophy and religion and in the collective human psyche—the Copernican revolution can be seen as constituting *the* epochal shift of the modern age. It was a primordial event, world-destroying and world-constituting.

In philosophy and epistemology this larger Copernican revolution took place in the dramatic series of intellectual advances that began with Descartes and culminated in Kant. It has been said that Descartes and Kant were both inevitable in the development of the modern mind, and I believe this is correct. For it was Descartes who first grasped and articulated the experience of the emerging autonomous modern self as being fundamentally distinct and separate from an objective external world that it seeks to understand and master. After Copernicus, humankind was on its own in the universe, its cosmic place irrevocably relativized; Descartes then drew out and expressed in philosophical terms the experiential consequence of that new cosmological context, starting from a position of fundamental doubt vis-à-vis the world, and ending in the *cogito*. In doing this, Descartes set into motion a train of philosophical events—leading from Locke to Berkeley and Hume and culminating in Kant—that eventually produced a great epistemological crisis. Descartes was in this sense the crucial midpoint between Copernicus and Kant, between the Copernican revolution in cosmology and the Copernican revolution in epistemology.

For if the human mind was in some sense fundamentally distinct and different from the external world, and if the only reality that the human mind had direct access to was its own experience, then the world apprehended by the mind was ultimately only the mind's interpretation of the world. Human knowledge of external reality had to be forever incommensurate with its goal, for there was no guarantee that the human mind could ever accurately mirror a world with which its connection was so indirect and mediated. Instead everything that this mind could perceive and judge would be to some undefined extent determined by its own character, its own subjective structures. The mind could experience only phenomena, not things-in-themselves; appearances, not an independent reality. In the modern universe, the human mind was on its own.

Thus Kant, building on his empiricist predecessors, drew out the epistemological consequences of the Cartesian *cogito*. Of course Kant himself set
forth cognitive principles, subjective structures, that he thought were
absolute—the a priori forms and categories—based upon the apparent cer-
tainties of Newtonian physics. As time passed, however, what endured from
Kant was not the specifics of his solution but rather the profound problem he
articulated. For Kant had drawn attention to the crucial fact that all human
knowledge is interpretive. The human mind can claim no direct mirror-like
knowledge of the objective world, for the object it experiences has already
been structured by the subject's own internal organization. The human being
knows not the world-in-itself but rather the world-as-rendered-by-the-
human-mind. Thus Descartes's ontological schism was both made more
absolute and superseded by Kant's epistemological schism. The gap between
subject and object could not be certifiably bridged. From the Cartesian
premise came the Kantian result.

In the subsequent evolution of the modern mind each of these fundamental shifts, which I am associating here symbolically with the figures of
Copernicus, Descartes, and Kant, has been sustained, elaborated, and pressed
to its extreme. Thus Copernicus's radical displacement of the human being
from the cosmic center was continued and reinforced by Darwin's relativiza-
tion of the human being in the scheme of evolution—no longer divinely
ordained, no longer absolute and secure, no longer the crown of creation, the
favored child of the universe, but rather just one more ephemeral species.
Placed in the vastly expanded cosmos of modern astronomy, the human being
now spins adrift, once the noble center of the cosmos, now an insignificant
denizen of a tiny planet revolving around an undistinguished star—you know
the familiar litany—at the edge of one galaxy amongst billions, in an indifferent and ultimately hostile universe.

So too was Descartes's schism between the personal and conscious human
subject and the impersonal and unconscious material universe ratified by subsequent scientific developments, from Newtonian physics all the way to contemporary big-bang cosmology, W and Z particles and grand unified
superforce theories. The world revealed by modern science has been a world
devoid of spiritual purpose, opaque, ruled by chance and necessity, without
intrinsic meaning. The human soul has not felt at home in the modern cosmos—the soul can hold dear its poetry and its music, its private metaphysics
and religion, but these find no certain foundation in the empirical universe.

And so too with the third of this modern trinity of alienation: Kant's recognition of the human mind's subjective ordering of reality, and thus finally the

relative and unrooted nature of human knowledge, was extended and reinforced by a host of subsequent developments, from Marx and Nietzsche to Weber and Wittgenstein, from anthropology, sociology of knowledge, and linguistics to cognitive psychology, literary criticism, quantum physics, and philosophy of science. The consensus is decisive: the world is in some essential sense a construct. Human knowledge is radically interpretive. There are no perspective-independent facts. Every act of perception and cognition is mediated, contextual, theory-soaked. Human language is unrooted in an independent reality. Meaning is rendered by the mind and cannot be assumed to inhere in the object, in the world beyond the mind, for that world can never be contacted without having already been saturated by the mind's own nature. That world cannot even be justifiably postulated. Radical uncertainty prevails, for in the end what one knows and experiences is to an indeterminate extent a projection.

Thus the cosmological estrangement of modern consciousness initiated by Copernicus and the ontological estrangement initiated by Descartes was in a sense completed by the epistemological estrangement initiated by Kant: a three-fold mutually enforced modern prison of alienation.

Now as an aside here I want to point out the striking resemblance between this state of affairs and the famous condition that Gregory Bateson described as the "double bind": the impossibly problematic situation in which mutually contradictory demands eventually lead a person to become schizophrenic. In Bateson's formulation, there were four basic premises necessary to constitute a double-bind situation between a child and a "schizophrenogenic" mother: (1) The child's relationship to the mother is one of vital dependency, thereby making it critical for the child to assess communications from the mother accurately. (2) The child receives contradictory or incompatible information from the mother at different levels, whereby for example her explicit verbal communication is fundamentally denied by the "metacommunication," the nonverbal context in which the explicit message is conveyed (thus the mother who says to her child with hostile eyes and a rigid body "Darling, you know I love you so much"). The two sets of signals cannot be understood as coherent. (3) The child is not given any opportunity to ask questions of the mother that would clarify the communication or resolve the contradiction. And (4) the child cannot leave the field, i.e. the relationship. In such circumstances, Bateson found, the child is forced to distort his or her perception of both the outer world and the inner feelings, with serious psychopathological consequences.

Now if we substitute in these four premises "world" for mother and "human being" for child we have the modern double bind in a nutshell: (1) The human being's relationship to the world is one of vital dependency, thereby making it critical for the human being to assess the nature of that world accurately. (2) The human mind receives contradictory or incompatible information about its situation with respect to the world, whereby its inner psychological and spiritual sense of things is incoherent with the scientific metacommunication. (3) Epistemologically the human mind cannot achieve direct communication with the world. And (4) existentially the human being cannot leave the field.

The differences between Bateson's double bind and the modern existential condition are more in degree than in kind: the modern condition is an extraordinarily encompassing and fundamental double bind, made less immediately conspicuous simply because it is so universal. We have the post-Copernican dilemma of being a peripheral and insignificant inhabitant of a vast cosmos, and the post-Cartesian dilemma of being a conscious purposeful and personal subject confronting an unconscious purposeless and impersonal universe, with these compounded by the post-Kantian dilemma of there being no possible means by which the human subject can know the universe in its essence. Thus we are evolved from, embedded in, and defined by a reality that is radically alien to our own, and moreover cannot ever be directly contacted in cognition.

This double bind of modern consciousness has been recognized in one form or another since at least Pascal: "I am terrified by the eternal silence of these infinite spaces." Our psychological and spiritual predispositions are absurdly at variance with the world revealed by our scientific method. We seem to receive two messages from our existential situation: on the one hand, strive, give oneself to the quest for meaning and spiritual fulfillment; but on the other hand, know that the universe, of whose substance we are derived, is entirely indifferent to that quest, soulless in character, and nullifying in its effects. We are at once aroused and crushed. For inexplicably, absurdly, the cosmos is inhuman, yet we are not. The situation is profoundly unintelligible.

Now if we follow Bateson's diagnosis, it should not be surprising what kinds of response the modern psyche has made to this situation as it attempts to escape the double bind's inherent contradictions. Either the inner world or the outer world is distorted: inner feelings are repressed and denied, as in apathy and psychic numbing, or they are inflated in compensation, as in narcissism and egocentrism; or the outer world is slavishly submitted to as the only reality, or it is aggressively objectified and exploited. There is also the strategy of flight, through various kinds of escapism: compulsive economic consumption, absorption in the mass media, fadism, cults, ideologies, nationalistic fervor, alcohol, drugs. When avoidance mechanisms cannot be sustained, there is anxiety, paranoia, chronic hostility, a sense of helpless victimization. And at the extreme there are the full-blown psychopathological reactions of the schizophrenic: self-destructive violence, delusional states, catatonia, automatism, mania, nihilism. The modern world knows each of these different reactions in various combinations and compromise formations, and its social and political life is notoriously so determined.

And is it any wonder that twentieth-century philosophy finds itself in the condition we now see? Of course modern philosophy has brought forth some courageous intellectual responses to the post-Copernican situation, but by and large the philosophy that has dominated our century and our universities resembles nothing so much as a severe obsessive-compulsive sitting on his bed repeatedly tying and untying his shoes because he never quite gets it right— while in the meantime Socrates and Hegel and Aquinas are already high up the mountain on their hike, breathing the bracing alpine air, seeing new and unexpected vistas.

But there is one crucial way in which the modern situation is not identical to the psychiatric double bind, and this is the fact that the modern human being has not simply been a helpless child, but has actively engaged the world and pursued a specific strategy and mode of activity—a Promethean project of freeing itself from and controlling nature. The modern mind has demanded a specific type of interpretation of the world, its scientific method has required explanations of phenomena that are concretely predictive, and thus impersonal, mechanistic, structural. To fulfill their purposes, these explanations of the universe have been systematically "cleansed" of all spiritual and human qualities. Of course we cannot be certain that the world *is* in fact what these explanations suggest; we can only be certain that the world is to an indeterminate extent *susceptible* to this way of interpretation. Kant's insight is a sword that cuts two ways. Although on the one hand it appears to place the world beyond the grasp of the human mind, on the other hand it recognizes that the impersonal and soulless world of modern scientific cognition is not necessarily the whole story. Rather it is the only kind of story that for the past three centuries the Western mind has considered intellectually justifiable. As Ernest Gellner has said: "It was Kant's merit to see that this compulsion [for mechanistic impersonal explanations] is in us, not in things." And "it was Weber's to see that it is historically a specific kind of mind, not human mind as such, that is subject to this compulsion."

Thus one crucial part of the modern double bind is not airtight. In the case of Bateson's schizophrenogenic mother and child, the mother more or less holds all the cards, for she unilaterally controls the communication. But the lesson of Kant is that the locus of the communication problem—i.e., the problem of human knowledge of the world—must first be viewed as centering in the human mind, not in the world as such. Thus it is theoretically possible that the human mind has more cards than it has been playing. The pivot of the modern predicament is epistemological, and it is here that we should look for an opening.

4. Hidden Wisdom by Roger Walsh

*Once again, we are reminded of the intellect's limitations, this time by recogniz-
ing that reality consists of many different inner states, each containing its own
wisdom. Speaking from the perspective of transpersonal psychology, Walsh points
to a consensus of opinion from spiritual traditions concerning the "eye of contemplation." As a complement to intellectual training, contemplatives train the
inner eye of awareness so as to experience, describe, and compare the subtle messages of state-specific knowledge that are usually overlooked.*

WESTERN PHILOSOPHERS USUALLY assume that intellectual training and analysis alone provide the royal road to understanding. However, transpersonal
philosophers—especially those of Asian traditions such as Vedanta, Sankhya,
Buddhism, and Taoism—think differently. They emphasize that while intellectual training is necessary, by itself it is not sufficient for deep understanding. They claim that the mind must also be given a multidimensional
contemplative or yogic training that refines ethics, emotions, motivation, and
attention.[1,2]

This training is designed to develop "the eye of contemplation" by inducing
specific states of consciousness in which one has "the keenness, subtlety and
quickness of cognitive response"[3] that are required for penetrating insights
into the nature of mind and reality. These insights collectively constitute the
transcendental wisdom variously known as *prajna* (Buddhism), *jnana* (Hinduism), *ma'rifah* (Islam), or *gnosis* (Christianity). This wisdom is the goal of
contemplative training and is said to liberate those who acquire it from delu-
sion and the suffering it produces.

This wisdom is described as a direct nonconceptual intuition that is
beyond words, concepts, and dualities; hence it is described as transverbal,
transrational, and nondual. "Not by reasoning is this apprehension attainable,"
say the Upanishads, and according to the Third Zen Patriarch "to seek Mind
with the [discriminating or logical] mind is the greatest of all mistakes." It is
a mistake because, in the words of the great Indian philosopher Radhakrishnan, "The real transcends, surrounds and overflows our miserable categories."[4]

Although intellectual analysis by itself is insufficient to acquire or comprehend this wisdom, one can subsequently derive intellectual ideas, psycholo-

gies and philosophies from this wisdom. Indeed, the perennial philosophy and the world's traditional transpersonal philosophies and psychologies probably were derived in just this way. Moreover, unless this wisdom is directly experienced in succeeding generations, traditions easily ossify into mere dogma.

So contemplatives first train the eye of contemplation in order to develop specific capacities and states of consciousness. Then they investigate, describe, and philosophize from the perspectives of both contemplative and ordinary states. This means that transpersonal philosophies and psychologies are multistate systems. Significant parts of their knowledge may therefore be state-specific and comprehensible only to those who have themselves adequately trained their eye of contemplation. The result is that their insights "cannot be judged by unenlightened people from the worm's eye view of book learning."[5]

For example, the idea that our sense of self, which we usually assume to be relatively stable and enduring, is actually constructed anew each moment out of a ceaseless flux of thoughts, images, and sensations may be an interesting concept when we read about it. But when seen directly in meditation it becomes undeniably clear, and by undercutting egocentricity it can be life-changing and helpful.

Aldous Huxley said, "Knowledge is a function of being."[6] Without contemplative training our being is not adequate for accessing such insights. According to the Buddhist economist E. F. Schumacher:

> If we do not have the requisite organ or instrument, or fail to use it, we are not *adequate* to this particular part or facet of the world with the result, as far as we are concerned, it simply does not exist.[7]

If it is true that without an open eye of contemplation, we are not fully adequate to the deeper profundities of transpersonal philosophies and psychologies, then what aspects of them are lost to us and how are we likely to respond to our truncated vision of them? One common response is simply to dismiss them as nonsensical. In such cases the entire wisdom of the traditions is lost to us.

In other cases the loss may be more insidious. For when we approach transpersonal disciplines without the requisite contemplative training, the more subtle, profound, state-specific depths tend to be overlooked. And what is crucial to understand is that we will not even recognize that we are overlooking these more profound depths of meaning.

This occurs because the higher "grades of significance" are lost. The easiest way of illuminating this term is by means of a classic example of the diverse responses and grades of significance that an object may elicit. For example, an animal may see an oddly shaped black and white object, a tribal person a rectangular flexible object with curious markings. To a Western child it is a book, while to an adult it may be a particular type of book, namely a book that makes incomprehensible, even ridiculous, claims about reality. Finally, to a physicist it may be a profound text on quantum physics.

What is important to see is that all the observers are partly correct in their characterization of the book, but all except the trained physicist are unaware how much more meaningful and significant the object is than they can recognize. And, most important, to the nonphysicist adult it is a book that seems incomprehensible, even ridiculous. What this example so nicely demonstrates is that when we cannot comprehend higher grades of significance, we can blithely believe that we have fully understood something whose true significance we have completely missed. As Schumacher pointed out:

> Facts do not carry labels indicating the appropriate level at which they ought to be considered. Nor does the choice of an inadequate level lead the intelligence into factual error or logical contradiction. All levels of significance up to the adequate level, i.e., up to the level of meaning in the example of the book, are equally factual, equally logical, equally objective, but not equally real. . . . When the level of the knower is not adequate to the level (or the grade of significance) of the object of knowledge, the result is not factual error but something much more serious: an inadequate and impoverished view of reality.[7]

This raises an arresting question: What higher grades of significance, what profound meanings and messages, does the world give us that we are overlooking? It is said that to a sage the leaves on the trees are like the pages of a sacred text, filled with transcendent meaning. We do not see things only as they are, but also as we are. Contemplative training changes the way we are and opens us to the hidden wisdom and higher grades of significance in transpersonal traditions, in the world, and in ourselves.

5. Technology of Transcendence
by Frances Vaughan and Roger Walsh

Here we are introduced to the idea that most of the important "new" psychological discoveries during the twentieth century were, in fact, revivals of far older ways of knowing. The task in the century ahead will be to develop our untapped human potential through these rediscovered inner technologies. The methods involved don't require further refinement of our logical mind, relying instead on six traditional processes that make up the art of transcendence.

WHEN HISTORIANS LOOK back on the twentieth century, they may find that two of the most important breakthroughs in Western psychology were not discoveries of new knowledge but recognitions of old wisdom.

First, psychological maturation can continue far beyond our arbitrary, culture-bound definitions of normality. There exist further developmental possibilities latent within us all. As William James pointed out, "Most people live, whether physically, intellectually or morally, in a very restricted circle of their potential being. They make use of a very small portion of their possible consciousness. . . . We all have reservoirs of life to draw upon, of which we do not dream."

Second, techniques exist for realizing transpersonal potentials. These techniques are part of an art or technology that has been refined over thousands of years in hundreds of cultures, and constitutes the contemplative core of the world's great religious traditions. This is the art or technology of transcendence, designed to catalyze transpersonal development. As such, it is based on two fundamental assumptions about the nature and potentials of the mind.

The first assumption is that our usual state of mind is suboptimal. In fact, the mind has been described as clouded, distorted, dreamlike, entranced and largely out of control. This has been recognized by psychologists and mystics of both East and West: Freud's culture-shaking recognition that "man is not even master in his own house . . . his own mind,"[1] echoed the Bhagavad Gita's despairing cry two thousand years earlier:

> *Restless man's mind is*
> *So strongly shaken*
> *In the grip of the senses:*

> *Gross and grown hard*
> *With stubborn desire. . . .*
> *Truly, I think*
> *The wind is no wilder.*[2]

In the words of Ram Dass, "We are all prisoners of our own mind. This realization is the first step on the journey to freedom."[3] Pir Vilayat Khan put it even more succinctly, "The bind is in the mind."

The second assumption is that although the untrained mind is clouded and out of control, it can be trained and clarified and this training catalyzes transpersonal potentials. The sages of both East and West, past and present, agree on this. Socrates said: "In order that the mind should see light instead of darkness, so the entire soul must be turned away from this changing world, until its eye can bear to contemplate reality and that supreme splendor which we call the Good. Hence there may well be an art whose aim would be to effect this very thing."[4] Likewise, according to Ramana Maharshi, "All scriptures without any exception proclaim that for salvation mind should be subdued."[5]

Although practices and techniques vary widely, there seem to be six common elements that constitute the heart of the art of transcendence: ethical training; development of concentration; emotional transformation; a redirection of motivation from egocentric, deficiency-based needs to higher motives, such as self-transcendence; refinement of awareness; and the cultivation of wisdom.

Ethics is widely regarded as an essential foundation of transpersonal development. Contemplative traditions, however, view ethics not in terms of conventional morality but rather as an essential discipline for training the mind. Contemplative introspection renders it painfully apparent that unethical behavior both stems from and reinforces destructive mental factors such as greed and anger. Conversely, ethical behavior undermines these and cultivates mental factors such as kindness, compassion, and calm. Ultimately, after transpersonal maturation occurs, ethical behavior is said to flow spontaneously as a natural expression of identification with all people and all life. For a person at this stage, which corresponds to Lawrence Kohlberg's highest stage of moral development, "whatever is . . . thought to be necessary for sentient beings happens all the time of its own accord."[6]

Attentional training and the cultivation of concentration are regarded as essential for overcoming the fickle wanderlust of the untrained mind. As E. F. Schumacher observed of attention, "No topic occupies a more central place in all traditional teaching; and no subject suffers more neglect, misunderstanding, and distortion in the thinking of the modern world."[7]

Attentional training is certainly misunderstood by Western psychology, which has unquestioningly accepted William James's century-old conclusion that: "Attention cannot be continuously sustained."[8] Yet James went further: "The faculty of voluntarily bringing back a wandering attention over and over again is the very root of judgment, character and will. No one is *compos sui* if he have it not. An education which would improve this faculty would be the education par excellence. . . . It is easier to define this ideal than to give practical direction for bringing it about."[9] Here, then, we have a stark contrast between traditional Western psychology, which says attention *cannot* be sustained, and the art of transcendence, which says that attention can and *must* be sustained if we are to mature beyond conventional developmental limits.

Being able to direct attention at will is so important because the mind tends to take on qualities of the objects to which it attends. For example, if we think of an angry person, we tend to feel angry; if of a loving person, we tend to feel loving. The person who can control attention can, therefore, control and cultivate specific emotions and motives. Ultimately, said the Indian sage Ramakrishna, the mind of such a person "is under his control; he is not under the control of his mind."[10]

Ethical behavior and attentional stability facilitate the third element of the art of transcendence: emotional transformation. There are three components to emotional transformation.

The first is the reduction of inappropriate destructive emotions such as fear and anger, a process which is well known in Western therapy. Of course, what is implied here is not repression or suppression but rather clear awareness of such emotions and consciously relinquishing them where appropriate.

The second component is the cultivation of positive emotions such as love, joy, and compassion. Whereas conventional Western therapies have excellent techniques for reducing negative emotions, they have virtually none for enhancing positive emotions such as these. In contrast, the art of transcendence contains a wealth of practices for cultivating these emotions to an intensity and extent undreamed of in Western psychology. Thus, for example, the Buddhist's compassion, the Bhakti's love, and the Christian's agape are said to reach their full flowering only when they unconditionally and unwaveringly encompass all creatures, without exception and without reserve.

This mindboggling intensity and scope of positive emotion is facilitated by a third component of emotional transformation: the cultivation of equanimity, an emotional imperturbability which allows love and compassion to remain unconditional and unwavering even under duress. This capacity is the Stoic's *apatheia,* the Christian Father's *divine apatheia,* the Buddhist's equanimity, the Taoist principle of "the equality of things," which leads beyond "the trouble of preferring one thing to another," and the contemporary philosopher Franklin Merrell-Wolff's "high indifference."

Ethical behavior, attentional stability, and emotional transformation all work together, along with practices such as meditation, to redirect motivation along healthier, more transpersonal directions. The net effect is a reduction in the intensity and compulsivity of motivation and a change in its direction, variety, and focus. Most important, the compulsive power of both addiction and aversion is reduced.

As motivation becomes less scattered and more focused, the things desired become more subtle, more internal; there is less emphasis on getting and more on giving. Desires gradually become less self-centered and more self-transcendent.

Traditionally this motivational shift was seen as "purification" or as "giving up attachment to the world." In contemporary terms it is movement up Maslow's hierarchy of needs, Arnold Toynbee's process of "etherealization," and the means for reaching the philosopher Kierkegaard's goal in which "purity of heart is to will one thing."

The reduction of compulsive craving is said to result in a corresponding reduction in intrapsychic conflict and suffering, a claim now supported by studies of advanced meditators.[11] In the words of the Athenian philosopher Epicurus, "If you want to make a man happy, add not to his riches but take away from his desires." This is not to imply that redirecting motives and relinquishing craving is necessarily easy. In Aristotle's estimation, "I count him braver who overcomes his desires than him who conquers his enemies; for the hardest victory is the victory over self."[12]

The great wisdom traditions agree that in our usual untrained state of mind, awareness and perception are insensitive and impaired: fragmented by attentional instability, colored by clouding emotions, and distorted by scattered desires. Accordingly we are said to mistake shadows for reality (Plato) because we see "through a glass darkly" (St. Paul), a "reducing valve" (Aldous Huxley), or "narrow chinks" (Blake). . . .

The fifth element of the art of transcendence, therefore, aims to refine perception and awareness and render them more sensitive, more accurate, and more appreciative of the freshness and novelty of each moment of experience. One of the primary tools for this is meditation. . . .

The sixth quality cultivated by the technology of transcendence is wisdom, which is something significantly more than knowledge. Whereas knowledge is something we have, wisdom is something we become. Developing it requires self-transformation. This transformation is fostered by opening defenselessly to the reality of "things as they are," including the enormous extent of suffering in the world. In the words of the psalms, this is the recognition that we are "as dust . . . our lives are but toil and trouble, they are soon gone, they come to an end like a sigh" (Psalm 90); "what man can live and never see death?" (Psalm 89).

In our own time, existentialism has emphasized this recognition most forcefully. With its graphic description of the inevitable existential challenges of meaninglessness, freedom, and death it has rediscovered aspects of the Buddha's first noble truth, which holds that unsatisfactoriness is an inherent part of existence. Both existentialism and the wisdom traditions agree that, in the words of Thomas Hardy, "if a way to the Better there be, it exacts a full look at the Worst."[13]

Whereas existentialism leaves us marooned in a no-exit situation of heightened awareness of existential limits and suffering, the art or technology of transcendence offers a way out. For existentialism, wisdom consists of recognizing these painful facts of life and accepting them with authenticity, resoluteness (Heidegger), and courage (Tillich). For contemplative traditions this existential attitude is a preliminary rather than a final wisdom and is used to redirect motivation away from trivial, egocentric pursuits toward the contemplative practices that lead to deeper wisdom. This deeper wisdom recognizes that the sense of being marooned in a noexit situation of limits and suffering can be transcended through transforming the self that seems to suffer. Such wisdom springs from the development of direct intuitive insight into the nature of mind, self, consciousness, and cosmos. This insight matures into the direct intuitive wisdom—beyond words, thoughts, concepts, or even images of any kind—which transforms and liberates. And with this liberation the goal of the art of transcendence is realized.

These, then, seem to be six essential, common elements, qualities or processes that constitute the heart of the art of transcendence. Of course different practices and traditions focus more on some processes than on others. For example, Indian philosophy divides practices into various yogas. All of them acknowledge ethics as an essential foundation. Raja yoga emphasizes meditation and the training of attention and awareness; Bhakti yoga is more emotional and focuses on the cultivation of love; Karma yoga uses work in the world to refine motivation; and Jnana yoga hones the intellect and wisdom. It seems, however, that to the extent a tradition is authentic—that is, capable of fostering transpersonal development and transcendence[14]—it will incorporate all the elements of the technology of transcendence.

Almost all paths include some form of meditation. Meditation is central because it works directly on so many processes essential to transpersonal development. At its best it stabilizes attention, transforms emotions and motivation, cultivates awareness, heightens sensitivity to unethical behavior, and fosters wisdom. If dreams are the royal road to the unconscious, meditation is the royal road to the transpersonal.

What then is meditation? The term refers to a family of practices that train attention in order to bring mental processes under greater voluntary control and to cultivate specific mental qualities such as awareness, insight, concentration, equanimity, and love. It aims for development of optimal states of consciousness and psychological well-being.

The term "yoga" refers to a family of practices with the same aims as meditation, but in addition to meditation, yogas encompass ethics, lifestyle, body posture, breathing, and intellectual study. The origins of meditation and yoga are lost in antiquity, but they are at least four thousand years old and perhaps considerably older, and specific practices have evolved over centuries.

There are many varieties of meditation and meditative experiences. The best known involve sitting quietly, but other practices include walking, dancing, and bringing conscious awareness to everyday activities. Meditation can focus on an almost infinite variety of objects, ranging from dead corpses to the breath to sublime mind states. Needless to say, these many practices result in a wide range of experiences. Even within a single tradition such as Sufism, different meditative practices have overlapping but also distinct effects.

These different practices are often divided into two major types: concentration and awareness practices. Concentration meditations attempt to focus attention unwaveringly on a single object such as the breath. Awareness practices, on the other hand, open awareness in a choiceless, nonjudgmental manner to whatever experiences arise.

The history of meditation in the West has had many distinct phases. At various times in their long histories, Judaism, Christianity, and Islam offered various meditative techniques, but they never attained the popularity and centrality that such techniques enjoy in Asian traditions such as Hinduism and Buddhism.

In the twentieth century, initial reports of the results of Asian meditation met with skepticism from Western psychologists and psychiatrists. This skepticism was especially strong in the psychoanalytic community, which for the most part dismissed meditation, along with practices such as shamanism and yoga, as primitive or regressive and diagnosed their practitioners as pathological. The eminent psychoanalyst Franz Alexander, for example, titled one of his papers "Buddhist Training as an Artificial Catatonia."[15] Yet as Ken Wilber has pointed out, the "facile equation of the mystic with the psychotic can be done only by demonstrating one's ignorance of the subtleties involved."[16] Alexander's proclamation now stands as a classic example of the "pre/trans fallacy" and mistaking the transpersonal for the prepersonal.

Since the 1960s, meditation has become widely accepted and there has been a veritable explosion of popular, professional, and research interest. It has been estimated that by 1980 over six million people in the United States alone had learned some form of meditation.

Part Two

Ancient Avenues
of Wisdom

*E*ach epoch of history has been preoccupied with different types of knowledge, and each has relied on a state of consciousness that could produce that wisdom. In the ancient world, still rooted in nonduality, it was understood that individuals operate within a greater intelligence, and the systems of knowledge persevering from that time reflect that inseparable linkage.

The social settings for unitive events, like the ancient oracles of Delphi, no longer exist, but we do have records of them in some of our greatest literature. Oracular guidance figures in the epics of Homer and the plays of Sophocles and Aeschylus. In the Greek religions, a priestess ritually unified her consciousness with a greater source of intelligence, so that her prophetic message emanated from another world. Nonduality is also reflected in the belief that a higher consciousness is expressed when a storyteller embodies his words, when a singer unites with her song, when a cook and the food are of one mind, and when individuals truly join with the tribe.

The systems of knowledge described in Part II are embedded in nonduality. The *I Ching,* for example, is an oracle in the sense that it is used for predictive purposes and to decipher hidden meanings in real world events. It was brought back into popularity in the early part of this century due to Jung's and others' interests in worldwide archetypal mythologies. Theosophy, a popular philosophical school embracing esoteric and mystical knowledge in the 1800s, also promoted nondual systems of knowing. In Britain, the Society of the Golden Dawn included many writers, intellectuals, and political figures of the day. Such societies helped to proliferate interest in nonordinary realities represented by systems like the Tarot, which is a modern-day version of an ancient oracle.

The New Age movement has brought back interest in divination, trance work, and ritual, accompanied by a special fascination with indigenous cultures and their modes of knowing and healing. However, much of this outpouring of research and anecdotal material about the planet's original cultures is only the superficial husk of the real teaching. Reading about a "field study" for example, may reveal the sequence of events in a ritual and how the participants responded, but such sensory-level descriptions do not explore the actual states of mind that make foresight and healing possible.

Likewise, a Tarot reading given today may use essentially the same deck of cards that made its appearance centuries ago, yet the quality of guidance still depends on the operator's capacity. Ordinary consciousness produces a mechanical rendition of memorized meanings for a spread. But when that same spread is contemplated from a unified state of mind, the reader's inner imagery can yield exponentially better information.

Despite all criticism, the New Age movement touches many people who eventually find their way to the deeper teachings that rely upon nondual awareness. The works of Joseph Campbell, Mircea Eliade, and Carl Jung have also contributed to revitalized interest in inner ways of knowing.

Perhaps nonordinary wisdom is best expressed through Shamanism, the oldest-known body of spiritual practices. Rooted in the dawn of human consciousness, this tradition understands that the powers, knowledge, and vital forces of the natural world can be experienced both as events "out there" and as a parallel reality within ourselves.

The authors in Part II focus on ancient paths to inner knowing that have endured over time. An exploration of these ancient systems will prepare us for the readings in parts V and VI, which show us how to rediscover the unified consciousness within which each system is grounded.

6.   The Tradition of Oracles and Channels
by Arthur Hastings

The process called channeling can be traced from the oracular traditions of Delphi, Tibet, and Biblical prophecy to the channeling phenomenon of the 1980s, when America experienced a resurgence of interest in the method. Variously called prophecy, oracle, revelation, spirit communication, possession, and the inspiration of muses, Hastings sees channeling as producing ideas, creative works, and personal guidance "from a source outside the individual personality, as if the person is serving as a channel for some other, nonphysical communicator."

What is currently called channeling has existed as a source of information since the beginning of recorded time. Here we see the interplay between a nonphysical communicator, and the channel's subjective personality, in what is perhaps the oldest demonstration of inner knowing on the planet.

AT THE ORACLE location was a shrine or temple and a priestess or priest who spoke for the god, or who would conduct a divination process. The questions asked of the oracles were concerned with personal questions as well as weighty matters of politics, war, worship, and philosophy. The following matters are some that were asked by common citizens of the oldest Greek oracle, that of Zeus at Dodona in Greece:

> Would it be better for Onasimos to get married now, or should he avoid it?
> Would it be advisable for Ariston to go to Syracuse?
> Timodamus asks whether he should invest his money in a trading fleet or in a business.
> Lysias wants to know if he will be successful in sea trade.[1]

The Dodona oracle was located in a grove of oak trees sacred to Zeus. The questions were written on thin lead plates, rolled, and put into a jar. The priestess would take one out, listen to the rustling of the trees in the wind, and pronounce the words she heard. These would be written down as the response of the god. For example, to the question of Timodamus, the oracle responded, "Stay in the town and open a business. . . ." Later, the oak tree voices were replaced by a priestess who went into a trance state to speak the words of Zeus.

The oracles were consulted on all major political, economic, and military matters; their answers were kept on record, and their reputation for accuracy was high. The Roman senator Cicero observed that the reputation of the oracles could not have been so high had they not been correct over the centuries. In addition to divination of the future, requests to the gods, and judgments on controversies, the answers sought were often counsel or guidance on decisions. There were several instances of apparent psychic functioning on record. A Greek military leader named Cimon sent a delegation to the oracle of Amon in Egypt. The oracle sent the delegation home, saying that Cimon had already gone to Amon. The delegation left, not understanding the pronouncement, until they learned that Cimon had died the very day they spoke with the oracle.[2]

DELPHI

There were many oracles in the Near East, each the site of a deity, including Ishtar, Hercules, Apollo, Athena, Artemis, Areas, Zeus, Amun, and Leto. The best known by moderns is the oracle of Apollo at Delphi in Greece, which had the recommendation "Know Thyself" written on the temple.[3] Other oracles of Apollo were at Claros and Dydima. From the myths, it seems that the Apollo cult took Delphi over from Ge, the Earth goddess. The spokesperson for the god remained a woman, who paid homage to the Earth in her prayer of invocation before she prophesied. She was known as the Pythia, perhaps after the python, sacred to Ge.

Questions would be brought to the oracle by petitioners who ranged from the leaders of the country to the common populace. The Pythia would go into a trance and be possessed by the god to speak the answer. The process was one of receiving information from outside the conscious mind as in mediumship, channeling, and prophecy.

The Ritual

The priestess entered the prophetic state with a ritual. She would first bathe ritually, then be led into the temple. The Pythia was robed and had a wool strip placed around her forehead. A laurel crown was placed on her head. A young goat was sprinkled with water. If it began shivering (a propitious sign), it was sacrificed. The priestess went into the inner room where she drank from waters of the stream Cassotis, which was supposed to stimulate her powers. She was given bay laurel leaves (sacred to Apollo) to chew. More laurel leaves were burned as incense, and there were other perfumes and smoke in the air. Then the priestess sat on the tripod, a seat with three legs, to prophesy.

We recognize this ritual as an altered-state induction procedure which would put the priestess into a trance state. Many religious and spiritual ceremonies embody ritual purification, incense, special clothing, and other evocative techniques to destabilize the normal state and create a trance state. The theory of this type of state change has been described by Charles Tart in his book *States of Consciousness*.[4] The state is created with the intention and expectation of being possessed by Apollo, and these expectations determine the nature of the trance and what happens in it, similar to the idea of demand characteristics in hypnosis, which are assumptions held by the individual that act like hypnotic suggestions.

According to a description by Apollonius of Tyana, the Pythia changed physically when she was possessed. Her chest swelled, she flushed then paled, and her limbs trembled convulsively more and more violently; her eyes flashed fire, she foamed at the mouth, and her hair stood on end. Then she tore off the strip of wool around her head and spoke a few words, which the attendant priests wrote down.[5] Other sources say that the priestess spoke in a different voice when prophesying.[6] As the god Apollo, she spoke in first person. Also, she originally gave answers in hexameter and elegaic couplets. In later centuries, the versification stopped, and the priests were responsible for putting the answer into rhyme.

We see here familiar aspects of trance channeling: an induction ritual that leads to an altered state; the personality of the individual being replaced by that of the god: the changes in posture, behavior, and voice; speaking in verse.

The Case of Croesus

An illustration of oracular advice is a series of messages given to King Croesus of Lydia, about 550 B.C., by the oracle of Apollo at Delphi. First, the king tested all the famous oracles by sending delegations to ask each what he was doing on the hundredth day after the delegation left. On the hundredth day, in his capital of Sardis, Croesus cut up a lamb and a tortoise and boiled them in a brass pot. Of all the oracles, only the Pythia at Delphi was correct, saying:

> Can I not number all the grains of sand,
> And measure all the water in the sea?
> Tho' a man speak not I can understand;
> Nor are the thoughts of dumb men hid from me.

A tortoise boiling with a lamb I smell:
Bronze underlies and covers them as well.[7]

Persuaded that Delphi was truly prophetic, Croesus asked his questions. First, should he attack Persia, an empire that was beginning to threaten his kingdom, and should he find an ally? Second, would he have a long reign?

The oracle answered, "After crossing the Halys [a river], Croesus will destroy a great empire." And he was told to ally himself with the most powerful of the Greek states. On the second question, the prophecy was that he should flee when a mule became the king of the Medes. Croesus interpreted all these as favorable, but his interpretation was colored by his hopes. Croesus did ally himself successfully with Sparta but, when he attacked the Persians, he was defeated; the empire that was destroyed was his own. The ruler that conquered him was Cyrus, not an animal but a mule in the sense that he was of mixed parentage, Mede and Persian.[8]

Croesus was wise to test the oracle before he posed his important questions. This is a practice that should be matter of fact with any psychic or prophetic claims. Indeed, channels themselves should be the first to test and evaluate the quality of their channeled messages.

PSYCHOLOGICAL FACTORS IN PROPHECIES

The answers that the oracle gave to Croesus were ambiguous, though this was not apparent to Croesus. Why were they phrased thus, when the oracle apparently had the capability for precise and matter of fact statements? Perhaps because the oracle was facing a difficult situation. Here was one of the most powerful and wealthy rulers in the world (hence the phrase "wealth of Croesus"). The correct answers to his questions were definitely against his interests and could incur his wrath. Remember that the Greeks had a propensity to kill the messenger who brought them bad news. On the other hand, if the oracle gave incorrect answers and predicted that Croesus would triumph when he would actually be defeated, the failure would be spectacular, with severe consequences for the Pythia's reputation. The resolution to the dilemma was to speak in a manner that gave the correct answer, but was semantically ambiguous. Croesus could interpret the answers in the framework of his desire for them to be favorable. Others would, in retrospect, see the true meanings and not blame the oracle. The responses were adapted to the complex needs of the "truth," the situation, and the audience.

This analysis is my speculation on the inner process of the oracle. I do not suggest that this situation was consciously analyzed at the time; analysis is not a job for ego consciousness, but is the sort of thing that is usually handled elsewhere in the mind (or perhaps outside the mind). It requires that the several needs, the conflicting points of view, and the consequences of alternatives are all taken into consideration, and the answers respond to whatever priorities are established among them.

Whether that is what happened with that prophecy or not, it is likely that messages of contemporary channels are processed in this way. I have listened to channeled messages that were arranged and phrased in terms that were most responsive to the particular audience in contrast to other audiences the entity had addressed. No messages from channels come through unadorned. All channeled information is modified by the channel and adapted to the audience, the circumstances, the purposes, and the consequences.

The part that Croesus played in the affair should not be overlooked. He was given a message that was not explicit. It was stated poetically, and the referent for "empire" was not clear. We have to say that it was his projection, no doubt unconscious, that the empire to be destroyed was Persian. It was an interpretation that linked with his hopes and so gained uncritical emotional confirmation. In the same manner, when channeled prophecies (or other messages) are ambiguous, they are likely to be interpreted to confirm a person's expectations, desires, or fears. This is also true of situations involving psychics, physicians, and others who are given authority, especially if the client's feelings about the situation have been suppressed or repressed.

THE ARK OF THE COVENANT AS AN ORACLE

The word "oracle" originally referred to the place where the gods spoke. By association, it became used for the person who spoke the words and even the messages themselves. In the original meaning, classical oracles were sites located in sacred groves, at springs, and at other locations in Greece, Africa, Babylonia, and other lands surrounding the Mediterranean. Rituals similar to those at Delphi and Dodona were used. People desiring answers would go to those sites, or send a representative, to ask their questions.

The Israelites, on the other hand, were a nomadic tribe and had no land of their own for oracles. Further, their deity had created a covenant with them that was exclusive; they could neither worship other gods nor make statues to take with them. Yet, their religion was one of revelation. How were they to receive the word of God?

There may have been a mode of revelation, using the process of channeling, that took place before the prophets began to emerge in Jewish history. The Ark of the Covenant, which the Israelites took with them as they traveled, may have served as a portable oracle shrine specifically for Yahweh. The Ark was a rectangular chest which was a cabinet for the Ten Commandments and, later, the Torah. It was considered the resting place of God, and it also was used as a pulpit.

On top of the chest was a cover of gold with a winged figure fastened at each end to protect it. Said the Lord to Moses, "There I shall come to meet you; there from above the throne of mercy [cover], from between the two cherubs that are on the Ark of the Testimony, I shall give you all my commands for the sons of Israel" (Exodus 25:23). This covering, or seat, was God's answering place. John Wyclyffe originally gave the name of this seat as "oracle" in his translation of the Bible.

Instructions for the sanctuary included special robes and a breastplate for the priest, incense, and a spice mixture for anointing the priests and equipment. The sanctuary was a tent; the Ark, altar, tables, and other equipment were made to be portable, to go with the people as they moved. The breastplate had on it something referred to as Urim and Thummim, also called an oracle. It is speculated that these were stones for divination, but knowledge of them is lost. Interestingly, Joseph Smith, prophet of the Mormon Church, said that he translated the Book of Mormon by using gazing stones called Urim and Thummim.

The Ark was thus a holy shrine which carried the presence of God. The divine instructions lay out ritual preparations, very similar to those that occurred later at Delphi. Perhaps their use could put the priest into a prophetic state in which he received the word of God. Thus, the Israelites could receive oracular communication from their own God wherever their travels took them. The priest could use the Ark as a pulpit, just as the Pythia spoke from the sacred tripod of Apollo. There was a social function to this portable shrine. It was a religious invention that replaced the elaborate temples of the Babylonians and Egyptians and the sacred oracle sites of the local gods.

In the Bible, there is no report of a priest going through the preparation ritual and then speaking the words of God. The writings do say that the voice of

God spoke from the Holy of Holies where the Ark was kept. If the Ark was an oracle, then this voice could have been the priest, embodying the deity or reporting the words of an inner voice. Now, the traditions around the Ark are lost, and whatever they were, its use now is as a cabinet for the scrolls.

TIBETAN ORACLES

Oracles were used in Tibet before Buddhist times, but were incorporated into the religious and political structure when the country was united into a central government. The earliest, according to Lama Govinda (1966) in *The Way of the White Clouds,* was in the monastery of Samye. The high priest would become possessed by the ancient guardian spirits of Tibet whenever the ceremony in their honor was performed. In this trance, they would speak through him and answer questions. In the time of the fifth Dalai Lama (1617–1682), the Nanchung oracle at the monastery of Drepung was recognized as the official state oracle of Tibet. It was consulted on locating reincarnations of high lamas and on important political decisions. Questions of less import could be asked after the business of state was completed. Many of the important monasteries in Tibet had their own oracles. Each of the oracle priests had to be confirmed by the state oracle after going through rigorous training and testing. The Tibetan government in exile in India still uses the state oracle. In 1987, Asian scholar David Komito told me that the position was held by a frail, elderly monk. When the monk enters the oracular process, he goes through an astonishing transformation into a frenzied, vigorous being with the appearance and behaviors of the protector deities.

Govinda gives a vivid description of an oracle session at the monastery of Dungkar Gompa in Tibet. The priest was clad in brocade robes and wore a jeweled crown. Monks chanted guttural invocations as cymbals, bells, and drums played. Incense from censers filled the temple. The oracle priest began to shake with convulsive movements, "as if the dark powers from the depth of the earth, the chthonic powers that governed humanity before the dawn of history, had seized his body and threatened to burst it."[9] His face changed to become like a terrifying deity.

A senior monk held up questions, written on pieces of paper and tightly folded. The oracle priest, possessed by one of the six protectors, seized a sword and swung it about with flashing speed. Five or six of the monk attendants battled with him and, by weight of numbers, forced him back to the throne. Finally, he became calmer. He spoke and his words were recorded. Then he was possessed by another of the guardians, and the process repeated. The ceremony continued for hours, leaving the priest exhausted. Later the oracle priest told Govinda that he remembered nothing of the experience, though physically the aftereffects lasted for days.

The similarities of the Tibetan and Delphic oracles are obvious. There was a special temple ritual, a frenzied possession by the deity, and responses to questions. Each incorporated more ancient traditions. Each was consulted on matters of state and important religious decisions. The process is one of possession in which the individual is taken over by the deity.

The Role of the Oracles

The decisions of Delphi and Nanchung demonstrate the important role that oracles can play. There was no important question in the Near East that was not submitted to Delphi when the oracle was at its height. It was understood to be the embodiment of Apollo and to indicate the will of the god for city-states, colonies, commerce, and religious matters. The responses of Apollo provided guidance and authority in matters where reason or knowledge were inadequate and, in many cases, the decision might otherwise have been made by force. The high regard in which the oracle was held indicates it did this with success. Likewise, the Tibetan oracles provide information and authority for important societal matters, an example being the finding of children who are identified as reincarnated lamas. Today, in addition to those of the Tibetan society, there are similar oracles in many cultures such as Brazil, parts of Africa, and Asia. It is noteworthy that these and possession oracles in all societies are also available for personal questions on health, family, business, and other matters. Anthropologists sometimes distinguish between macro-decisions at the level of society or government and micro-decisions with regard to individual lives. The oracles lent their knowledge and authority to needs at both levels.

7. Synchronistic Knowing: Understanding Meaningful Coincidence by Jean Shinoda Bolen

The Tao has many names, each of which refers to a unifying principle that underlies our perception of constantly changing events. Jung has been a primary exponent of synchronistic happenings as manifestations of "an acausal connecting principle called Tao." He theorized that people, animals, plants, and inanimate objects are all linked through a collective unconscious, which shows itself through meaningful coincidences and events. These occurrences are constantly taking place in unrecognized ways, but when an observer notices and gives meaning to a coincidence, then the "unknowable" becomes known.

JUNG WROTE ABOUT synchronicity fairly late in his professional life. His major exposition, "Synchronicity: An Acausal Connecting Principle," was published in 1952, when he was in his midseventies. He described it as an effort "to give a consistent account of everything I have to say on the subject," in order to "open up a very obscure field which is philosophically of greatest importance." It is a very complex, multifootnoted elaboration of an essay, "On Synchronicity," that had been given as a lecture the year before. Possibly because this monograph is difficult reading, possibly because the concept itself is difficult to grasp by intellect alone and requires an intuitive facility, synchronicity has been more in the closet than out in the world.

In 1930, Jung had introduced the "synchronistic principle" in a memorial address for his friend, Richard Wilhelm, the sinologist who translated many ancient Chinese texts. His first description of synchronicity however was in the foreword to the Wilhelm-Baynes translation of the *I Ching* or *Book of Changes* in 1949. In the thirty years preceding, Jung had made other fleeting mentions of synchronicity in his lectures and writing. This was a concept long incubated.

"Synchronicity" is a descriptive term for the link between two events that are connected through their meaning, a link that cannot be explained by cause and effect. To illustrate synchronicity, Jung described an incident with a patient, a woman who "always knew better about everything" and whose analysis consequently was not going very well.

> After several fruitless attempts to sweeten her rationalism with a somewhat more human understanding, I had to confine myself to the hope that something unex-

pected and irrational would turn up, something that would burst the intellectual retort into which she had sealed herself. Well, I was sitting opposite her one day with my back to the window, listening to her flow of rhetoric. She had an impressive dream the night before, in which someone had given her a golden scarab—a costly piece of jewelry. While she was still telling me this dream, I heard something behind me gently tapping on the window. I turned around and saw that it was a fairly large flying insect that was knocking against the window-pane from outside in the obvious effort to get into the dark room. This seemed to me very strange. I opened the window immediately and caught the insect in the air as it flew in. It was a scarabaeid beetle, whose gold-green color most nearly resembles that of a golden scarab. I handed the beetle to my patient with the words, "Here is your scarab." This experience punctured the desired hole in her rationalism and broke the ice of her intellectual resistance. The treatment could now be continued with satisfactory results.

For the scarablike beetle to come into the room at that moment was an eerie coincidence for this woman. Meaningful coincidences such as this reach in to touch a deep feeling level in the psyche. This woman needed a transforming emotional experience, which the scarab provided. Interestingly, the event symbolically paralleled her situation. The scarab is an Egyptian symbol of rebirth or transformation—"it" needed to enter the analysis. When the scarabaeid beetle entered the room, transformation of a rigid attitude could begin, new growth could happen.

Synchronicity requires a human participant, for it is a subjective experience in which the person gives meaning to the coincidence. "Meaning" differentiates synchronicity from a synchronous event. A synchronous event is anything simultaneous, events that occur at the same moment. Clocks are synchronized, airplanes are scheduled to take off at the same time, several people walk into the same auditorium at the same moment, but no one sees anything significant in these "coincidences." In synchronicity, however, the meaningful "coincidence" occurs within a subjective time frame. The person links the two events together, and the events need not occur simultaneously, although this is often the case.

Jung described three types of synchronicity. In the first category, there is *a coincidence between mental content (which could be a thought or feeling) and outer event.* This seemed to be the case in an incident between myself and my then four-year-old daughter. I was in the kitchen in the midst of dinner preparation and mentioned to my husband Jim that I needed some flowers for the table. The children were playing outside, quite out of range of hearing. Moments later Melody came in through the length of the house, a bouquet of pink geraniums in her hands, saying "Here, Mommy." The incident of the scarab beetle exemplifies this category, in which the outer event uncannily reflects what is happening psychologically in that moment.

In the second group of synchronistic events, *a person has a dream or vision, which coincides with an event that is taking place at a distance (and is later verified).* It is an awareness of what is happening without using any of the five senses. For example, my grandfather had an uncanny way of knowing when an old friend or relative would die. The person would appear to him in a dream or in a waking vision, carrying a suitcase. In this way, he would know that they were leaving and moving on. My mother remembers his remarking on several occasions that so-and-so died—my grandfather had "seen" him on his way with a suitcase. Then, often weeks later, news would come verifying what Grandfather already knew clairvoyantly. Because he had come to America from Japan, a considerable distance separated my grandfather in New York City from relatives and many old friends. The news took a relatively long time to travel via standard means, by sea over the Pacific, by land to the East Coast. A historical event in this category is Swedenborg's "Vision of the Great Fire" in Stockholm, in which he described what he "saw" to others. Days later, the news arrived of the actual event, which had occurred at the time when he had had the vision and as he had described it.

In the third synchronistic category, *a person has an image (as a dream, vision, or premonition) about something that will happen in the future, which then does occur.* When I was pregnant, my husband Jim was sure about the sex of each child to come, based on a strong psychic impression, and I had the intuition that he really did know. So sure were we that common sense did not prevail— we had only a girl's name, Melody Jean, picked for our first child, our daughter, and only a boy's name for our son, Andre Joseph, who arrived less than two years later. And President Lincoln, just prior to his assassination, reported having dreams in which he saw his body lying in state, which is a historical example of the coincidence between a dream and a future happening.

In each situation, an actual event coincided with a thought, vision, dream, or premonition. My own examples are not particularly dramatic and may not be at all convincing to someone else, yet they stand out in my memory because of the feelings that accompanied the events: the sense of the bond between all of us—that Melody and I were tuned into one another, that Jim would know "who" I was carrying. The accompanying sense of connection is what was meaningful to me when the outer event coincided with the thought or premonition. Synchronicity is the principle that Jung postulates as the link connecting psyche and event in a meaningful coincidence, the participant determining (through purely subjective feelings) whether the coincidences are "meaningful." To *fully* appreciate what a synchronistic event is, one may need to personally experience an uncanny coincidence and feel a spontaneous emotional response—of chills up the spine, or awe, or warmth—feelings that often accompany synchronicity. Ideally, there should be no way to account for the coincidence rationally or by pure chance.

Some important differences exist between synchronicity and causality. Causality has to do with *objective* knowledge: Observation and reasoning are used to explain how one event arises directly out of another. When a rock is thrown at a window and the window breaks, cause and effect are involved. It does not matter who does the throwing, when or where it happens, or who is watching. Causality says that a rock thrown with enough force will break a glass window. In contrast, synchronicity has to do with *subjective* experience—if a person has a sudden premonition warning him or her to move away from a window and if seconds later a rock flies through it, the awareness of the premonition makes the broken window a synchronistic event. The timing is significant to the person, for whom the inner psychological premonitory feeling was in some unknown way linked to an outer event, which then followed.

To appreciate cause and effect, one needs the ability to observe outer events and to think logically. To appreciate a synchronistic event, one needs the ability to note an inner subjective state, a thought, feeling, vision, dream, or premonition and to intuitively link it with a related outer event. Synchronicity is a *co*-incidence of events that is meaningful to the participant; thus each synchronistic experience is unique. Causality is a sequence of events that can be logically explained and is generally repeatable.

Jung maintained that the collective unconscious or the archetypal layer of the unconscious (two terms for the same phenomenon) was involved in synchronistic events. While he agreed with Freud that we each have a personal unconscious that owes its existence to personal experience and would contain whatever was forgotten or repressed, Jung also described a deeper layer of the unconscious, which he called the *collective unconscious* and which he considered universal and inborn.

What the collective unconscious is and what archetypes are took Jung hundreds of pages to elaborate. Two volumes of his collected works—Volume 9,

Part 1: *The Archetypes and the Collective Unconscious,* and Volume 9, Part 2: *Aion*—provide the nucleus of Jung's theory. So it is presumptuous, but necessary, to explain archetypes in a few paragraphs here, in order to show the relationship between archetypes and synchronicity.

Jung describes archetypes as "patterns of instinctual behavior," saying that "There are as many archetypes as there are typical situations in life. Endless repetition has engraved these experiences into our psychic constitution." Examples of archetypal situations are those such as birth and death, marriage, mother and child bonds, or heroic struggles. Themes of relationship and conflict raised in Greek tragedies, myths, or modern plays often concern archetypal situations. It is because they touch a common chord in us all that they have universal appeal. The common chord is this archetypal layer.

Yet another definition of archetypes that Jung uses refers to "primordial images," or archetypal figures that become activated and then clothed with personally derived emotional coloration. This occurs when an emotional situation develops that corresponds to a particular archetype. For example, a person may go to hear a lecture from an elderly man, whose presence and words evoke an emotional response to the archetype of the Wise Old Man. Immediately, that man becomes "numinous" or awesome; he is experienced as being wise and powerful; every word uttered by him seems charged with significance. Accepted as the Wise Old Man, whatever he says is not examined critically. Considered as a source of wisdom, his every word, however mundane, seems a pearl of wisdom. The archetype has become personified—clothed as this particular man, who is given all the attributes of the archetype. Other examples of archetypal figures are the divine child, all-giving mother, patriarchal father, temptress, or trickster—all are symbolic, recurring figures in dreams, literature, and religions.

When the archetypal level of the collective unconscious is touched in a situation, there is emotional intensity as well as a tendency for symbolic expression. Then the usual everyday level of experience becomes altered; there is more "magic" in the air, one can become "inspired," or be "on a crusade." Colloquial expressions acknowledge this change in psychological level: "What the devil got into him anyway?" or "He got caught in the grip of an idea" or "She went out of her mind with fear or rage."

When this emotionally charged archetypal level is active, then dream images of great intensity and symbolic meaning may arise, and synchronistic events are more likely to occur. Both dreams and synchronistic events are expressed symbolically, which shows their common connection in the collective unconscious. However, this does not "explain" how or why synchronicity occurs—it merely notes that there is a connection between synchronicity and an active archetype in the collective unconscious.

Jung described the relationship between the collective unconscious and synchronistic events in a 1945 letter to Dr. J. B. Rhine, the noted extrasensory perception researcher. Jung said that the collective unconscious behaved "*as if it were one and not as if it were split into many individuals*" and as manifesting itself "*not only in human beings but also at the same time in animals and even in physical conditions.*" Jung then gave an example to illustrate this:

> I walked with a woman patient in the wood. She tells me about the first dream in her life that had made an everlasting impression on her. She had seen a spectral fox coming downstairs in her parental home. At this moment, a real fox comes out of the trees not forty yards away and walks quietly on the path ahead of us for several minutes. The animal behaves as if it were a partner in the situation.

This is one of those eerie synchronicities that seem to be saying that what is being discussed in that moment is highly emotionally charged and important. What the fox represented must have been a central issue in her family situation.

In his autobiography, *Memories, Dreams and Reflections,* Jung described the synchronistic event that had the greatest personal significance for him. It had occurred at the end of a lengthy and lonely period that followed his break with Freud. He had differed with Freud on a major premise, saying that incest was a symbolic rather than a literal problem, as Freud held. This "excommunicated" Jung from the psychoanalytic movement, leaving him without colleagues. Jung saw his patients, and continued to work on understanding the psyche in isolation. His theoretical differences brought his very significant friendship with Freud to an end and resulted in his expulsion from the professional community around Freud. He described this as "*a period of inner uncertainty, a state of disorientation.*" It was a time when he had not yet found his own footing. Instead of listening to patients with a theory in mind, he resolved to listen to their dreams and fantasies with a completely open mind, merely asking them, "What occurs to you in connection with that?" or "How do you mean that, where does it come from, and what do you think about it?" He did the same with his own dreams, delved into his own childhood memories, and followed an impulse to build a miniature town at the edge of a lake while his thinking clarified. In exploring the contents from his unconscious—his dreams, visions, and fantasies—he drew pictures and came across psychic material that was the same as found in children, mental patients, and mythic imagination. This repetition of motifs and images in individuals and in the world's literature pointed toward the concept of collectively held archetypes.

He then became engrossed with mandalas, which figure prominently in Eastern mystical religions and in the spontaneous drawings of people in turmoil, and tried to understand what they symbolized. (Mandalas are drawings that have a center point, often a circle within a square.) The idea gradually emerged that the mandala represented a meaning-giving center of the personality—which Jung called the Self and which was for him, the goal of psychic development.

He conceptualized the Self as a midpoint related to both ego and unconscious, yet equivalent to neither; a source of energy that urges the person to "become what one is"; an archetype that provides a sense of order and meaning in the personality. In *Memories, Dreams, and Reflections,* he said that if the goal of psychological development is the Self then "*there is no linear evolution (except at the beginning of life); there is only the circumambulation of the self.*"

While working on this concept, Jung had a dream about a well-fortified golden castle. He was painting this image in the center of a mandala, which was Chinese in feeling, when he received *The Secret of the Golden Flower* from Richard Wilhelm with a request that he write a commentary on it. Jung was moved by the event, which was a tremendously meaningful coincidence and writes,

> I devoured the manuscript at once, for the text gave me undreamed-of confirmation of my ideas about the mandala and the circumambulation of the center. That was the first event which broke through my isolation. I became aware of an affinity, I could establish ties with something and someone. In remembrance of this coincidence, this synchronicity, I wrote underneath the picture which had made so Chinese an impression upon me: "In 1928, when I was painting this picture, showing the golden, well-fortified castle, Richard Wilhelm in Frankfurt sent me the thousand-year-old text on the yellow castle, the germ of the immortal body."

The break with Freud had occurred some sixteen years previously. Jung had during these years had no support for his ideas. To find in an ancient Chinese text a view that paralleled his own conceptions was confirmation of the value of his solitary studies into the nature of the psyche. This synchronistic event must have brought with it a sense that what he had been working on these many years, had meaning after all, dispelling doubts about the choices he had made. His theoretical differences had isolated him, and the decision to delve into the psyche had so preoccupied him that he had withdrawn from the university where he had lectured for eight years and had the expectation of a smooth academic career. This sense of isolation that had resulted from these choices was changed by the synchronistic event. Now he felt an affinity to others.

8. Foreword to the **I Ching or Book of Changes** by Carl Jung

Of all the systems originating in mythic antiquity, the Book of Changes *is perhaps the most revered. Utterly unique in its descriptive imagery, it was at the outset a collection of linear signs used to predict the outcome of future events. In antiquity, oracles were everywhere in use, and the fundamental concept of the* I Ching, *the oldest among them, uses eight trigrams, each symbolizing a transitional state. When the trigrams are applied to predicting real world events, they produce descriptive passages focused on the inherent transitions that affect an event over time. Unlike Western thought, which centers attention on the characteristics and objects that distinguish an event, the* I Ching *predicts the flow and direction of an event's movement through time.*

Richard Wilhelm, the sinologist and translator of the I Ching, *wrote about the consciousness that shaped the book:*

It has occupied the attention of the most eminent scholars of China down to the present day. Nearly all that is significant in the three thousand years of Chinese history has either taken its inspiration from this book, or has exerted an influence on the interpretation of its text. . . . Not only the philosophy of China but its science and statecraft as well have never ceased to draw . . . from [its] wisdom. . . . Even the policy makers of so modern a state as Japan . . . refer to it . . . in difficult situations.*

I CAN ASSURE my reader that it is not altogether easy to find the right access to this monument of Chinese thought, which departs so completely from our ways of thinking. In order to understand what such a book is all about, it is imperative to cast off certain prejudices of the Western mind. It is a curious fact that such a gifted and intelligent people as the Chinese has never developed what we call science. Our science, however, is based upon the principle of causality, and causality is considered to be an axiomatic truth. But a great change in our standpoint is setting in. What Kant's *Critique of Pure Reason* failed to do, is being accomplished by modern physics. The axioms of causality are

---

* Wilhelm, R., *The I Ching or Book of Changes* (New Jersey: Princeton University Press, 1950), pp. x/vii–x/viii.

being shaken to their foundations: we know now that what we term natural laws are merely statistical truths and thus must necessarily allow for exceptions. We have not sufficiently taken into account as yet that we need the laboratory with its incisive restrictions in order to demonstrate the invariable validity of natural law. If we leave things to nature, we see a very different picture: every process is partially or totally interfered with by chance, so much so that under natural circumstances a course of events absolutely conforming to specific laws is almost an exception.

The Chinese mind, as I see it at work in the *I Ching,* seems to be exclusively preoccupied with the chance aspect of events. What we call coincidence seems to be the chief concern of this peculiar mind, and what we worship as causality passes almost unnoticed. We must admit that there is something to be said for the immense importance of chance. An incalculable amount of human effort is directed to combating and restricting the nuisance or danger represented by chance. Theoretical considerations of cause and effect often look pale and dusty in comparison to the practical results of chance. It is all very well to say that the crystal of quartz is a hexagonal prism. The statement is quite true in so far as an ideal crystal is envisaged. But in nature one finds no two crystals exactly alike, although all are unmistakably hexagonal. The actual form, however, seems to appeal more to the Chinese sage than the ideal one. The jumble of natural laws constituting empirical reality holds more significance for him than a causal explanation of events that, moreover, must usually be separated from one another in order to be properly dealt with.

The manner in which the *I Ching* tends to look upon reality seems to disfavor our causalistic procedures. The moment under actual observation appears to the ancient Chinese view more of a chance hit than a clearly defined result of concurring causal chain processes. The matter of interest seems to be the configuration formed by chance events in the moment of observation, and not at all the hypothetical reasons that seemingly account for the coincidence. While the Western mind carefully sifts, weighs, selects, classifies, isolates, the Chinese picture of the moment encompasses everything down to the minutest nonsensical detail, because all of the ingredients make up the observed moment.

Thus it happens that when one throws the three coins, or counts through the forty-nine yarrow stalks, these chance details enter into the picture of the moment of observation and form a part of it—a part that is insignificant to us, yet most meaningful to the Chinese mind. With us it would be a banal and almost meaningless statement (at least on the face of it) to say that whatever happens in a given moment possesses inevitably the quality peculiar to that moment. This is not an abstract argument but a very practical one. There are certain connoisseurs who can tell you merely from the appearance, taste, and behavior of a wine the site of its vineyard and the year of its origin. There are antiquarians who with almost uncanny accuracy will name the time and place of origin and the maker of an *objet d'art* or piece of furniture on merely looking at it. And there are even astrologers who can tell you, without any previous knowledge of your nativity, what the position of sun and moon was and what zodiacal sign rose above the horizon in the moment of your birth. In the face of such facts, it must be admitted that moments can leave long-lasting traces.

In other words, whoever invented the *I Ching* was convinced that the hexagram worked out in a certain moment coincided with the latter in quality no less than in time. To him the hexagram was the exponent of the moment in which it was cast—even more so than the hours of the clock or the divisions of the calendar could be—inasmuch as the hexagram was understood to be an indicator of the essential situation prevailing in the moment of its origin.

This assumption involves a certain curious principle that I have termed synchronicity,[1] a concept that formulates a point of view diametrically opposed to that of causality. Since the latter is a merely statistical truth and not absolute, it is a sort of working hypothesis of how events evolve one out of another, whereas synchronicity takes the coincidence of events in space and time as meaning something more than mere chance, namely, a peculiar interdependence of objective events among themselves as well as with the subjective (psychic) states of the observer or observers.

The ancient Chinese mind contemplates the cosmos in a way comparable to that of the modern physicist, who cannot deny that his model of the world is a decidedly psychophysical structure. The microphysical event includes the observer just as much as the reality underlying the *I Ching* comprises subjective, i.e., psychic conditions in the totality of the momentary situation. Just as causality describes the sequence of events, so synchronicity to the Chinese mind deals with the coincidence of events. The causal point of view tells us a dramatic story about how *D* came into existence: it took its origin from *C*, which existed before *D*, and *C* in its turn had a father, *B*, etc. The synchronistic view on the other hand tries to produce an equally meaningful picture of coincidence. How does it happen that *A'*, *B'*, *C'*, *D'*, etc., appear all in the same moment and in the same place? It happens in the first place because the physical events *A'* and *B'* are of the same quality as the psychic events *C'* and *D'*, and further because all are the exponents of one and the same momentary situation. The situation is assumed to represent a legible or understandable picture.

Now the sixty-four hexagrams of the *I Ching* are the instrument by which the meaning of sixty-four different yet typical situations can be determined. These interpretations are equivalent to causal explanations. Causal connection is statistically necessary and can therefore be subjected to experiment. Inasmuch as situations are unique and cannot be repeated, experimenting with synchronicity seems to be impossible under ordinary conditions.[2] In the *I Ching,* the only criterion of the validity of synchronicity is the observer's opinion that the text of the hexagram amounts to a true rendering of his psychic condition. It is assumed that the fall of the coins or the result of the division of the bundle of yarrow stalks is what it necessarily must be in a given "situation," inasmuch as anything happening in that moment belongs to it as an indispensable part of the picture. If a handful of matches is thrown to the floor, they form the pattern characteristic of that moment. But such an obvious truth as this reveals its meaningful nature only if it is possible to read the pattern and to verify its interpretation, partly by the observer's knowledge of the subjective and objective situation, partly by the character of subsequent events. It is obviously not a procedure that appeals to a critical mind used to experimental verification of facts or to factual evidence. But for someone who likes to look at the world at the angle from which ancient China saw it, the *I Ching* may have some attraction.

My argument as outlined above has of course never entered a Chinese mind. On the contrary, according to the old tradition, it is "spiritual agencies," acting in a mysterious way, that make the yarrow stalks give a meaningful answer.[3] These powers form, as it were, the living soul of the book. As the latter is thus a sort of animated being, the tradition assumes that one can put questions to the *I Ching* and expect to receive intelligent answers. Thus it occurred to me that it might interest the uninitiated reader to see the *I Ching* at work. For this purpose I made an experiment strictly in accordance with the Chinese conception: I personified the book in a sense, asking its judgment about its present situation, i.e., my intention to present it to the Western mind.

Although this procedure is well within the premises of Taoist philosophy, it appears exceedingly odd to us. However, not even the strangeness of insane delusions or of primitive superstition has ever shocked me. I have always tried to remain unbiased and curious—*rerum novarum cupidus.* Why not venture a dialogue with an ancient book that purports to be animated? There can be no harm in it, and the reader may watch a psychological procedure that has been carried out time and again throughout the millennia of Chinese civilization, representing to a Confucius or a Lao-tse both a supreme expression of spiritual authority and a philosophical enigma. I made use of the coin method, and the answer obtained was hexagram 50, Ting, THE CALDRON.

In accordance with the way my question was phrased, the text of the hexa-gram must be regarded as though the *I Ching* itself were the speaking person. Thus it describes itself as a caldron, that is, as a ritual vessel containing cooked food. Here the food is to be understood as spiritual nourishment. Wilhelm says about this:

> The *ting*, as a utensil pertaining to a refined civilization, suggests the fostering and nourishing of able men, which redounded to the benefit of the state. . . . Here we see civilization as it reaches its culmination in religion. The *ting* serves in offering sacrifice to God. . . . The supreme revelation of God appears in prophets and holy men. To venerate them is true veneration of God. The will of God, as revealed through them, should be accepted in humility.

Keeping to our hypothesis, we must conclude that the *I Ching* is here testify-ing concerning itself.

When any of the lines of a given hexagram have the value of six or nine, it means that they are specially emphasized and hence important in the inter-pretation. In my hexagram the "spiritual agencies" have given the emphasis of a nine to the lines in the second and in the third place. The text says:

> *Nine in the second place means:*
> *There is food in the* ting.
> *My comrades are envious,*
> *But they cannot harm me.*
> *Good fortune.*

Thus the *I Ching* says of itself: "I contain (spiritual) nourishment." Since a share in something great always arouses envy, the chorus of the envious[4] is part of the picture. The envious want to rob the *I Ching* of its great possession, that is, they seek to rob it of meaning, or to destroy its meaning. But their enmity is in vain. Its richness of meaning is assured; that is, it is convinced of its positive achievements, which no one can take away. The text continues:

> *Nine in the third place means:*
> *The handle of the* ting *is altered.*
> *One is impeded in his way of life.*
> *The fat of the pheasant is not eaten.*
> *Once rain falls, remorse is spent.*
> *Good fortune comes in the end.*

The handle [German *Griff*] is the part by which the *ting* can be grasped [*gegriffen*]. Thus it signifies the concept[5] (*Begriff*) one has of the *I Ching* (the *ting*). In the course of time this concept has apparently changed, so that today we can no longer grasp (*begreifen*) the *I Ching*. Thus "one is impeded in his way of life."We are no longer supported by the wise counsel and deep insight of the oracle; therefore we no longer find our way through the mazes of fate and the obscurities of our own natures. The fat of the pheasant, that is, the best and richest part of a good dish, is no longer eaten. But when the thirsty earth finally receives rain again, that is, when this state of want has been overcome, "remorse," that is, sorrow over the loss of wisdom, is ended, and then comes the longed-for opportunity. Wilhelm comments: "This describes a man who, in a highly evolved civilization, finds himself in a place where no one notices or recognizes him. This is a severe block to his effectiveness."The *I Ching* is complaining, as it were, that its excellent qualities go unrecognized and hence lie fallow. It comforts itself with the hope that it is about to regain recognition.

The answer given in these two salient lines to the question I put to the *I Ching* requires no particular subtlety of interpretation, no artifices, no unusual knowledge. Anyone with a little common sense can understand the meaning of the answer; it is the answer of one who has a good opinion of himself, but whose value is neither generally recognized nor even widely known. The answering subject has an interesting notion of itself: it looks upon itself as a vessel in which sacrificial offerings are brought to the gods, ritual food for their nourishment. It conceives of itself as a cult utensil serving to provide spiritual nourishment for the unconscious elements or forces ("spiritual agencies") that have been projected as gods—in other words, to give these forces the attention they need in order to play their part in the life of the individual. Indeed, this is the original meaning of the word *religio*—a careful observation and taking account of (from *relegere*)[6] the numinous.

The method of the *I Ching* does indeed take into account the hidden individual quality in things and men, and in one's own unconscious self as well. I have questioned the *I Ching* as one questions a person whom one is about to introduce to friends: one asks whether or not it will be agreeable to him. In answer the *I Ching* tells me of its religious significance, of the fact that at present it is unknown and misjudged, of its hope of being restored to a place of honor—this last obviously with a sidelong glance at my as yet unwritten foreword,[7] and above all at the English translation. This seems a perfectly understandable reaction, such as one could expect also from a person in a similar situation.

But how has this reaction come about? Because I threw three small coins into the air and let them fall, roll, and come to rest, heads up or tails up as the case might be. This odd fact that a reaction that makes sense arises out of a technique seemingly excluding all sense from the outset, is the great achievement of the *I Ching*. The instance I have just given is not unique; meaningful answers are the rule. Western sinologues and distinguished Chinese scholars have been at pains to inform me that the *I Ching* is a collection of obsolete "magic spells." In the course of these conversations my informant has sometimes admitted having consulted the oracle through a fortune teller, usually a Taoist priest. This could be "only nonsense" of course. But oddly enough, the answer received apparently coincided with the questioner's psychological blind spot remarkably well.

I agree with Western thinking that any number of answers to my question were possible, and I certainly cannot assert that another answer would not have been equally significant. However, the answer received was the first and only one; we know nothing of other possible answers. It pleased and satisfied me. To ask the same question a second time would have been tactless and so I did not do it: "the master speaks but once." The heavy-handed pedagogic approach that attempts to fit irrational phenomena into a preconceived rational pattern is anathema to me. Indeed, such things as this answer should remain as they were when they first emerged to view, for only then do we know what nature does when left to herself undisturbed by the meddlesomeness of man. One ought not to go to cadavers to study life. Moreover, a repetition of the experiment is impossible, for the simple reason that the original situation cannot be reconstructed. Therefore in each instance there is only a first and single answer.

To return to the hexagram itself. There is nothing strange in the fact that all of Ting, THE CALDRON, amplifies the themes announced by the two salient lines.[8] The first line of the hexagram says:

> *A* ting *with legs upturned.*
> *Furthers removal of stagnating stuff.*
> *One takes a concubine for the sake of her son.*
> *No blame.*

A *ting* that is turned upside down is not in use. Hence the *I Ching* is like an unused caldron. Turning it over serves to remove stagnating matter, as the line says. Just as a man takes a concubine when his wife has no son, so the *I Ching* is called upon when one sees no other way out. Despite the quasi-legal status of the concubine in China, she is in reality only a somewhat awkward makeshift; so likewise the magic procedure of the oracle is an expedient that may be utilized for a higher purpose. There is no blame, although it is an exceptional recourse.

The second and third lines have already been discussed. The fourth line says:

> *The legs of the* ting *are broken.*
> *The prince's meal is spilled*
> *And his person is soiled.*
> *Misfortune.*

Here the *ting* has been put to use, but evidently in a very clumsy manner, that is, the oracle has been abused or misinterpreted. In this way the divine food is lost, and one puts oneself to shame. Legge translates as follows: "Its subject will be made to blush for shame." Abuse of a cult utensil such as the *ting* (i.e., the *I Ching*) is a gross profanation. The *I Ching* is evidently insisting here on its dignity as a ritual vessel and protesting against being profanely used.

The fifth line says:

> *The* ting *has yellow handles, golden carrying rings.*
> *Perseverance furthers.*

The *I Ching* has, it seems, met with a new, correct (yellow) understanding, that is, a new concept (*Begriff*) by which it can be grasped. This concept is valuable (golden). There is indeed a new edition in English, making the book more accessible to the Western world than before.

The sixth line says:

> *The* ting *has rings of jade.*
> *Great good fortune.*
> *Nothing that would not act to further.*

Jade is distinguished for its beauty and soft sheen. If the carrying rings are of jade, the whole vessel is enhanced in beauty, honor, and value. The *I Ching* expresses itself here as being not only well satisfied but indeed very optimistic. One can only await further events and in the meantime remain content with the pleasant conclusion that the *I Ching* approves of the new edition.

I have shown in this example as objectively as I can how the oracle proceeds in a given case. Of course the procedure varies somewhat according to the way the question is put. If for instance a person finds himself in a confusing situation, he may himself appear in the oracle as the speaker. Or, if the question concerns a relationship with another person, that person may appear as the speaker. However, the identity of the speaker does not depend entirely on the manner in which the question is phrased, inasmuch as our relations with our fellow beings are not always determined by the latter. Very often our relations depend almost exclusively on our own attitudes, though we may be quite unaware of this fact. Hence, if an individual is unconscious of his role in a relationship, there may be a surprise in store for him; contrary to expectation, he himself may appear as the chief agent, as is sometimes unmistakably indicated by the text. It may also occur that we take a situation too seriously and consider it extremely important, whereas the answer we get on consulting the I Ching draws attention to some unsuspected other aspect implicit in the question.

Such instances might at first lead one to think that the oracle is fallacious. Confucius is said to have received only one inappropriate answer, i.e., hexagram 22, GRACE—a thoroughly aesthetic hexagram. This is reminiscent of the advice given to Socrates by his daemon—"You ought to make more music"—whereupon Socrates took to playing the flute. Confucius and Socrates compete for first place as far as reasonableness and a pedagogic attitude to life are concerned; but it is unlikely that either of them occupied himself with "lending grace to the beard on his chin," as the second line of this hexagram advises. Unfortunately, reason and pedagogy often lack charm and grace, and so the oracle may not have been wrong after all.[8]

9. Shamanism by Roger Walsh

Roger Walsh describes the arduous training that enables a shaman to mediate between the known world of the tribe and the unseen forces upon which the tribe depends. In the difficult conditions of indigenous life, survival depends on people who possess shamanic power. No Bushman would undertake a long trek through the desert unless there was some surety of water at a distant oasis. Likewise, seafaring cultures wouldn't attempt an arduous journey by water unless guided by the abilities of someone gifted in weather prediction.

Shamanic knowing appears in dreams and at the apex of ceremonies that induce concentrated attention. Often practical, such information is vital to group survival, and is transmitted in the context of an individual tribe's mythical and cosmological framework.

WHEN THE HERO has answered the call to adventure and found a teacher, the period of training and discipline begins. In this period the mind is trained, the body toughened, cravings are reduced, fears faced, and strengths such as endurance and concentration are cultivated. This is usually a slow and lengthy process where success may be measured in months and years and patience is not only a virtue but a necessity. The goal is to hone both body and mind so as to awaken to, and be an effective instrument of, spirit. The process has been pithily summarized by Chuang Tzu, one of the greatest of the Taoist sages:

> First gain control of the body
> and all its organs. Then
> control the mind. Attain
> one-pointedness. Then
> the harmony of heaven
> will come down and dwell in you.
> You will be radiant with Life.
> You will rest in Tao. [1]

The shaman's instructions come from both inner and outer worlds. In the outer world it consists of apprenticeship to a master shaman. From the teacher the apprentice learns both theory and practice: the myths and cosmology, rituals and techniques of the shamanic culture. These provide the means by which the apprentice shaman's experiences are cultivated, interpreted, and made meaningful within the tribal and shamanic traditions.

In the inner world the apprentice learns to cultivate and interpret dreams, fantasies, visions, and spirits. Ideally, both inner and outer worlds align to mold the novice into a mature shaman who can mediate effectively between these worlds, between the sacred and profane, the spiritual and mundane.

The length of apprenticeship may vary from as little as days to months or years. After the novice has been accepted, his first task may be a ritual purification in which he must confess any breaches of taboo or other offenses.[2] After this the actual instruction by the teacher, aided of course by the teacher's spirits, begins.

Much must be learned. On the theoretical side the apprentice must become a mythologist and cosmologist. To become an effective "cosmic traveler" he must learn the terrain of this multi-layered, interconnected universe in which he will quest for power and knowledge. He must also become familiar with its spiritual inhabitants—their names, habitats, powers, likes and dislikes, how they can be called, and how they can be controlled. For it is these spirits whom he will battle or befriend, who will help or hinder him as he does his work. It is they who represent and embody the power at work in the cosmos, and it is his relationship with them that will determine his success. So the cosmology the would-be shaman learns is no dry mapping of inanimate worlds but a guide to a living, conscious, willful universe.

Much of this cosmic terrain and the guidelines for relating to it are contained in the culture's myths. Indeed, throughout most of human history myths have provided the major cultural guidelines for the conduct of life. It is only in our own time that major cultures have lacked a common, coherent myth— a grand, unifying picture, story, and explanation of the cosmos. Indeed this lack of a common myth may be a major factor in the fragmentation and alienation that haunts so much of the contemporary world. Much may depend on our ability to create a new myth appropriate to our time and needs.

Joseph Campbell suggests that myths serve four major functions: developmental, social, cosmological, and religious. Their developmental function is to provide guidelines for individuals as they mature through life's stages. Their social function is to support the social structure and provide a shared understanding of life and relationship. Their cosmological and religious roles are to provide an image and understanding of the cosmos and of humankind's role and responsibility in it.[3]

Myths serve the shaman in all four ways. This is not surprising since many myths may have originated in shamanic journeys and reflect the terrain discovered there. They guide the shaman's development, give him his place in society and cosmos and indicate how he is to relate to them. In addition, myths provide the belief system he and his patients will share. This may be crucial since contemporary research suggests that a shared belief system may be a vital part of an effective therapeutic relationship.

In addition to learning myths, the would-be shaman must learn diagnostic and healing practices, master the arts of entering altered states and of journeying, and acquire his own helping spirits.

These helping spirits constitute the shaman's inner teachers. They may appear to him in dreams, daydreams, images, journeys, or visions. Consequently, much of the shaman's training concerns learning how to cultivate the circumstances and states of consciousness that will coax the spirits to reveal themselves and their messages. The most dramatic of these circumstances include ascetic practices and periods of isolation.

Ascetic practices are the atom bombs of religious discipline. These powerful tools are said to strengthen and purify practitioners by forcing them to confront their limits, fears, and self-deceptions. They are tools of high risk and high gain, for although they can be beneficial, they can also be misused.

Traditionally, ascetic practices are said to strengthen and purify. They may strengthen warrior qualities such as will, courage, and endurance; remove both physical and mental impurities; and foster clarity and concentration of mind.[4] The sum total of these benefits is power—power of body, mind, and spirit. It is power to control one's faculties and responses, power to overcome temptations and obstacles, power over spirits, and power to serve and benefit others.

Like any spiritual path, asceticism has its traps. Feelings of righteousness are common, as is puritanical denial of the beauty and joy of life.[5] Another trap is extremism, since asceticism can be carried to dubious and dangerous extremes, even to the point of self-torture, mutilation, and death. But assuming that ascetic practices can also confer benefits, the logical question is, how do they do this?

Several possible mechanisms exist. Those who succeed in meeting challenges have been found to enhance their sense of self-esteem and effectiveness.[6] Thus the ascetic who masters extreme challenges might well be expected to develop an exceptional sense of personal power.

Holding fast to their goals despite the pull of conflicting desires and fears means that ascetics give little reinforcement to these motives. Unreinforced motives tend to diminish and even disappear. This weakening of conflicting drives, which is a goal of most religions, is traditionally called "purification." Some traditions claim that, in the higher reaches of spiritual mastery, competing desires can become so stilled that the mind rests in peace, free of all conflict. This claim has recently received support from studies of advanced Buddhist meditators whose unique and remarkable Rorschach test patterns showed "no evidence of sexual or aggressive drive conflicts."[7] While there is little evidence that shamans strive for this remarkable degree of purification, they may confront and overcome diverse fears and desires, thus attaining unusual degrees of concentration and power.

Assuaging guilt may also play a role in the effectiveness of asceticism. If practitioners believe they are sinful and must pay for their sins, then asceticism may seem a logical way to do so. While such logic and practices may work to some extent, they are also very tricky. Self-punishment may assuage guilt temporarily but may also strengthen the belief in the necessity and appropriateness of both guilt and punishment.

Ascetic practices occur in varying degrees in different parts of the world. Almost absent in some places, they take extreme forms in parts of India and Japan. For centuries Japanese ascetics have undertaken practices of almost incomprehensible, life-threatening proportions.

Many of these Japanese ascetics have been described as shamans.[8] If we look closely, however, relatively few of them seem to meet our definition of shamanism. No distinction is made between shamans and mediums; beyond that, contemporary shamanism in Japan seems to have degenerated significantly from former times. Few contemporary Japanese shamans enter altered states and actually journey. It appears that most simply act out the classic trance and journey in symbolic rituals.

> Today this trance occurs only rarely. The capacity for this kind of dissociation, and for the visionary journey which goes with it, seems to have diminished in recent centuries, and today the magic journey is most commonly accomplished by symbolic action in fully waking consciousness.[9]

This is an example of what might be called the ritualization of religion: the process in which transcendence-inducing practices degenerate into ineffective rituals, direct experience gives way to symbols of experience, and the understanding and appreciation of effective altered states are lost.

Whatever its current limitations, Japanese shamanism has historically been highly ascetic, and some ascetic practices persist even today. The three major types include dietary restriction, cold, and solitude.

In its mildest form dietary restriction involves the avoidance of certain foods, such as meat, salt, or cooked substances, that are believed to inhibit the acquisition of power. In its most extreme form it involves fasting to the point of death. One such extreme is the mind-boggling discipline of "tree eating."

Though its practitioners were not really shamans, the discipline is valuable in showing the extremes to which some ascetic practices have been carried. Practitioners would vow to follow the discipline for one thousand, two thousand, or even three thousand days.

> During the first part of the discipline their diet consisted of nuts, bark, fruit, berries, grass and sometimes soy in fair abundance. The quantity of these things was then reduced, until by the end of their allotted period they had undergone a total fast of many days. Ideally, if the discipline were properly calculated, the man should die from starvation, upright in the lotus posture, on the last day of his avowed fast. His body should have been reduced to skin and bone.[10]

Such a practice was obviously not for the faint of heart.

A second major austerity is exposure to cold. Common in both Arctic areas and Japan, this technique is considered very effective in developing power. Once again the severity of the practices can reach almost incomprehensible extremes.

> To stand under a waterfall, preferably between the hours of two and three in the morning and preferably during the period of the great cold in midwinter, is believed to be an infallible method of gaining power."[11] Indeed, one female ascetic reported that such a practice "no longer felt in the least cold to her. It rather promoted an unrivalled concentration of mind . . . which formed the very basis of her ascetic power.[12]

The third major ascetic practice, periods of solitary withdrawal from society, is common to diverse religious traditions. Such periods mark the lives of many great saints and religious founders. Witness Jesus' 40 days of fasting in the wilderness, Buddha's solitary meditation, and Mohammed's isolation in a cave. Such practices have been part of the training of Eskimo shamans, the Christian desert fathers, Hindu yogis, and Tibetan monks who may be walled away in caves for up to 13 years.

The reason for seeking solitude is essentially to allow attention to be redirected away from the distractions of the world and toward the spiritual. This spiritual realm is ultimately found to reside within the seeker—for example, "The Kingdom of Heaven is within you"; "Look within, Thou art the Buddha"—but to find it requires intense contemplation and introspection.

Concentration must be cultivated, sensitivity to one's inner world deepened, the mind quietened, and the clamor of competing desires stilled.

"Know thyself" is the motto of these practices. The demands and distractions of society usually hinder profound inner searching and self-knowledge. Consequently, periodic withdrawal and solitude may be essential. As Wordsworth explained so poetically:

> *The world is too much with us; late and soon,*
> *Getting and spending, we lay waste our powers;*
> *Little we see in Nature that is ours;*
> *We have given our hearts away. . . .*

Shamans were the first to appreciate the far-reaching benefits of solitude for psychological and spiritual development. They were the first to learn from direct experience that, to use their own words, "The power of solitude is great and beyond understanding."[13]

The numerous trials faced by those willing to confront isolation and themselves in this way have been the subject of countless spiritual biographies. The Eskimo shaman Aua, whose parents' rituals and taboos were outlined earlier, described his period of solitude as follows.

> Then I sought solitude, and here I soon became very melancholy. I would sometimes fall to weeping, and feel unhappy without knowing why. Then, for no reason, all would suddenly be changed, and I felt a great, inexplicable joy, a joy so powerful that I could not restrain it, but had to break into song, a mighty song, with only room for the one word: joy, joy! And I had to use the full strength of my voice. And then in the midst of such a fit of mysterious and overwhelming delight I became a shaman, not knowing myself how it came about. But I was a shaman. I could see and hear in a totally different way.[14]

Note the extreme mood swings and lack of control. These are common initial reactions to solitude and can be surprisingly powerful. After my own first retreat I wrote of experiencing "sudden apparently unprecipitated wide mood swings to completely polar emotions. Shorn of all my props and distractions there was just no way to pretend that I had more than the faintest inkling of self-control over either thoughts or feelings."[15]

Those who face themselves in solitude soon come to appreciate just how restless and out of control the untrained mind is. They soon come to understand Sigmund Freud's claim that "man is not even master in his own house . . . in his own mind"[16] and why "all scriptures without any exception proclaim that for attaining salvation mind should be subdued."[17] Solitude and fasting are traditional ways of subduing the mind.

Not content with the rigors of solitude, fasting, or cold alone, shamans sometimes combine all these, as in the following account by an Eskimo shaman, Igjugarjuk. While still young he received his call to adventure in the form of mysterious dreams. "Strange unknown beings came and spoke to him, and when he awoke, he saw all the visions of his dream so distinctly that he could tell his fellows all about them. Soon it became evident to all that he was destined to become an angakoq [a shaman] and an old man named Perqanaoq was appointed his instructor. In the depth of winter, when the cold was most severe, Igjugarjuk was placed on a small sled just large enough for him to sit on, and carried far away from his home to the other side of Hikoligjuaq. On reaching the appointed spot, he remained seated on the sled while his instructor built a tiny snow hut, with barely room for him to sit cross-legged. He was not allowed to set foot on the snow, but was lifted from the sled and carried into the hut where a piece of skin just large enough for him to sit on served as a carpet. No food or drink was given him; he was exhorted to think only of the Great Spirit and of the helping spirit that should presently appear—and so he was left to himself and his meditations.

"After five days had elapsed, the instructor brought him a drink of lukewarm water, and with similar exhortations, left him as before. He fasted now for fifteen days, when he was given another drink of water and a very small piece of meat, which had to last him a further ten days. At the end of this period, his instructor came for him and fetched him home. Igjugarjuk declared that the strain of those thirty days of cold and fasting was so severe that he 'sometimes died a little.' During all that time he thought only of the Great Spirit, and endeavored to keep his mind free from all memory of human beings and everyday things. Toward the end of the thirty days there came to him a helping spirit in the shape of a woman. She came while he was asleep and seemed to hover in the air above him. After that he dreamed no more of her, but she became his helping spirit. For five months following this period of trial, he was kept on the strictest diet, and required to abstain from all intercourse with women. The fasting was then repeated; for such fasts at frequent intervals are the best means of attaining to knowledge of hidden things."[18]

Igjugarjuk's conclusion from all this was that "the only true wisdom lives far from mankind, out in the great loneliness, and it can be reached only through suffering. Privation and suffering alone can open the mind of a man to all that is hidden to others."[19]

Igjugarjuk would therefore probably have agreed with the French existentialist Albert Camus that "when a man has learned—and not on paper—how to remain alone with his suffering, how to overcome his longing to flee, then he has little left to learn."[20]

So practices such as solitude and fasting enhance access to the inner world and its images, visions, dreams, and spirits. The range of these inner experiences is vast, but commonalities emerge across cultures. For the successful candidate these practices climax in certain experiences which indicate that a degree of shamanic mastery has been attained. Two of the most frequent shamanic culmination experiences—those of being immersed in light and of death-rebirth—are examined in the next chapter.

10. *Aboriginal Men of High Degree by A. P. Elkin*

The intuitives of indigenous societies are commonly required to show evidence of their ability. Tribal communities depend on their shamans to heal, to describe past and future events, to find the hidden, clarify the mysterious, and to sense the unknown. The indigenous practitioner is expected to show evidence of skill and reliability before being entrusted with the task of assisting others on the inner journey.

Citing field work in Aboriginal society, Professor Carl Elkin reports on the extraordinary faculties demonstrated by "clever men." He stresses the point that a medicine person simply possesses human faculties of perception to a greater degree than others, making them "unusually normal." He describes psychic displays of walking on fire, clairvoyance, fast traveling, and a physical magic cord, all of which phenomena are echoed in the worldwide oral traditions of other indigenous societies.

A MAN GROWS in knowledge by attending initiations and various cult-ceremonies and by learning from the "masters." Eventually he plays a leading part in the dreamtime rituals, on sacred ground, painted with arm blood or red ochre sanctified by the chanting that accompanies its application, and carrying or beholding the sacred symbols. On these occasions it is realized by both himself and all present that he is no longer himself; he is the great dreamtime hero whose role he is re-enacting, if only for a few minutes.

The function and purpose of these rituals are complex. They serve to strengthen in all present the realization of the dreamtime and the presence and power of its cult-heroes. They also dramatically remind and impress everyone present with all the sanctity and authority of traditional tribal behavior. In some cases, too, they are believed to cause the natural species to increase in their wonted way, so that man may live. But in addition to these effects, the rituals, with their dreamtime heroic associations, create and maintain in the participants unity of emotion, thought, and action; they renew sentiments that make for social continuity and cohesion; and so they bring about a highly desirable condition of social well-being and individual certainty and courage.[1]

THE PROBLEMS OF DAILY LIFE

Initiation into the secret and sacred ritual and mythology of the tribe provides an authoritative background, a solid footing, and a sure hope for life. It gives general support and guidance to man in most moral and social situations. But it does not help him to cope specifically with the problems, desires, and set-backs of daily life, for example:

1. misfortune; bad luck; lack of success in love, hunting, or fighting; ill-ness; or death;

2. lack of knowledge of what is occurring out of sight and at a distance that may affect us unless we are forewarned and can take precautions;

3. ignorance of what the spirits of the dead or mischievous or evil spirits are likely to work on us;

4. the desire to obtain this or that object or goal, the realization of which is fraught with various uncertainties and contingencies.

In Aboriginal life these problems, setbacks, and desires are met in two ways. The first is the way of magic, with its rites, spells, paraphernalia, and concen-tration of thought. If it is designed to cause injury to an individual or social group, it is called black magic or sorcery; but if it is used to prevent evil or to produce good or well-being, it is called white magic.

The second way of meeting life's problems leads to the realm of psychic powers (and presumed psychic powers): hypnotism, clairvoyance, medi-umship, telepathy, telesthesia, and the conquest of space and time.

All persons can, and indeed do, possess to a degree some of these powers. For example, in most tribes everybody can practice some forms of black magic and through dreams and traditionally formalized systems of presentiments know or learn what is happening at a distance that is of significance to them-selves and their friends. Thus, to see in a vision of the night a person's dream totem (that is, the natural species or phenomenon that is his symbol in dreams) is to know that something is to happen to him or be done by him in relation to the dreamer. In many tribes, the various parts of the body are mapped out to symbolize in each case a prescribed type of classificatory relation, such as father, mother, sister's child, and so on. If an involuntary twitching occurs in a muscle in the part associated with the class of father, the person immediately abstracts himself from all surrounding interests and, letting his head droop for-ward, as I have seen, enters a condition either of receptivity or of free associ-ation. After a time, he becomes satisfied that such and such a person in the prescribed relationship will arrive before long. The information has "come" to him.[2]

To the Aborigines, there is nothing extraordinary about gaining informa-tion in these ways. Anyone can do so. But if he gets into difficulty or into doubt, for example, about the authenticity of a dream revelation or a presentiment, he can consult a specialist. For there are specialists; these are the medicine men, the clever men, the *karadji*, to use the term longest known to us. They are men of high degree. . . .

PSYCHIC DISPLAYS

Many of the manifestations of psychic powers are for practical ends, to cure the sick, detect the sorcerer, gather information of social importance, visit the sky to release water stored there and so make rain, influence people at a distance, and protect the group. But in addition, specialists occasionally give displays of their power to impress on others the high degree of knowledge and power they have reached and so build up faith in their efficiency, an asset in the day of need. Initiations are favorite times for these exhibitions, no doubt because the young initiates are in a highly suggestible state and will be duly impressed. This definitely occurred in southeast Australia, where medicine men played a very important part in initiation.[3]

WALKING ON FIRE

During one display in western New South Wales, after the bull-roarer had been swung, thus creating a mystic atmosphere, for it is the voice of Baiame (the sky cult-hero), the men present were told to sit around and stare into a big fire on the sacred ground. As they stared, they saw a clever man roll into the fire and scatter the coals. He then stood up among the rest of the men, who noticed that he was not burned, nor were the European clothes that he wore damaged. The informant and the others were quite satisfied the doctor was in the fire. In 1944 some Weilwan men told me that they had seen this same doctor "walk through the fire" naked and unhurt.

Aborigines, on ceremonial occasions, are able, in their excitement, to stamp on and scatter the burning coals of a fire without any apparent harm, and novices in initiation are sometimes tossed into a big smoke fire. But these displays of fire-rolling and fire-walking were thought to go further. It is, moreover, in line with the claim and the belief that medicine men can travel in a flame of fire or send fire from their bodies along invisible cords to objects to which they had attached the cords. This power arose from a flame of fire having been sung into them by Baiame at their making.[4]

THE USE OF MAGIC CORD

During their making in southeast Australia, a magic cord is slung into the doctors. This cord becomes a means of performing marvelous feats, such as sending fire from the medicine man's insides, like an electric wire. But even more interesting is the use made of the cord to travel up to the sky or to the tops of trees through space. At the display during initiation—a time of ceremonial excitement—the doctor lies on his back under a tree, sends his cord up, and climbs up it to a nest on top of the tree, then across to other trees, and at sunset, down to the ground again. Only men saw this performance, and it is preceded and followed by the swinging of the bull-roarers and other expressions of emotional excitement.[5] In the descriptions of these performances recorded by R. M. Berndt and myself, the names of the doctors are given and such details as the following: Joe Dagan, a Wongaibon clever man, lying on his back at the foot of a tree, sent his cord directly up, and "climbed" up with his head well back, body outstretched, legs apart, and arms to his sides. Arriving at the top, twelve meters up, he waved his arms to those below, then came down in the same manner, and while still on his back the cord re-entered his body.

Apparently, in this case, his body floated up and down in the horizontal position with no movement of his hands or legs, and the explanation must be sought in group suggestion of a powerful nature.

DISAPPEARING AND REAPPEARING

Another form of psychic display was to disappear from one spot suddenly and appear in another, or to pass into or out of a tree. Thus one man (J. K.) said that at his initiation, a clever doctor (C. J.) was standing near the novices, when quite suddenly he disappeared, and then was seen standing with his back to them about 140 meters away, turning from time to time to look at them. "He was doing this to show them all he was very clever."

Another doctor hit a tree and disappeared into it, like stone sinking into muddy water. The reverse of this is given in the following episode: J. K. was about to doze off one morning while the billy was boiling, when he was awakened by an iguana touching his foot. Looking at it, he noticed that it turned its head around in the direction of some trees. So he sang out to his two brothers who were nearby, "That old fellow (M. D.) must be about here," for he knew that M. D. had an iguana inside him (that is, as a familiar). Standing up, he looked at the iguana, which suddenly ran back to a tree and disappeared. From this, they knew that M. D. must be inside that tree. Then they heard M. D. call out in a low voice, "Can you see me?" But they could not, until he gradually came out of the tree, which closed up without leaving a mark. He then walked up to them and said he had sent out his spirit helper to see whether they would recognize it.

Aborigines regarded dreams as material occurrences, and this may have been a dream experience. The narrator, however, says he was wide awake; if so, the clever fellow (M. D.) must have exercised some psychical power over the three men.

CREATING ILLUSIONS

Another incident illustrates the power of creating illusions in the minds of a group, but this time not merely for display but to protect one's own group. Two medicine men, having sent their group on ahead, lit a big fire and, lying like logs on either side, sang a magical song. The enemy saw and heard them, but when they rushed in and speared the "men," the singing stopped, and they saw only two logs. In the distance they could see the two doctors walking along. After this experience had been repeated several times, the enemy realized that they were being played with by very clever men and so went home.

This may be only an elaboration of an able elusion of an enemy raiding party, and wonders apart, medicine men usually did play an important part on both the raiding and the defending sides. Magical help was essential.[6]

FAST TRAVELING

Medicine men are believed to be able to travel at a very fast pace. This is obvious enough if the claim is to fly in sleep or in a vision to distant places, or to send their familiars on such journeys. But they can also run at a surprising pace for any distance, faster than anyone can run, and without getting tired or out of breath. They apparently run less than a meter above the ground. Indeed, it has been said that the air has been made soft and solid, and that it moves along, carrying them with it. The explanation given by other Aborigines is that "these clever men can make their spirits take them along very quickly." Information regarding this form of progression comes from southeast Australia, especially western New South Wales, and eastern South Australia.[7]

Aborigines are noted for their extraordinary feats of walking long distances, at what we regard as remarkable speed. Hunting and raiding on foot fits them for this. But the medicine man's powers are said to exceed this and to be more than physical.

MEDITATION

At the back of these claims to various psychic powers, for whatever they are worth, is the fact that Aborigines spend much time with their own thoughts, reflecting on dreams, and being ready, at any moment, to enter a condition of receptivity. The quietness and silence of so much of their life, the absence of rush and of urgent appointments, and the fewness of their numbers facilitate this occupation with the psychic. Moreover, their totemistic and animistic view of life predisposes them to it.

Some persons, however, specialize in meditation as well as in psychic experiences. All men of high degree have practiced it, but some do so to the exclusion of becoming adepts in other branches of magical and psychical endeavor. The temptation is to think that an Aborigine sitting down, apparently dreaming, is doing nothing. But he may be engaged in serious meditational and psychic discipline. It is to this aspect of their life that I desire to draw special attention.

The following is a description by an Aboriginal informant of an old man meditating. It is translated freely from the native text in Yaralde.[8]

> When you see an old man sitting by himself over here in the camp, do not disturb him, for if you do he will "growl" at you. Do not play near him, because he is sitting down by himself with his thoughts in order "to see." He is gathering those thoughts so that he can feel and hear. Perhaps he then lies down, getting into a special posture, so that he may see when sleeping. He sees indistinct visions and hears "persons" talk in them. He gets up and looks for those he has seen, but, not seeing them, he lies down again in the prescribed manner, so as to see what he had seen before. He puts his head on the pillow as previously so as to see [have a vision] as before. Getting up, he tells his friends to strengthen that power [miwi] within them, so that when they lie down they will see and feel [or become aware of] people not present, and in that way they will perceive them.

This describes how certain persons, abstracting themselves from what was happening around them and concentrating on the psychic power within them, practiced something akin to recollection. Lying down in the prescribed posture, they saw and "heard" what was happening at a distance. In other words, they were clairvoyant. Indeed, during such periods of meditation and vision, when this power and his own thoughts were as one, the clever man would see visions unconnected with earthly life. He would go to the world of ancestral beings.

This power, called *miwi* by the Yaralde of the Lower Murray, is said to be present in all persons but to be especially developed by a few. All manifestations of psychic power are dependent on it—including white and black magic. Old people can use it so as to know who is coming and what is going to happen, whereas the especially gifted person, after much practice, can perform the quite remarkable acts already described. This miwi is said to be located in the pit of the stomach. And even as I wrote this, at Walgett, in August 1944, among the Weilwan tribal remnants there, I was told how they seem to know events of importance to them before it seems feasible that they should do so. And several of them have told me that the clever man (*wiringin*) sent something out of his body (pointing to the stomach) to see things. Moreover, this something might even be a materialization of himself, which could be seen by at least some persons kilometers away where it had been "sent," such persons being sensitives.

COMPARISON WITH TIBET

Some light on our Aboriginal men of high degree can be obtained by a comparison with those from Tibet, a country characterized by psychic specialization. There the great yogi, possessed of clairvoyant vision, is said to be able to observe the physiological processes of his own body. He requires no mechanical devices in order to traverse air or water or land, for he tells us that he can quit his gross physical body and visit any part of the earth or pass beyond the stratosphere to other worlds with a speed greater than light. As a result of his discipline and training, he can acquire fleetness of foot, lightness of body, and immunity to harm by fire. He can become immune also to severe cold, the result of practicing the yoga of psychic heat. This includes concentration and visualization of fire at the meeting point of the nerves at the psychic center. The latter is situated four fingers below the navel. It is "the hidden abode of the sleeping Goddess Kundalini, the personification of the Serpent-Power, of the latent mystic fire-force of the body."[9] And there, too, are located the miwi, the cord, and the rainbow serpent or other familiar in the case of the Australian man of high degree.

Let us remember, too, one of the favorite exercises of the yogi, the "man of the rule": sitting in a prescribed way on a prescribed type of couch, gazing at the end of his nose and not looking around about him, he becomes impassive to the perceptions of the senses and enjoys boundless happiness.[10]

Part Three

From Imagination
to Inner Knowing

*I*t's consoling to realize that the ancient avenues to wisdom, described in Part II, were never really lost. Instead of denying them outright, our rational mind simply categorized them as "subjective," thereby luckily preserving them. The rational mind tends to dichotomize, so today we distinguish between "objective" cognitive understanding, and subjective inner knowing. The rational mind is conscious while dreams are unconscious, science represents adult understanding while fairy tales are the knowing of childhood. In our culture, the pursuit of inner knowing is a diversion from the more important tasks of work and professionalism. Experiments are scientific and dramatic plays are art, activity in the office or classroom is secular while rituals are sacred, and so on.

Because its vocabulary is characterized by subjective impressions laden with emotion and imagination, inner knowing is less amenable to research models that can be replicated by others. Yet according to the philosopher Thomas Aquinas, imagination is central to inner knowing because it is the only human faculty that unifies body, mind, and spirit with the past, present, and future. The evolutionary process has seen to it that imagination begins immediately in childhood, forming a deep root of human consciousness.

Before conceptual powers are firmly established, a child's time is filled with daydreams, wishes, reveries, and play. But far from being a plaything of childhood, imagination is the raw stuff, the basic material, the primary faculty of perception for nonordinary knowing. The rational mind may categorize knowledge transmitted through dreams, art, metaphor, ritual, and emotional connections as subjective and personal, yet the faculty of imagination cannot be dismissed, because it is part of our very being.

Dreams exemplify the potent vocabulary of metaphor, which is the language of inner knowing. Rather than being mere fictitious fantasies, dreams produce powerful information that can be verified when we wake and analyze the communication. If in this world we are forced to see ourselves as separate from others, in the imaginal world we are at one with each other and the environment. Dreams are not like thoughts, where we feel separate from what we think. They are instead, spontaneously lived events, filled with directly experienced messages, mainly in the form of feelings and visual metaphors. In the universe of the imagination, we are touched, moved, broken, thrilled, and swept away from our familiar sense of separation from people and things. We

become different aspects of ourselves in a dream, inhabiting scenes and scenarios laden with meaning. We even become other people, seeing ourselves
from their point of view, and all this takes place within a unitive state of mind
where there's no sense of separation, no emotional filter, and we can't retract
our awareness.

Dreaming dissolves the customary psychological defenses that cushion reality while we are awake. Things happen to us, instead of us making things happen. Dreamers rarely anticipate or control what shows up before it appears,
reminding us of childhood, when the world acts upon us and we are affected
by whatever comes our way.

But once grown, we live in a private, emotionally guarded world that seems
removed from a greater reality. We think of imagination that was once so active
as "something I made up," or "just another daydream, a silly fantasy." Indeed,
as adults, we think in concepts almost continuously, reducing the potent
vocabulary of imagination to the level of guided imagery, mere counterparts
for thought.

But fortunately, at night, everything changes. For when we dream, we're
again in the state of mind of a child. The authors in Part III focus on different
aspects of the dichotomy between reason and imagination. They help us see
that reason allows us to decipher the meaning contained in imaginative
impressions—and that reason can also obstruct the faculties of imagination.

Though our access to feelings and imagery typically diminishes as we
mature in the rational world, we never lose contact with inner faculties of
imagination and can always find ways to educate them.

Here, six contemporary writers describe familiar ways of knowing that do
not rely on intellect or analysis. They tell us that through dreams, fairy tales,
active imagination, and even our own emotions, we can learn a great deal
about ourselves and our environment. These nonintellectual conduits of information are recognized, if not respected, by our science-based culture, because
they have played their part in our life experiences since childhood.

11. Experiential Knowing by Abraham H. Maslow

In this classic piece from the literature of consciousness, Maslow reminds us that whether we like it or not, we find ourselves in a dualistic world. Here we are compelled to practice what he calls "spectator knowing," which creates a split between the knower and the known, even producing an "alienation of the knower from his known."

In contrast, Maslow develops ten characteristics of what he calls "full experiencing," where the observer's awareness shifts to "become" what is known, rather than remaining in the stance of a separate spectator. Drawing on extensive work with peak experience, he sees experiential knowing as "I-Thou knowledge" or "fusion knowledge"—both ways of describing the nondual state of mind in which we fully comprehend each other.

SPECTATOR KNOWLEDGE ABOUT THINGS

What does the orthodox scientist mean by "knowing"? Let us remember that at the beginning of science the word "knowing" meant "knowing of the external physical world," and for the orthodox scientist it still does. It means looking at something that is not you, not human, not personal, something independent of you the perceiver. It is something to which you are a stranger, a bystander, a member of the audience. You the observer are, then, really alien to it, uncomprehending and without sympathy and identification, without any starting point of tacit knowledge that you might already have. You look through the microscope or the telescope as through a keyhole, peering, peeping, from a distance, from outside, not as one who has a right to be in the room being peeped into. Such a scientific observer is not a participant observer. His science can be likened to a spectator sport, and he to a spectator. He has no necessary involvement with what he is looking at, no loyalties, no stake in it. He can be cool, detached, emotionless, desireless, wholly other than what he is looking at. He is in the grandstand looking down upon the goings on in the arena; he himself is not in the arena. And ideally he doesn't care who wins.

He can be and should be neutral if he is looking at something utterly strange to him. It is best for the veridicality of his observations that he lay no bets, be neither for nor against, have no hopes or wishes for one outcome rather than another. It is most efficient, if he seeks a truthful report, that he move toward being nonaligned and uninvolved. Of course we know that such neutrality and noninvolvement is theoretically almost impossible. Yet movement *toward* such an ideal is possible, and is different from movement *away* from it.

It will help communication with those who have read Martin Buber if I call this I-It knowledge by contrast with the I-Thou knowledge that I shall try to describe. I-It knowledge is sometimes all you can do with things, with objects that have no human qualities to be identified with and to be understanding about. . . .

I do not mean here that this alien knowledge of the alien is the best that can be managed, even for things and objects. More sensitive observers are able to incorporate more of the world into the self, i.e., they are able to identify and empathize with wider and wider and more and more inclusive circles of living and nonliving things. As a matter of fact, this may turn out to be a distinguishing mark of the highly matured personality. It is likely that some degree of such identification makes possible some corresponding degree of experiential knowledge, by becoming and *being* what is to be known rather than remaining totally the outside spectator. Since this identification can be subsumed under "love" broadly defined, its ability to increase knowledge from within may be considered for research purposes an instance of improvement of knowledge by love. Or perhaps we might formulate a general hypothesis to read so: love for the object seems likely to enhance experiential knowledge of the object, with lack of love diminishing experiential knowledge of the object, although it may very well increase spectator knowledge of that same object.

An obvious illustration supported by common sense experience might be this. Researcher A is really fascinated with schizophrenics (or white rats or lichens). Researcher B, however, is much more interested in manic-depressive insanity (or monkeys or mushrooms). We may confidently expect that Researcher A will (a) freely choose or prefer to study schizophrenics, etc., (b) work better and longer at it, be more patient, more stubborn, more tolerant of associated chores, (c) have more hunches, intuitions, dreams, illumination about them, (d) be more likely to make more profound discoveries about schizophrenia, and (e) the schizophrenics will feel easier with him and say that he "understands" them. In all these respects he would almost certainly do better than Researcher B. But observe that this superiority is in principle far greater for acquiring experiential knowledge than it is for acquiring knowledge about something, or spectator knowledge, even though Researcher A probably could do a bit better at that, too.

So far as spectator knowledge of the alien is concerned, any competent scientist or research assistant may confidently be expected to accumulate knowledge about *anything* in a normal, routine way, e.g., external statistics. As a matter of fact, this is exactly what happens a great deal today in an age of "projects," grants, teams, and organizations. Many scientists can be hired to do one disconnected, passionless job after another, just as a good salesman prides himself on being able to sell anything, whether he likes it or not, or as a horse pulls whatever wagon he happens to get hitched to.

This is one way of describing the Cartesian split between the knower and the known that the existentialists, for instance, speak of today. We might also call it the "distancing" or perhaps even the alienation of the knower from his known. It must be clear from what has gone before that I can conceive of other kinds of relationships between knower and known or between perceiver and percept. I-Thou knowledge, knowledge by experiencing, knowledge from within, love knowledge, Being-Cognition, fusion knowledge, identification knowledge—all these have been or will be mentioned. Not only do these other forms of knowing exist, but also they are actually better, more efficaious, more productive of reliable and valid knowledge *if* we are trying to acquire knowledge of a particular person or even persons in general. If we wish to learn more about persons, then this is the way we'd better go about it.

SOME PROPERTIES AND CHARACTERISTICS OF EXPERIENCING

Fullest and richest experiencing of the kind described by the Zen Buddhists, the general semanticists, and the phenomenologists includes at least the following aspects (my own primary source of data here are studies of peak experiences):

1. The good experiencer gets "utterly lost in the present," to use Sylvia Ashton-Warner's beautiful phrase. He loses his past and his future for the time being and lives totally in the here-now experience. He is "all there," immersed, concentrated, fascinated.

2. Self-consciousness is lost for the moment.

3. The experiencing is timeless, placeless, societyless, historyless.

4. In the fullest experiencing, a kind of melting together of the person experiencing with that which is experienced occurs. This is difficult to put into words but I shall try below.

5. The experiencer becomes more "innocent," more receptive without questioning, as children are. In the purest extreme the person is naked in the situation, guileless, without expectations or worries of any kind, without

"shoulds" or "oughts," without filtering the experience through any a priori ideas of what the experience should be, or of what is normal, correct, proper, right. The innocent child receives whatever happens without astonishment, shock, indignation, or denial and without any impulse to "improve" it. The full experience inundates the "helpless," will-less, amazed, and unselfishly interested experiencer.

6. One especially important aspect of full experiencing is the abeyance of importance-unimportance. Ideally the experience is not structured into relatively important or unimportant aspects, central or peripheral, essential or expendable.

7. In the good instance fear disappears (along with all other personal or selfish considerations). The person is then nondefensive. The experience rushes in upon him without hindrance.

8. Striving, willing, straining tend to disappear. Experience happens without being made to happen.

9. Criticism, editing, checking of credentials or passports, skepticism, selecting and rejecting, evaluating—all tend to diminish or, in the ideal, to disappear for the time being, to be postponed.

10. This is the same as accepting, receiving, being passively seduced or raped by the experience, trusting it, letting it happen, being without will, noninterfering, surrendering.

11. All of this adds up to laying aside all the characteristics of our most prideful rationality, our words, our analysis, our ability to dissect, to classify, to define, to be logical. All of these processes are postponed. To the extent that they intrude, to that extent is the experience less "full." Experiencing of this sort is much closer to Freud's primary process than to his secondary processes. It is in this sense nonrational—although it is by no means antirational.

12. On Fairy Tales by Bruno Bettelheim

Fairy tales are the language that children use to make sense of the world. It's a language of image and feelings and moods, and if it weren't for imagination and fairy tales, Bettelheim argues, children would have no way to deal with the prominent shadow issues of their personalities. Irrational anxieties, angry fantasies, fear of abandonment, selfish outbursts, and other monstrous rumblings have to be made sense of. And so by way of fairy tales, unconscious urges are allowed into awareness, and given a structure so they can be worked through in the imagination.

This encourages adults as well to use the tradition of stories and tales as a healing agent. Rather than shy away from existential anxieties about maturity, aging, and death, the structure of a tale reveals the value of meeting these dilemmas head on by imaginatively identifying with traditional solutions that suggest a better course of action.

MY INTEREST IN fairy tales is not the result of such a technical analysis of their merits. It is, on the contrary, the consequence of asking myself why, in my experience, children—normal and abnormal alike, and at all levels of intelligence—find folk fairy tales more satisfying than all other children's stories.

The more I tried to understand why these stories are so successful at enriching the inner life of the child, the more I realized that these tales, in a much deeper sense than any other reading material, start where the child really is in his psychological and emotional being. They speak about his severe inner pressures in a way that the child unconsciously understands, and—without belittling the most serious inner struggles which growing up entails—offer examples of both temporary and permanent solutions to pressing difficulties. . . .

[I am now] explor[ing] in greater detail and depth why folk fairy tales are so valuable in the upbringing of children. My hope is that a proper understanding of the unique merits of fairy tales will induce parents and teachers to assign them once again to that central role in the life of the child they held for centuries.

FAIRY TALES AND THE EXISTENTIAL PREDICAMENT

In order to master the psychological problems of growing up—overcoming narcissistic disappointments, oedipal dilemmas, sibling rivalries; becoming able to relinquish childhood dependencies; gaining a feeling of selfhood and of self-worth, and a sense of moral obligation—a child needs to understand what is going on within his conscious self so that he can also cope with that which goes on in his unconscious. He can achieve this understanding, and with it the ability to cope, not through rational comprehension of the nature and content of his unconscious, but by becoming familiar with it through spinning out daydreams—ruminating, rearranging, and fantasizing about suitable story elements in response to unconscious pressures. By doing this, the child fits unconscious content into conscious fantasies, which then enable him to deal with that content. It is here that fairy tales have unequaled value, because they offer new dimensions to the child's imagination which would be impossible for him to discover as truly on his own. Even more important, the form and structure of fairy tales suggest images to the child by which he can structure his daydreams and with them give better direction to his life.

In child or adult, the unconscious is a powerful determinant of behavior. When the unconscious is repressed and its content denied entrance into awareness, then eventually the person's conscious mind will be partially overwhelmed by derivatives of these unconscious elements, or else he is forced to keep such rigid, compulsive control over them that his personality may become severely crippled. But when unconscious material *is* to some degree permitted to come to awareness and worked through in imagination, its potential for causing harm—to ourselves or others—is much reduced; some of its forces can then be made to serve positive purposes. However, the prevalent parental belief is that a child must be diverted from what troubles him most: his formless, nameless anxieties, and his chaotic, angry, and even violent fantasies. Many parents believe that only conscious reality or pleasant and wish-fulfilling images should be presented to the child—that he should be exposed only to the sunny side of things. But such one-sided fare nourishes the mind only in a one-sided way, and real life is not all sunny.

There is a widespread refusal to let children know that the source of much that goes wrong in life is due to our very own natures—the propensity of all men for acting aggressively, asocially, selfishly, out of anger and anxiety. Instead, we want our children to believe that, inherently, all men are good. But children know that *they* are not always good; and often, even when they are, they would prefer not to be. This contradicts what they are told by their parents, and therefore makes the child a monster in his own eyes.

The dominant culture wishes to pretend, particularly where children are concerned, that the dark side of man does not exist, and professes a belief in an optimistic meliorism. Psychoanalysis itself is viewed as having the purpose of making life easy—but this is not what its founder intended. Psychoanalysis was created to enable man to accept the problematic nature of life without being defeated by it, or giving in to escapism. Freud's prescription is that only by struggling courageously against what seem like overwhelming odds can mean succeed in wringing meaning out of his existence.

This is exactly the message that fairy tales get across to the child in manifold form: that a struggle against severe difficulties in life is unavoidable, is an intrinsic part of human existence—but that if one does not shy away, but steadfastly meets unexpected and often unjust hardships, one masters all obstacles and at the end emerges victorious.

Modern stories written for young children mainly avoid these existential problems, although they are crucial issues for all of us. The child needs most particularly to be given suggestions in symbolic form about how he may deal with these issues and grow safely into maturity. "Safe" stories mention neither death nor aging, the limits to our existence, nor the wish for eternal life. The fairy tale, by contrast, confronts the child squarely with the basic human predicaments.

For example, many fairy stories begin with the death of a mother or father; in these tales the death of the parent creates the most agonizing problems, as it (or the fear of it) does in real life. Other stories tell about an aging parent who decides that the time has come to let the new generation take over. But before this can happen, the successor has to prove himself capable and worthy. The Brothers Grimm's story "The Three Feathers" begins: "There was once upon a time a king who had three sons. . . . When the king had become old and weak, and was thinking of his end, he did not know which of his sons should inherit the kingdom after him." In order to decide, the king sets all his sons a difficult task; the son who meets it best "shall be king after my death."

It is characteristic of fairy tales to state an existential dilemma briefly and pointedly. This permits the child to come to grips with the problem in its most essential form, where a more complex plot would confuse matters for him. The fairy tale simplifies all situations. Its figures are clearly drawn; and details, unless very important, are eliminated. All characters are typical rather than unique.

Contrary to what takes place in many modern children's stories, in fairy tales evil is as omnipresent as virtue. In practically every fairy tale good and evil are given body in the form of some figures and their actions, as good and evil are omnipresent in life and the propensities for both are present in every man. It is this duality which poses the moral problem, and requires the struggle to solve it.

Evil is not without its attractions—symbolized by the mighty giant or dragon, the power of the witch, the cunning queen in "Snow White"—and often it is temporarily in the ascendancy. In many fairy tales a usurper succeeds for a time in seizing the place which rightfully belongs to the hero—as the wicked sisters do in "Cinderella." It is not that the evildoer is punished at the story's end which makes immersing oneself in fairy stories an experience in moral education, although this is part of it. In fairy tales, as in life, punishment or fear of it is only a limited deterrent to crime. The conviction that crime does not pay is a much more effective deterrent, and that is why in fairy tales the bad person always loses out. It is not the fact that virtue wins out at the end which promotes morality, but that the hero is most attractive to the child, who identifies with the hero in all his struggles. Because of this identification the child imagines that he suffers with the hero his trials and tribulations, and triumphs with him as virtue is victorious. The child makes such identifications all on his own, and the inner and outer struggles of the hero imprint morality on him.

The figures in fairy tales are not ambivalent—not good and bad at the same time, as we all are in reality. But since polarization dominates the child's mind, it also dominates fairy tales. A person is either good or bad, nothing in between. One brother is stupid, the other is clever. One sister is virtuous and industrious, the others are vile and lazy. One is beautiful, the others are ugly. One parent is all good, the other evil. The juxtaposition of opposite characters is not for the purpose of stressing right behavior, as would be true for cautionary tales. (There are some amoral fairy tales where goodness or badness, beauty or ugliness play no role at all.) Presenting the polarities of character permits the child to comprehend easily the difference between the two, which he could not do as readily were the figures drawn more true to life, with all the complexities that characterize real people. Ambiguities must wait until a relatively firm personality has been established on the basis of positive identifications. Then the child has a basis for understanding that there are great differences between people, and that therefore one has to make choices about who one wants to be. This basic decision, on which all later personality development will build, is facilitated by the polarizations of the fairy tale.

Furthermore, a child's choices are based, not so much on right versus wrong, as on who arouses his sympathy and who his antipathy. The more simple and straightforward a good character, the easier it is for a child to identify with it and to reject the bad other. The child identifies with the good hero not because of his goodness, but because the hero's condition makes a deep positive appeal to him. The question for the child is not "Do I want to be good?"

but "Who do I want to be like?" The child decides this on the basis of projecting himself wholeheartedly into one character. If this fairy-tale figure is a very good person, then the child decides that he wants to be good, too.

Amoral fairy tales show no polarization or juxtaposition of good and bad persons; that is because these amoral stories serve an entirely different purpose. Such tales or type figures as "Puss in Boots," who arranges for the hero's success through trickery, and Jack, who steals the giant's treasure, build character not by promoting choices between good and bad, but by giving the child the hope that even the meekest can succeed in life. After all, what's the use of choosing to become a good person when one feels so insignificant that he fears he will never amount to anything? Morality is not the issue in these tales, but rather, assurance that one can succeed. Whether one meets life with a belief in the possibility of mastering its difficulties or with the expectation of defeat is also a very important existential problem.

The deep inner conflicts originating in our primitive drives and our violent emotions are all denied in much of modern children's literature, and so the child is not helped in coping with them. But the child is subject to desperate feelings of loneliness and isolation, and he often experiences mortal anxiety. More often than not, he is unable to express these feelings in words, or he can do so only by indirection: fear of the dark, of some animal, anxiety about his body. Since it creates discomfort in a parent to recognize these emotions in his child, the parent tends to overlook them, or he belittles these spoken fears out of his own anxiety, believing this will cover over the child's fears.

The fairy tale, by contrast, takes these existential anxieties and dilemmas very seriously and addresses itself directly to them: the need to be loved and the fear that one is thought worthless; the love of life, and the fear of death. Further, the fairy tale offers solutions in ways that the child can grasp on his level of understanding. For example, fairy tales pose the dilemma of wishing to live eternally by occasionally concluding: "If they have not died, they are still alive." The other ending — "And they lived happily ever after" — does not for a moment fool the child that eternal life is possible. But it does indicate that which alone can take the sting out of the narrow limits of our time on this earth: forming a truly satisfying bond to another. The tales teach that when one has done this, one has reached the ultimate in emotional security of existence and permanence of relation available to man; and this alone can dissipate the fear of death. If one has found true adult love, the fairy story also tells, one doesn't need to wish for eternal life. This is suggested by another ending found in fairy tales: "They lived for a long time afterward, happy and in pleasure."

An uninformed view of the fairy tale sees in this type of ending an unrealistic wish-fulfillment, missing completely the important message it conveys to the child. These tales tell him that by forming a true interpersonal relation, one escapes the separation anxiety which haunts him (and which sets the stage for many fairy tales, but is always resolved at the story's ending). Furthermore, the story tells, this ending is not made possible, as the child wishes and believes, by holding on to his mother eternally. If we try to escape separation anxiety and death anxiety by desperately keeping our grasp on our parents, we will only be cruelly forced out, like Hansel and Gretel.

Only by going out into the world can the fairy-tale hero (child) find himself there; and as he does, he will also find the other with whom he will be able to live happily ever after; that is, without ever again having to experience separation anxiety. The fairy tale is future-oriented and guides the child—in terms he can understand in both his conscious and his unconscious mind—to relinquish his infantile dependency wishes and achieve a more satisfying independent existence.

Today children no longer grow up within the security of an extended family, or of a well-integrated community. Therefore, even more than at the times fairy tales were invented, it is important to provide the modern child with images of heroes who have to go out into the world all by themselves and who, although originally ignorant of the ultimate things, find secure places in the world by following their right way with deep inner confidence.

The fairy-tale hero proceeds for a time in isolation, as the modern child often feels isolated. The hero is helped by being in touch with primitive things—a tree, an animal, nature—as the child feels more in touch with those things than most adults do. The fate of these heroes convinces the child that, like them, he may feel outcast and abandoned in the world, groping in the dark, but, like them, in the course of his life he will be guided step by step, and given help when it is needed. Today, even more than in past times, the child needs the reassurance offered by the image of the isolated man who nevertheless is capable of achieving meaningful and rewarding relations with the world around him.

13. *Dreaming Consciousness by Montague Ullman, M.D.*

When awake, we are preoccupied with the external environment and locate ourselves within it by means of language. During sleep, we scan an internal environment and orient ourselves by means of imagery, symbol, and story.

Feelings serve as a connective tissue between people, while we are awake, but when the free flow of feelings is disrupted, Ullman sees dreams as resolving that tension by restoring emotional connections. There are no rational defenses in a dream, and we therefore face ourselves more honestly, in a way that we cannot while awake.

Dreaming also serves our survival needs as a species, by cutting through illusions, making us aware of our best and basest motivations, and restoring the balance between personal identity and the need to live with others. Again, we are reminded of the intelligence communicated through imagination, this time through the eyes of a brilliant spokesperson for dreams as a unitive state of mind that connects us to others.

THE UNIQUE VALUE of dreams for our waking life rests on the fact that we do something asleep and dreaming that we cannot do nearly as well while awake. We look at ourselves with greater honesty and in greater depth. This ability rests on what I consider to be the three cardinal features of dreaming consciousness. . . . The first is the fact that dreaming is connected with current concerns. As we go through the day, feelings and moods evolve that register with greater or lesser clarity. In general, feelings serve as a kind of connective tissue between ourselves and others. When feelings flow freely and appropriately, they do not leave any troublesome residue. When, however, that free flow is impeded by a tension that we fail to resolve, there is a tear or rupture, so to speak, in this connective tissue. The aftereffects persist as a kind of background Greek chorus reminding us that there is some unfinished emotional business from our past that needs attention.

While dreaming, we not only have the opportunity but also face the necessity to look further into the situation. The way we do this is the second unique feature of dreaming consciousness. We take the feeling provoked by this break in the connective tissue and run it through our memory bank to gather more information and clues about its historical source in our particular life story. That is why references to the past so often find their way into the dream. The more available the information, the more accurately we can assess the extent and significance of the break. In addition, our backward search reminds us of the many coping mechanisms we have at our disposal to deal with it.

The third and most significant quality of dreaming consciousness is its utter honesty. It may seem strange to think of the bizarre and confusing pictures we create at night in terms of honesty. To understand it, we must take a closer look at the situation we are in when our sleeping brain gets the signal to be aroused and start dreaming. At that point, the dreamer has been aroused from a state of seeming unconsciousness. He is also very much alone, having temporarily suspended his connections to the outside world and the cushioning support it offers. The consciousness then shaping itself is geared to three implicit questions:

- What is happening to me?
- How has it come to be this way?
- What can I do about it?

In other words, the dreamer is reorienting himself to his life at that moment and to his subjective state in particular. When we orient ourselves to our surroundings while awake, we do so by means of language. That remarkable tool . . . is a two-edged sword. We can use it to communicate honestly, or we can use it to deceive ourselves and others. Many unconscious strategies of self-deception are resorted to in the waking state when we do not wish to be confronted by what is distasteful or frightening.

We have no such leeway when we dream. This is because we have a most important question to decide, and we are left completely to our own devices to come up with an answer. We cannot look it up in a book or get help from anyone else. The question we are faced with is whether, in the light of the residual tension that now occupies us, Is it safe to remain asleep and alone or is it important enough for us to awaken and return to a more familiar landscape? This is a decision that involves a more radical change of state than we are ever called on to make when we are awake. It also requires a greater degree of honesty.

When I talk about the honesty that underlies the images we create while dreaming, I do not mean to imply that we are transformed into superhonest creatures endowed with halos. Rather, we allow ourselves to catch an honest glimpse of our subjective state, one that displays whatever self-deceptive tendencies may be at work. This truthful encounter with ourselves, warts and all, makes the remembered dream a powerful therapeutic instrument. I will have more to say about the inexorable quality of this honesty later on in my discussion of the connection of dreaming consciousness to the survival of the species.

What we have not yet addressed is why dreaming consciousness takes the form of imagery to carry out its potentially alerting function. Characteristically, dreaming occurs during the rapid eye movement (REM) stage of sleep. This is controlled by subcortical mechanisms, and from a phylogenetic standpoint, it is considered the most archaic stage of sleep. The ability to think in imagery seems to be carried over from our prehistory. That such imagery is so closely linked to the repetitive physiological stages of arousal during sleep, the REM stage, suggests that the imagery serves an alerting function.[1] The need for this may have come about because from a phylogenetic standpoint, it may not have been safe enough, in the presence of predators, to remain unconscious for too long a period of time. Lower animals have the same periods of arousal during sleep that characterize the dreaming stage in humans. Animals are more immediately dependent on their natural environment than are humans, and their survival is contingent on possible dangers from that environment. As primitive people evolved into social beings, their concerns shifted gradually from the possibility of physical danger from the outside to dangers inherent in maintaining the fabric of social existence. The problem of survival was transformed to what was happening in the social environment. This, in turn, was contingent on the quality and nature of one's connections to others. Social dangers become more manifest through the play of feelings and mood, contingent on the vicissitudes of social intercourse. To display concerns of that kind, the simple literal imaging mode, presumably possible for lower animals, had to be transformed into a more sophisticated use of imagery that ultimately led to the use of the image as a visual metaphor. Vigilance with respect to physical danger has been transformed into social vigilance.

This formulation stresses the underlying identity between waking consciousness and dreaming consciousness. Both are concerned with the effect of impinging stimuli. Both involve the challenge of novelty. Awake, we scan an external environment. Asleep, we scan an internal environment. When we are awake, perception begins with sensitivity to form and motion and is directed outward. When we are asleep and dreaming, perception begins with sensitivity to feelings triggered by recent intrusive events and is directed inward. Awake, we strive toward conceptual clarity as a guide to action in the world. In the case of dreaming, there is a flow of imagery that both expresses and contains feelings. The "action" that results is an internal one affecting the level of arousal. Both forms of consciousness serve a communicative function. Awake and through the power of language, we are able to keep in touch with others. Asleep and dreaming, we use a different language to tell ourselves stories about ourselves that we have not heard before.

In summary, dreaming consciousness serves the same function as waking consciousness with regard to laying the foundation for interconnectedness between members of the human species. It does so under different circumstances, deals with different content, and processes that content in a different way. In each of us, there is an incorruptible core of being, sensitive to the way we hurt ourselves or others and concerned with undoing the fragmentation that has resulted. We have not done too well as yet in preserving our animal heritage of being at one with nature or our human responsibility to be at one with each other. Our dreams are constant reminders of the infinite number of ways we have managed to get derailed and, at the same time, provide us with the opportunity to get back on track.

I regard waking consciousness as an evolutionary adaptation that enables us to move into the future as social creatures bent on shaping our own cultural and social destinies. At our disposal in this endeavor are the memories of our past; the free play of our imaginations; the range of our desires; and the energy, hope, and creativity that we bring to this task.

The building tool for conscious social adaptations is language, a somewhat unreliable tool. Lies can be presented as truths, and all kinds of deceptions can ensue. In other words, there is nothing so compelling about the nature of waking consciousness that would ensure its success as an instrument for survival. Not only individuals but whole nations have been deceived into thinking the emperor is parading through town wearing beautiful clothes. Might dreams be the child in us protesting the deception? Rycroft[2] refers to the "innocence of dreams," an innocence we otherwise seem to have lost. Might dreaming consciousness serve our survival needs as a species by the way it cuts through illusions and, with considerable drama and a good deal of hyperbole, calls attention to both our basest and our loftiest attributes?

There is, of course, a two-way equilibrium between the survival of the species and the survival of the individual. Our biological heritage moves us in the direction of a concern with species survival. Our cultural heritage provides us with a collective setting within which we attempt to fulfill our individual destinies. Dreaming consciousness, rooted in both domains, reflects both the priority of species survival as well as the significance of the role played by the individual. If this view is correct, then dreaming is an unconscious ally in the struggle of the species to survive and an ally in the struggle of the individual to fulfill a role in society that favors species survival. That role goes beyond the purely biological to include cultural and social goals as well. The range of our personal experience is sifted through a "survival filter" when we dream in a way that highlights those aspects of that experience that are either strengthening or hindering our capacity for collaborative ties with others. Seen in this light, dreaming is an even more reliable ally than waking consciousness in that there are no spurious ego needs to pander to. It is more spontaneous, more insistent, more compelling. . . .

What concerns us here is the facilitating role that dreams can play in fostering greater harmony than now exists among us. Dreams speak not only to the disconnections in the immediate life of the dreamer, but through the social stereotypes that find their way into the dream, they also address issues that confront society as a whole. The honesty of the dream points to what is irrational and prejudicial in society and ourselves. . . .

If we take the trouble to permit those nocturnal reflections to find their place in our waking world, they provide us with a starting point in the continuing struggle to transcend our limitations. The nature of our interdependence is such that, as personal connections evolve more solidly, there are effects that reverberate upward toward ever-larger social units. Dreams can point us in the right direction. They reveal our strengths, acknowledge our weaknesses, expose our deceits, and liberate our creativity. They deserve far greater attention than they now receive. . . .

In a manner somewhat analogous to Chomsky's[3] view of our intrinsic structural preparation for language, I prefer to postulate an inborn structural preparation for a nocturnal language capable of communicating to ourselves any tears in the social fabric of our existence. No one taught us this language, but we all speak it fluently. Our dreaming self has never lost sight of the fact that we are all members of a single species, and it makes use of this intrinsic capacity to keep reminding us of that fact.

An early pioneer of the psychoanalytic movement, Trigant Burrow,[4] wrote extensively on what he referred to as species or phylic consciousness. He spoke of the preconscious stage of development, referring to the sense of total union experienced by the infant with its environment. For him, the preconscious stage of unity between mother and child offered a template for all future relatedness. His emphasis was on how, in our subsequent development, we fail to preserve this common biological heritage and no longer feel linked in a total way to our natural and human environment. Burrow felt that our vulnerability to this kind of split began with our mastery of language and capacity for symbolic expression. . . .

We certainly have succeeded in fragmenting ourselves as a species. In our long struggle to become civilized, we have exploited fully every conceivable line of cleavage that can separate human beings from one another. Not only have we failed to overcome geographical boundaries, we continue to throw up barriers on the basis of religion, class, race, sex, and so on. The failure to master the use of a technology capable of destroying each other, as well as life on the planet is both symbolic of this fragmenting process and, unfortunately, an accurate and true picture of where our history as a species has brought us. Our artists and writers reflect and rebel against the fragmentation; our scientists, through their increasing specialization, play into it; our philosophers worry about it; and our politicians seek in vain for solutions. Religion offers an ideal but fails in practice. The rise of interest in Eastern philosophies seems at one and the same time to be a retreat from the problems and an attempt to transcend them.

An individual human being can lead a self-centered and selfish life, live to a ripe old age, and die peacefully in bed. From all indications, that possibility does not exist for humankind considered as a whole. The nations of the world are just beginning to face the reality that, only through cooperation and collaboration, will it be possible for all to inhabit the same planet. . . .

The relationship of dreams to connectedness emerges clearly in the course of group dream work. In the presence of a safe atmosphere generated by the nonintrusive nature of the process, social defenses melt away or, at any rate, don't interfere with the deep-level sharing and sense of communion that is generated. Group members respond at a feeling level to someone else's imagery. Although this is understandable in terms of sharing a similar social milieu and facing similar life issues, it may also point to a deeper way that imagery has of linking people together, something more akin to a shared aesthetic response. Group dream work discloses an agency that works against fragmentation. Trust, communion, and a sense of solidarity develop rapidly in a dream-sharing group. There is an interweaving of lives at so profound a level that the feeling of interconnectedness becomes a palpable reality.

These considerations have led me to the speculative notion that while asleep and dreaming, we engage with a much broader aspect of our nature, one that goes beyond the concern of the individual. Our dreaming psyche seems to be aware of the vital significance for species survival of maintaining collaborative ties to each other. Somewhere within us, there is the awareness that, if unchecked, disunity carries within it the seeds of divisiveness and potential destruction. Only through constructive and affectionate bonding can this fragmentation be overcome and the species endure. In this sense, dreams may be seen as arising from a built-in mechanism concerned with the survival of the species. The individual's concern with the maintenance of connectedness is part of this larger concern—namely, the issue of species connectedness, the preservation of the individual being necessary for the preservation of the species. While dreaming, we seem to transcend individual boundaries to move toward our place in a larger whole. . . .

Our freedom as human beings can be achieved only through and with other people. Our evolutionary path has made us social creatures. There is no backing away from that reality. The only way forward is to create circumstances within ourselves and outside ourselves that will allow for the same natural sense of freedom in a social environment as our fellow creatures enjoy in their natural environment. Ultimately, this will depend on whether or not we can ever heal the devastating fragmentation I have referred to. At the moment, this is a distant goal, but the path there exists and the dreaming part of one's psyche grasps it intuitively. It concerns itself with all that limits or stands in the way of the free flow of affectionate ties to our fellow human beings. This is what concerns us as we sleep and dream.

14. *Psychoanalysis and the Art of Knowing by Erich Fromm*

In this seminal piece from the analytic tradition, written in the late 1950s as part of a series of lectures on psychoanalysis and Zen Buddhism, Erich Fromm struggles with analysts' need to bridge the gap between detached observation and becoming "observant participants" with their patients. Here we witness the estrangement between the Western dichotomy of conscious/unconscious functioning and the far broader spectrum of awareness described in spiritual tradition.

Can you imagine Dr. Fromm introducing his colleagues to the notion of "becoming" their patients, rather than analyzing the content of their free associations? I witnessed a similar culture clash in the late seventies, in a debate in which Charles Tart, one of the authors in this book, rose to defend the radical concept of state-specific knowing at a meeting of the American Association for the Advancement of Science. As in the case of Fromm's fascination with Zen, Tart's valuing of his inner experience above the current cognitive model was also hotly contested.

WE MAY BEGIN by saying that the average person, while he thinks he is awake, actually is half asleep. By "half asleep" I mean that his contact with reality is a very partial one; most of what he believes to be reality (outside or inside of himself) is a set of fictions which his mind constructs. He is aware of reality only to the degree to which his social functioning makes it necessary. He is aware of his fellowmen inasmuch as he needs to cooperate with them; he is aware of material and social reality inasmuch as he needs to be aware of it in order to manipulate it. *He is aware of reality to the extent to which the goal of survival makes such awareness necessary.* (In contradistinction in the state of sleep the awareness of outer reality is suspended, though easily recovered in case of necessity, and in the case of insanity, full awareness of outer reality is absent and not even recoverable in any kind of emergency.) The average person's consciousness is mainly "false consciousness," consisting of fictions and illusion, while precisely what he is not aware of is reality. We can thus differentiate between what a person *is* conscious of, and what he *becomes* conscious of. He *is* conscious, mostly, of fictions; he can *become* conscious of the realities which lie underneath these fictions.

There is another aspect of unconsciousness which follows from the premises discussed earlier. Inasmuch as consciousness represents only the small sector of socially patterned experience and unconsciousness represents the richness and depth of universal man the state of repressedness results in the fact that I, the accidental, social person, am separated from me the whole human person. I am a stranger to myself, and to the same degree everybody else is a stranger to me. I am cut off from the vast area of experience which is human, and remain a fragment of a man, a cripple who experiences only a small part of what is real in him and what is real in others.

Thus far we have spoken only of the distorting function of repressedness; another aspect remains to be mentioned which does not lead to distortion, but to making an experience unreal by *cerebration*. I refer by this to the fact that I believe I see—but I only *see words;* I believe I feel, but I only *think feelings.* The cerebrating person is the alienated person, the person in the cave who, as in Plato's allegory, sees only shadows and mistakes them for immediate reality.

This process of cerebration is related to the ambiguity of language. As soon as I have expressed something in a word, an alienation takes place, and the full experience has already been substituted for by the word. The full experience actually exists only up to the moment when it is expressed in language. This general process of cerebration is more widespread and intense in modern culture than it probably was at any time before in history. Just because of the increasing emphasis on intellectual knowledge which is a condition for scientific and technical achievements, and in connection with it on literacy and education, words more and more take the place of experience. Yet the person concerned is unaware of this. He thinks he sees something; he thinks he feels something; yet there is no experience except memory and thought. When he thinks *he* grasps reality it is only his brain-self that grasps it, while he, the whole man, his eyes, his hands, his heart, his belly, grasp nothing—in fact, *he* is not participating in the experience which he believes is *his.*

What happens then in the process in which the unconscious becomes conscious? In answering this question we had better reformulate it. There is no such thing as "the conscious" and no such thing as "the unconscious." There are degrees of consciousness-awareness and unconsciousness-unawareness. Our question then should rather be: what happens when I become aware of what I have not been aware of before? In line with what has been said before, the general answer to this question is that every step in this process is in the direction of understanding the fictitious, unreal character of our "normal" consciousness. To become conscious of what is unconscious and thus to enlarge one's consciousness means to get in touch with reality, and—in this sense—with truth (intellectually and affectively). To enlarge consciousness means to wake up, to lift a veil, to leave the cave, to bring light into the darkness.

Could this be the same experience Zen Buddhists call "enlightenment"?

While I shall return later to this question, I want at this point to discuss further a crucial point for psychoanalysis, namely, the *nature of insight and knowledge* which is to affect the transformation of unconsciousness into consciousness.[1] Doubtlessly, in the first years of his psychoanalytic research Freud shared the conventional rationalistic belief that knowledge was intellectual, theoretical knowledge. He thought that it was enough to explain to the patient why certain developments had taken place, and to tell him what the analyst discovered in his unconscious. This intellectual knowledge, called "interpretation," was supposed to effect a change in the patient. But soon Freud and other analysts had to discover the truth of Spinoza's statement that *intellectual* knowledge is conducive to change only inasmuch as it is also *affective* knowledge. It became apparent that intellectual knowledge as such does not produce any change, except perhaps in the sense that by intellectual knowledge of his unconscious strivings a person may be better able to control them—which, however, is the aim of traditional ethics, rather than that of psychoanalysis. As long as the patient remains in the attitude of the detached scientific observer, taking himself as the object of his investigation, he is not in touch with his unconscious, except by *thinking* about it; he does not *experience* the wider, deeper reality within himself. Discovering one's unconscious is, precisely, *not* an intellectual act, but an affective experience, which can hardly be put into words, if at all. This does not mean that thinking and speculation may not precede the act of discovery; but the act of discovery itself is always a *total* experience. It is total in the sense that the whole person experiences it; it is an experience which is characterized by its spontaneity and suddenness. One's eyes are suddenly opened; oneself and the world appear in a different light, are seen from a different viewpoint. There is usually a good deal of anxiety aroused before the experience takes place, while afterwards a new feeling of strength and certainty is present. The process of discovering the unconscious can be described as a series of ever-widening experiences, which are felt deeply and which transcend theoretical, intellectual knowledge.

The importance of this kind of *experiential knowledge* lies in the fact that it transcends the kind of knowledge and awareness in which the subject-intellect observes himself as an object, and thus that it transcends the Western, rationalistic concept of knowing. (Exceptions in the Western tradition, where experiential knowledge is dealt with, are to be found in Spinoza's highest form of knowing, intuition; in Fichte's intellectual intuition; or in Bergson's creative consciousness. All these categories of intuition transcend subject-object split knowledge . . .). . . .

One more point in our brief sketch of the essential elements in psychoanalysis needs to be mentioned, *the role of the psychoanalyst*. Originally it was not different from that of any physician "treating" a patient. But after some years the situation changed radically. Freud recognized that the analyst himself needed to be analyzed, that is, to undergo the same process his patient was to submit to later. This need for the analyst's analysis was explained as resulting from the necessity to free the analyst from his own blind spots, neurotic tendencies, and so on. But this explanation seems insufficient, as far as Freud's own views are concerned, if we consider Freud's early statements, quoted above, when he spoke of the analyst needing to be a "model," a "teacher," being able to conduct a relationship between himself and the patient which is based on a "love of truth," that precludes any kind of "sham or deception." Freud seems to have sensed here that the analyst has a function transcending that of the physician in his relationship to his patient. But still, he did not change his fundamental concept, that of the analyst being the detached observer—and the patient being his *object* of observation. In the history of psychoanalysis, this concept of the detached observer was modified from two sides, first by Ferenczi, who in the last years of his life postulated that it was not enough for the analyst to observe and to interpret; that he had to be able to love the patient with the very love which the patient had needed as a child, yet had never experienced. Ferenczi did not have in mind that the analyst should feel erotic love toward his patient, but rather motherly or fatherly love or, putting it more generally, loving care.[2] H. S. Sullivan approached the same point from a different aspect. He thought that the analyst must not have the attitude of a detached observer, but of a *"participant observer,"* thus trying to transcend the orthodox idea of the detachment of the analyst. In my own view, Sullivan may not have gone far enough, and one might prefer the definition of the analyst's role as that of an *"observant participant,"* rather than that of a participant observer. But even the expression "participant" does not quite express what is meant here; to "participate" is still to be outside. The knowledge of another person requires being inside of him, to *be* him. The analyst understands the patient only inasmuch as he experiences in himself all that the patient experiences; otherwise he will have only intellectual knowledge *about* the patient, but will never really know what the patient experiences, nor will he be able to convey to him that he shares and understands his (the patient's) experience. In this productive relatedness between analyst and patient, in the act of being fully engaged with the patient, in being fully open and responsive to him, in being soaked with him, as it were, in this center-to-center relatedness, lies one of the essential conditions for psychoanalytic understanding and cure.[3] The analyst must become the patient, yet he must be himself; he must forget that he is the doctor, yet he must remain aware of it. Only when he accepts this paradox, can he give "interpretations" which carry authority because they are rooted in his own experience. The analyst analyzes the patient, but the patient also analyzes the analyst, because the analyst, by sharing the unconscious of his patient, cannot help clarifying his own unconscious. Hence the analyst not only cures the patient, but is also cured by him. He not only understands the patient, but eventually the patient understands him. When this stage is reached, solidarity and communion are reached.

This relationship to the patient must be realistic and free from all sentimentality. Neither the analyst nor any man can "save" another human being. He can act as a guide — or as a midwife; he can show the road, remove obstacles, and sometimes lend some direct help, but he can never do for the patient what only the patient can do for himself. He must make this perfectly clear to the patient, not only in words, but by his whole attitude. He must also stress the awareness of the realistic situation which is even more limited than a relationship between two persons necessarily needs to be; if he, the analyst, is to live his own life, and if he is to serve a number of patients simultaneously, there are limitations in time and space. But there is no limitation in the here and now of the encounter between patient and analyst. When this encounter takes place, during the analytic session, when the two talk to each other, then there is nothing more important in the world than their talking to each other — for the patient as well as for the analyst. The analyst, in years of common work with the patient, transcends indeed the conventional role of the doctor; he becomes a teacher, a model, perhaps a master, provided that he himself never considers himself as analyzed until he has attained full self-awareness and freedom, until he has overcome his own alienation and separateness. The didactic analysis of the analyst is not the end, but the beginning of a continuous process of self analysis, that is, of ever-increasing awakeness.

15. *Active Imagination in Practice by Janet Dallett*

For most of us, the first task in self-development lies in establishing some form of communication between conscious life (ego awareness) and our own unconscious. In this lucid description of the classic Jungian process of active imagination, we are given a primary tool for building that relationship.

Citing the four steps of the process outlined by analyst Marie-Louise von Franz, Dallett expands on the technique, recognizing that the unconscious communicates in symbols, images, and stories. Whereas everyone follows the same four steps, each person's ego-unconscious relationship is entirely original, forming its own unique pattern.

IN ONE OF the very few papers published about active imagination, B. Hannah writes:

> Whenever man has tried to come to terms with an invisible, supernatural and apparently eternal reality . . . he has instinctively evolved . . . some form of meditation or dialogue that corresponds in a greater or lesser degree with what Jung has called active imagination.[1]

Her treatment of the subject in spiritual terms resonates with my own sense that active imagination is most meaningfully defined as a *dialogue with the gods.* If this definition were understood fully, with all the meaning implicit in it, no more would have to be said. The rest of this chapter can be seen simply as an amplification of it.

There are some immediate implications of seeing active imagination as a dialogue with the gods. First of all, there must be at least two participants, separate from each other. One of the participants in active imagination is the conscious ego, rooted in external reality. It is impossible to relate to the world of imagination if you are simply caught and floating in it. . . .

In addition to the ego, whose importance is indisputable, the other partners in the dialogue of active imagination consist of the gods as they express themselves through the psyche. Gods include also what religion has traditionally called devils. It is possible to say that the other parties in the dialogue are the archetypes of the collective unconscious. That sounds more scientific than "the gods. . . ."

The word *gods* gives an emotional jolt, conveying something of the reality of a dialogue with the unconscious. The gods (and demons) are autonomous factors, rooted in a different reality (the reality of spirit, not necessarily the material world), that can express themselves through the imagination. As William Blake has said, imagination is the "divine body" in all of us.

Once the partners in the dialogue have been identified, the definition next implies that in active imagination there is a *relationship* between them. Some of the same considerations apply to this inner relationship as to relationships between people in the outside world. For example, full regard for the other's separateness and idiosyncrasies is essential. In the inner relationship, the unconscious must be permitted to be what it is, and not forced into ego or external reality notions of how it ought to behave. At the same time, the ego must hold firmly to its own reality. This is as difficult in inner as in outer relationships.

Another similarity to outer relationships is that many aspects of the inner relationship are personal and private, not to be discussed indiscriminately with others. It can be very important to discover when to keep to yourself what is going on between you and yourself, and when to talk about it.

Furthermore, if you make a promise, it is as much a violation to break it in the inner world as in the outer; if you try to control or to have power over your partner, inner or outer, it is no longer possible to relate; and an inner relationship can no more be forced to obey rational considerations than can an outer one.

The word *active* in active imagination is crucial. As in any relationship, if one partner (the ego) does not participate actively, the other (the unconscious) simply fills the vacuum by running on its own way, unchecked and unchanged, possibly taking over completely. Then there is no relationship. This is the case, for example, when a person is passively obsessed by fantasies.

There are many examples in literature and drama of the kind of relationship to divinity that expresses itself in active imagination. One of my favorites has long been the scenes in *Fiddler on the Roof* in which the father, Tevya, carries on down-to-earth, no-nonsense discussions with God. These provide a most authentic example of the actively participating relationship between God and man.

More recently, the film *Close Encounters of the Third Kind* impressively expresses both the emotional intensity of active imagination when it is fully engaged and some very specific aspects of it. In this film, visitors from another planet fill their human contacts with a sense of urgent necessity to paint or sculpt a specific image, a picture of the mountain where they land on earth and can be met. Others experience the same compelling drive to work out the mathematical-musical-color language that the aliens speak. These means of expression constitute the only way in which communication with the "others" can be established. Similarly, the voice of the unconscious in the dialogue of active imagination often pushes to be given form in some quite specific way, whether it be sculpture, painting, dance, music, or some other medium besides words.

One last direct implication of our definition of active imagination is the requirement for consciousness of the power and vastness of one of the partners in the dialogue, the gods, with whom a relationship is not to be undertaken lightly. Caution and religious respect for the other is a prerequisite of this encounter.

THE COMPONENTS OF ACTIVE IMAGINATION

Von Franz has spoken about four steps into which the process of active imagination can be divided.[2] These steps offer a conceptually convenient way to break up the process in order to look at it more closely, although it is unlikely that anyone ever actually does active imagination in such an orderly fashion.

1. The first step is what von Franz calls "stopping the mad mind." The thoughts of ego-consciousness must first be set aside in order to give the unconscious a chance to enter.

2. The unconscious begins to come in, usually in the form of fantasies, images, or emotions. These are written down or given some other external form at this point.

3. The ego reacts. There is a confrontation with the unconscious material that has come up.

4. Conclusions are drawn and put to work in life.

The First Step

. . . To permit that other point of view to come up, most people must find a way to set aside the critical, judging mode of the ego. At this stage the ego must simply observe, uncritically, what comes up, remaining alert but not filtering out anything. Something akin to the alpha state of unfocused attention is cultivated. About this Jung comments:

> We must be able to let things happen in the psyche. . . . Consciousness is forever interfering, helping, correcting, and negating, never leaving the psychic processes to grow in peace. . . . To begin with, the task consists solely in observing objectively how a fragment of fantasy develops.[3]

I once had a dream that expresses nicely what not to do. In the dream I planted some young trees, and right away, the next day, got worried that not enough nutrients would reach their roots. So I dug up the trees in order to see how the roots were doing! That is the kind of thing the ego does to interfere with the very growth process it intends to nurture.

A number of things can facilitate the first step of active imagination and help the interfering ego to stand aside. Naturally occurring situations of unfocused attention like tooth brushing, shaving, washing dishes, ironing, or jogging can be used to good advantage. Long before a patient is ready to engage the process fully, he or she can carry around a small notebook or tape recorder to catch the fragments of fantasy that impinge upon consciousness. The first thing is simply to notice the psyche's activity.

A ritual can help one to get into active imagination. When I first began to do active imagination, I would light a candle, turn down the lights, and sit in a particular way in a particular chair. Now, after many years, the act of sitting down at a typewriter is sufficient ritual.

Often a dream ends at a moment when it might easily be continued in imagination, or there may be a particularly powerful dream image to relate to. Then, getting back into the imagery and mood of the dream facilitates the beginning of active imagination.

Finally, working with graphic or plastic material rather than words may help reduce ego interference. The hands can do what they want without help from the head.

What is really required at this first stage is the attitude of the child at play. The hardest thing for adults to learn about play is to take it seriously. They usually feel they can indulge in play only after having taken care of serious business. Yet play is a serious matter for the child, who continually creates, destroys, and re-creates new worlds. Recognizing the importance of this kind of play is essential for active imagination, as well as for many other endeavors.

When, at the age of thirty-five, I returned to graduate school, I dreamed that I had to go to my childhood home and bring back with me a set of children's building blocks. At the time I did not fully appreciate how vital it was going to be to recapture the playful-serious creative perspective symbolized by the blocks, to help my spirit survive the deadly earnest, overrational atmosphere of graduate school. . . .

Jung wrote: "The creative activity of imagination frees man from his bondage to the 'nothing but' and *raises him to the status of one who plays*" (italics added).[4] This is the status that must be gained before active imagination can begin, with the play that so often initiates the process.

The Second Step

As the voice of the unconscious emerges, it is given expression. Whether in writing or some other medium, it is essential to give outer form to the material. Otherwise it is too easy simply not to hear (or see) what passes through, to be just a little dishonest about what the voice really said, of what the image really was, or how you truly felt at that moment. There is nothing more damaging to the psyche than self-deception. You can deceive your neighbor, your spouse, even your analyst, and get away with it; but when you deceive yourself, you simply become the victim of your unacknowledged inferiorities.

Active imagination is defined by the relationship between ego and unconscious, not by the particular medium employed. The unconscious can be expressed in an infinite number of ways, including poetry, stories, direct dialogue, verbal description of images, clay, painting, dance, photographs, movies, music, and collage. Doing these things does not in itself constitute active imagination. The ego must react to what has been expressed, draw conclusions, and put them to work in life before the process can be said to be complete.

Deciding what medium to use is an individual matter, and I can offer only a few hints from my experience. In general, whatever is comfortable or feels right at a given moment is fine. If someone is skilled in one medium (for example, a painter or a writer), it is usually better to begin active imagination in a different medium. Skill too easily serves ego control rather than expression of the unconscious. As Freud observed, mistakes usually express the unconscious and interfere with the ego's intentions. Skill interferes with mistakes! On the other hand, someone who is particularly afraid of the unconscious may be able to ease into the work by using a medium over which some personal control is possible.

Clay has the advantage of being down-to-earth and far from the head. It makes the process very concrete and real. Writing, on the other hand, may facilitate more cognitive understanding.

In my own active imagination, the medium I use depends partly on the state of the content. When I am in an emotional state, or when the content is deeply unconscious and newly emergent, or both, I prefer some graphic or plastic material. When I have come closer to understanding a message from the unconscious, writing works best for me.

The Third Step

Once the voice of the unconscious has been given form, the ego can confront it. It is only from this moment that we can legitimately speak of the process as active imagination, and it is only now that the personality can be deeply changed by it: Now is the time for the ego's questions, reservations, doubts, and judgments, as well as its emotions and its understanding. Now the ego must react to what has come.

At this stage it becomes essential to come to know the reality of the psyche. In its responses, the ego must recognize the inner event as being just as real as any outer event, even though it is in a different realm. If, in outer reality, a strange man appears and says, "Follow me," it is not a good idea to do so without knowing something about him; it is no wiser in inner reality. If a rattlesnake bites someone in the outer world, pretending it did not happen will not undo it. The same is true in the inner world. Inner events have real effects.

The figures of the unconscious express the reality of their own realm, but they are often unaware of human reality until the ego informs them about it. The ego has to confront the unconscious with the limitations and conditions of its human world. Once, when considerably greater inner demands were being made upon me than I had the strength to meet, I was startled to hear my analyst say, "Sometimes you have to say no to the Self." It was a revelation to discover that I could talk back and inform the inner figures about my limitations. It was still more startling to find that when I did talk back, enormously important changes came out of the clash between the yes and the no of the conflict.

Here, at the third step, it is necessary to take an ethical attitude toward what comes from the unconscious. It is difficult to move from watching the images like a movie to responding emotionally and making judgments about the contents. Part of the change is that now it is necessary to try to understand what the contents mean, in addition to appreciating their form. . . .

The individual's ethical participation in active imagination protects him from inflation by the archetypes of the collective unconscious—that is, from identifying with the gods. Without the commitment of confrontation, it is all too easy to become seized by the power principle, to use the unconscious for ego purposes rather than forming a relationship with it. This can have terrible consequences. . . .

The Fourth Step

Once the ego has confronted the voice of the unconscious, the final step—drawing conclusions and putting them to work in life—requires full acceptance of the responsibility for oneself. It means that one can no longer live unconsciously, as if one did not know what one has learned from working with the unconscious. What began as the play of a child leads now to the most profound ethical consequences in terms of how an individual life is lived. This is the hardest part, and the step that is too often not taken.

People often ask how a dialogue with images and emotions of the unconscious can lead to an ethical demand in life. A simple illustration follows. Because this did happen simply and rapidly, it is easier to describe than most pieces of active imagination, which are usually slower, deeper, and harder to grasp.

At a certain time in my life I had become profoundly exhausted, physically and emotionally, from doing more than my introverted nature could tolerate. I was at the end of my rope but did not know it. In this condition I made a collage. Getting to the first step of active imagination was no problem. I was already walking around in a half-conscious state that permitted unconscious contents to come through easily. From a large selection of pictures I rapidly chose some that appealed to a certain spot in my stomach, and pasted them to cardboard without thinking about what I was doing. Then I stood back and looked at it.

The central image was a young woman asleep in a hammock. The surrounding images were predominantly sad, dark, primitive women, children, animals, and people in introverted, prayerful, and self-reflective postures. As I looked at the collage, I descended into profound sadness and realized for the first time that I was exhausted. I saw that I had been ignoring my instincts, my femininity, my inner children, and my introverted nature. I knew that I should take time off from work and other obligations. Then the protests of the ego came in: I couldn't possibly do that, I was needed by my patients, I had many commitments for which I felt indispensable, and so on.

The depth at which these images touched me convinced me that I truly needed time in which to renew myself, but I did not take it. Within a few days I had developed a severe cold, which forced me to spend several days in bed, meeting the obligation to myself that I had not met voluntarily. In this case I had had the insight to draw the right ethical conclusion, but had failed to carry it out. Then life took care of the fourth step for me.

Part Four

Personal Accounts
of Inner Knowing

Throughout history, individuals have solved apparently impossible problems during moments of intense inner clarity. Variously called inspiration, peak performance, creative insight, and higher creativity, such moments produce illuminated understanding, which can then be shaped, revised, and carried forward by skill alone. Unlike insights achieved by force of intellect, many reports of nonordinary knowing have an out-of-the-blue quality of "Where did this come from?" The next thought is usually "Can this be true?" coupled with a fierce desire to check out the information.

Inner messages characteristically feel "new," in the sense that they don't flow from an established line of thought. Although the problem may have been under investigation for years, the new knowing is typically fresh. Breakthrough solutions sometimes appear in dreams, sometimes in the midst of a spiritual practice, and sometimes they just pop up. But regardless of how inner wisdom makes itself known, the real question is about replicating the state of mind where it is likely to occur.

In the West, we tend to see a dichotomy between creativity and reason, leading to the notion that inspiration is attached to the artistic process or "soft" sciences like psychology. Yet some historic mental lightning bolts initiated crucial inventions that altered the course of science and industry. The sewing machine, for instance, invented by Elias Howe, was developed from material appearing in a dream, as was Dmitri Mendeleev's periodic table of elements, the one we had to memorize in chemistry class. Although scientific in nature, these inspirations were first received inwardly and only later verified by experimental analysis.

This part offers personal accounts from people who found a way to return to the place of inner knowing. All of them have used this gateway to enhance their professional contributions: as writers, scientists, mathematicians and, in one case, the practice of bow hunting. In the true spirit of the oral tradition, they "give evidence" of having made an authentic inner connection by producing inspired work.

I find stories like these to be fundamentally encouraging. To me the personal reports of people speaking from the conviction of their own beliefs are the best possible teachers. They help us to see that extraordinary wisdom can be put to immediate practical use. They are neither odd nor weird or neurotic, and they help to make our own intuitive path more accessible.

16. *Indigenous Teaching by Hyemeyohsts Storm*

For the first time in history we have access to most of the world's religious, heal-
ing, and consciousness-altering disciplines. Now we are attempting to assimilate
that knowledge by entering the worldview of radically different traditions.

Hyemeyohsts Storm is a contemporary medicine teacher carrying a lineage of
knowledge that reaches back thousands of years in the Americas. His ground-
breaking book, Seven Arrows, *went through forty-six well-deserved printings.*
In this excerpt, he describes the medicine teacher, Estcheemah, as she instructs her
apprentices Lightningbolt and Liberty. The apprentices are being taught to enter
the living consciousness of the natural world through the vehicle of bow hunting.
Liberty's education is especially telling, in that during the time of her appren-
ticeship, she was also a student at the University of California.

TWO STRAW BALES [had been set up] for Liberty's target practice. She shot her
bow all day, speaking to herself and commanding her mind to be focused and
attentive. She went over and over the new Medicine Wheel, thinking of each
aspect of what had been shared with her.

By the second evening, Liberty began to understand, as her hunger
increased, what Estcheemah had told her about the Sacred Give-Away of the
plants and animals to all humans. No longer was the fact of her dependence
on the plants and animals simply intellectual. Her hunger spoke to her, as did
her bow and arrows—as did her will and Self thinking. Death and Life are forever inseparable, she could hear in her thinking. The plants and animals are
sacred children of Mother Earth and give you your Life, her thinking continued with amazing clarity.

Why did so few people appreciate the Beauty of the Sacred Give-Away of
the animals and plants? She realized how pretentious she had been about their
gift of Life to her. Believing that food comes from money and supermarkets is
madness, she scolded herself. Liberty vowed to never turn her back on the
great giving of her Mother Earth again. She would start by appreciating and
recognizing the Present of Life she was given every time she ate or drank from
Mother Earth's wondrous Garden of Life and Death.

The next morning Lightningbolt woke Liberty at dawn. They spoke very
little and immediately began to hunt. Liberty remained in the lead, looking
around her. However, it wasn't until the Sun was high in the sky that she spot-

ted a beautiful little furry creature with long brown ears underneath a large berry bush. Liberty bent down on one knee and fitted her arrow into her bow, taking aim. However, Liberty was nervous and her arm was shaking when she released the arrow. It flew five feet above the rabbit's head and disappeared. "Liberty, calm your Self. Be present," she commanded herself in a strong voice. Then she took a deep breath, fitting another arrow into her bow. This time, much more steadily, she took aim.

"If that rabbit meant the difference between Life and Death, you would be very clear about what you were about to do," Lightningbolt had cautioned her.

Liberty shot, and this time her arrow found its mark. The rabbit sprang into the air, pierced through the heart.

Liberty was dumbfounded. She was so amazed by what she had done that she let the bow fall from her hand to the ground. She was flushed with excitement, but in the same breath she was feeling panic and fear.

"We usually trap them," said Estcheemah, suddenly behind her. "At this moment Death meets with you, Liberty. Allow your Heart to understand what you did, but also let your Mind think clearly about what you have done."

"I am surprised," said Liberty, struggling to not cry and to not laugh. She carefully picked up the dead rabbit and examined it. "You know, it's amazing how beautiful a rabbit is. I never looked at a dead one before. I've never even seen a chicken killed. It's incredible!"

"It is deep-reaching," Estcheemah said, sitting down on the ground beside her. "We women feel beyond this moment. We wonder and are amazed because laughter and excitement are present, and deep appreciation."

"I don't know what to say, Estcheemah." Liberty brightened, yet felt a tear slip from her eye. "This experience has helped me feel a lot of things deep within me that I have never known before."

"Yes, that is so true," Estcheemah said, rising. "Come, we will return to the camp. Lightningbolt took you in a large circle around our camp. We are very close. In fact, you have been so close I have watched you hunt most of the morning—just as the rabbits did."

Liberty was shocked. She looked in disbelief and saw that what Estcheemah was saying was true! She had imagined that she was twenty-five miles away from the camp.

"Yes, it is remarkable," Estcheemah explained while they walked to the camp. "You have come from a culture that does not understand the profound or the subtle. Can you imagine people having a rabbit-killing school? The teachers would have the students take a number and wait in long lines to kill hundreds of rabbits and never see that they were in a slaughterhouse. War is something like that. Most humans have no imagination. Those same teachers would have people take numbers and stand in line to be born and to die."

"I'm not going to stand in any stupid line!" Liberty said with determination. "I'm going to do my own thinking, even if it kills me."

"Honor woman," Estcheemah challenged her, "or you will stand in a perpetual line that can only end in the grave."

The following morning, Liberty was determined. Arrows buzzed like angry bees, but not one rabbit was scratched.

She was running down a small draw after a rabbit when she heard Lightningbolt call to her.

"What?" she yelled back, feeling her exasperation after missing again.

"Don't run them to death!" he yelled back. "Hey, what's the matter? Why are you so tense?"

She walked to the top of a small hill and sat down to think and to have a look around. Far below her and half a mile away, the Ocean beamed with blue loveliness and grandeur.

"Where is your Focus Evaluation, Liberty?" she asked herself.

Lightningbolt climbed the hill and sat down beside her. "Estcheemah sent me to speak with you. To be a powerful huntress you must imagine the world of the being you are hunting. You are running around like mad. Slow down. Are you within the mind of the Big Rabbit Knowing? Where are your friends? Where do the animals drink and eat? What do they eat? What do they build and what do they hunt? What are their habits? Come on, Liberty, be with them. Are they night creatures or do they hunt during the day?

"These are the questions you must ask to be a good huntress. Quiet yourself. Enter the world of your animal family, the Big Rabbit Mind. Allow their Mind World to become part of you. Feel your time and the presence of your place. Move as they move, let your whiskers grow and touch the forest. Let Earth and Her Energies guide you. Be the Huntress, not the student. Listen to your Self and be present with Life.

"The Mother Earth knows humans must kill the plants and animals to live. She gives us the choice of how we will do this. How we approach Life and Death makes all the difference. Do we kill with appreciation for the gift of Life? Do we kill swiftly with care and balance? Are we clean and respectful, taking only what we need?

"Liberty, imagine within the presence of your lessons of Life. This is your forest. Your mind, your imagination, can be your Medicine Guide. This can be a higher, nobler part of your thinking, the Medicine Part of your Self. The forest will teach you what you need to know if you imagine with Her and listen."

Lightningbolt rose slowly and left, taking his time walking back down the hill. She watched him until he was out of sight, then slung her bow over her shoulder and began to hunt.

She walked for hours, imagining and then seeing the rabbits in her forest world. It was evening when she became more fully aware of the signs of their presence, and this excited her.

Liberty was crouching behind some cattail reeds at a small pond when she saw a beautiful white-and-black doe rabbit. The rabbit turned and stared directly at Liberty, motionless and proud, ears alert and eager.

A quiet knowing entered Liberty's consciousness. What was it? Was she sensing something? Liberty looked around to see if anything or anyone else was near. No, only herself and the rabbit. An understanding slowly became part of Liberty's thinking. It was a perfect knowing that told her that the rabbit was going to have young. Liberty let go of her anxiousness and sat down. Yes, it was the rabbit who had touched her with this knowing. There was no doubt about it.

"You will live, beautiful mother rabbit," Liberty said out loud. "I know you gave me one of your family yesterday. Because of you and all the plants and animals, I will live. I thank you. I will always remember your teaching me, mother rabbit." Liberty strode back to her camp, feeling another kind of victory. . . .

Liberty began to question her Self and the culture she lived in. The headband she wore was no longer simply a fashion. It had become a practical part of her attire. Her bow became her friend and felt as smooth and strong as her own muscles. On the third day, she shot a duck. The duck dinner was delicious, and Liberty began to feel a new strength.

"I wish you to tell Lightningbolt the reasons you sought me out," Estcheemah asked Liberty. "All right?"

"Yes, I'll be happy to," she answered. "When I found Estcheemah I was overjoyed to find a woman I could communicate with.

"Lightningbolt, I sought out Estcheemah because I had had an incredibly painful experience. I am very happy that I learned what I did, but I am glad that the pain is now in my past.

"I was planning to go to the University of California at Berkeley. I was saving money I made by working in a law office that summer. But then I began to have terrible pains in my stomach. I had missed my menstrual cycle for three months, and I was afraid I was pregnant.

"My Aunt Thelma arranged for me to see a woman gynecologist. When the doctor examined me, I saw that she was very alarmed, and this really scared me. She sent me to a surgeon. He informed me that I had what he called a 'dermoid cyst' in my right ovary. He said it was the size of a grapefruit and would have to be removed immediately. That same evening I had my operation.

"A few days later I learned that I'd had a parthenogenic pregnancy. What that means is that my egg started to divide and to develop into an embryo all by itself . . . without the introduction of any sperm. In other words, I got myself pregnant. He said that I had been self-pregnant for ten years or more. The embryo-cyst lay dormant in my ovary until I began to have my menstrual cycle. Then it began to grow."

"You had a tumor?" Lightningbolt asked.

"Yes," she answered. "But all the evidence showed that it had once been an embryo. The doctor was happy that it was not cancerous. He told me that he doubted if I would ever have a menstrual cycle again or be able to have children—and that there was nothing he knew that would help. I was told to not make love, and that I probably would not heal for at least five years. I was crushed.

"My depression was terrible. I felt so alone and frightened. I entered the university with a cane and had to change my bandages daily.

"Then I began to search for healing. I ran into every kind of nut possible. I tried acupuncture, vegetarianism, meditation, religion, Silva mind control, sound therapy, and psychology—in fact, psychology became my major. But all of them failed miserably.

"Four years later I was still in trouble and weighed only ninety-five pounds. But, after four years of searching, I had become very discriminating, and I realized that all the healers and all the techniques I had experienced were useless.

"Then three women friends suggested that I go backpacking with them fifty miles into the Sierras to see the eclipse of the Moon. Because I was raised in L.A. I was very excited about going into the wilderness. After a grueling, very challenging two days—and blistered feet—I arrived in the most beautiful place in the world.

"There was an exquisite lake. And rising behind Her were twin pyramid-shaped mountains, reflected perfectly in Her pristine waters. That night I walked alone . . . limping and thinking. I had never seen such Beauty.

"This was the first time in my life I realized that the Earth might actually be alive. The following night, one of my friends suggested that we build a fire and do some kind of ceremony in celebration of the lunar eclipse.

"We were all very ignorant . . . so we made it up. One of the women had a rattle and began to pass it around the circle. We all agreed to sing all night and pray.

"I watched the Moon turn a deep red as I prayed. I realized at this moment that somehow the Moon actually had something to do with every woman's menstrual cycle.

"I had heard about the Goddess at the university. The professors thought She was a psychological archetype. All the books actually called Life a 'cult.' They said that the Goddess 'cult' existed in the past, and that Goddess Life was no longer present. There was no real information to be had.

"But that night, when I looked at the red Moon I knew that if I was ever going to be healed, I would have to pray and speak directly to the Mother Earth and to the Moon. Only Goddess Life would heal me.

"For the first time in my life I addressed the Moon as though She would understand me . . . no differently than if I were talking with my aunt.

"I felt a sudden deep rage coming from within me, and I asked the Moon why She would allow this to happen to me. I broke down and sobbed. When I calmed, I made a pledge. I told the Moon, 'If you are really alive, show me. If I am healed, then I will dedicate my life to seeing that other women will know the female side of Creation—and that Mother Earth is alive.'"

Lightningbolt grabbed her hand. "That is sad and really beautiful."

"As I sat in classes for the next three weeks," Liberty continued, "I slowly began to realize that my professors didn't know a damn thing about what they were saying! They talked on and on about goddesses as 'archetypes in the psyche.' They never once realized that She really is alive! On the fourth day after my Ceremony and my talk with Mother Moon, I went into the bathroom after my physics class and discovered that I had my monthly cycle, my moon cycle."

17. Conversation with Isabel Allende
by Janet Lynn Roseman

In this discussion of her creative process, writer Isabel Allende shows how she tunes into the interior voices that direct her work. She describes how characters, prophecy, dreams, and past events are interconnected features of stories that seem to be "somewhere floating" and waiting to be written.

In the highly personal language that typifies such accounts, Allende sees her connection to inner knowing as filled with emotion and healing. She finds that feelings and story combine to express prophetic events through the voices of her characters, but far from being frightened by the way in which inner knowing presents itself, she treasures the authenticity of her connection.

When I read your books, it strikes me that you are a shaman, in the sense of being a bridge offering information from the other worlds to here. How do you respond to that?
I have the feeling that I don't write my books, that the story is somewhere floating. My job is to be quiet, to be silent and alone, ready to tune into those voices and write the story. But the story is not mine. That's why, when a book of mine is made into a movie, even if I don't like that movie, I don't feel connected with it; since the story wasn't mine to begin with. I heard it first, but I didn't make it up. The story doesn't belong to me. I am always scared when I start a new book, because I have a feeling that maybe this time I won't be able to hear the voices, that I will not be able to write. Because to me, writing is not a craft. It's not something that I can repeat if I have the formula or repeat if I have been successful. I don't know anything about writing. Every book is different and every book has to be invented from the very beginning.

What happens when you start a book?
When I start a book I am in total limbo. I don't have any idea where the story is going or what is going to happen or why I am writing this. I only know that I am writing this because, in a way that I can't even understand at the time, I am connected to this. I have chosen that story because it was important to me in the past or it will be in the future. I believe that [the events in my books] have happened before or will happen in the future.

Does that scare you?

I do have a feeling of fear, in a way, because I feel that I am responsible for [what is] happening. In the years that I have been writing, I have seen that very often there is a connection, a prophetic writing that later turns out to be true. When I am doing it, I don't know what I am writing. Now, I am more careful, because I have these feelings inside me that I am writing something that will happen.

Would you edit something out that wasn't pleasant?

Sometimes I can't, because of the story or the characters, whose personalities I can't control. I can't edit it out, unfortunately. I can maybe tell it, but I can't control it. I want the characters to be happy, to get married, and to have a lot of children and live happily ever after, but it never happens that way. . . .

Do you have any particular rituals that you engage in?

. . . I try to separate myself from the noise. Life is noise. In order to hear those voices and to understand the stories that are floating, I need silence. That silence is not something that I can get easily. I am not only talking about the silence without the phone ringing, I am talking about the silence in my head that the writing requires. For that, I have developed certain tiny rituals; for example, I light a candle at my desk and I have a photograph of my daughter, my grandmother, and my mother. Those are the three feminine spirits that inspire me and help me and protect me. Two of them are dead [but] . . . my mother is alive in Chile. I light a candle and I ask them to be with me. . . .

How was the writing for you yesterday? Did it go well?

I sat down and I started writing something with the feeling that my heart wasn't there, that it was a good story, probably a very commercial book, but I wasn't connected to the story. So last night I had a strange feeling that I had not really done anything. I woke up suddenly in the middle of the night with this need to write something else. I started writing something like a letter to my agent that I knew I would never send, but I had the freedom to write what I really wanted to write. I started something quite different, and most probably that's going to be the book and not [the first manuscript I started].

I would think the book with the emotional connection would provide you with more pleasure in the process.

It's not pleasure that I am looking for, it's a connection. It's that magic. I can't explain it. The novel I started writing yesterday is not connected with anything in my past, and I have the feeling that it is not connected with anything in my future. It is just a good story. There is always joy in telling a good story, but you can't justify the enormous effort that writing is just because it's a pleasure to tell the story. I need to feel that I am exorcising something, that I am trying to understand something. But the [second] story is like a gate or a door that I have to cross in order to enter into a place that is part of my inner world, where I have to explore something of myself and my life. Maybe I will explore it through those characters, which are totally fictitious, but the things that happen to them are connected to me.

I know that dreams are very important in your work and your life. Can you tell me more about that?
I talk about the dreams every day, all the time, with my mother and my husband. I write to my mother every day or we talk on the phone and we tell our dreams. We believe that there is another world, the world of dreams, that is like a world inside our minds where we store information that we don't know we have. During the day, I overhear conversations, I see flashes, but I don't record them in conscious memory. Unconsciously, I store them inside. When I dream, I have access to that storage place where events are. I use that information, when I can remember it, when I wake up. Very often, when I am writing, I dream about children, and it is always related to my work—the child is the work. What happens to the child in the dream is happening to the work in real life.

Can you give me an example of how the child in your dream and your work are related?
I dreamed that a child is in a room and the door is closed. I can't reach the child. I open the door and there is another door and another door. It's a recurring dream, and when I wake up I know that there is something wrong in the writing, that the writing is very removed from my feelings. I need to get closer. Other times I dream that the child cries with the voice of an old man and I know that there is something wrong with the voice of the narration.

Do you believe in "women's intuition"?
I think that *people* have intuition, and in some cultures women are allowed to explore their intuition more than men. If you go to Asia, you will never hear that term. It's just intuition. It's something that I think we all have, but some people develop it more. It's an awareness of how many means we have to perceive the world. In the Western world, especially in the last century, we relate to the world through the eyes, through what we see. What we see is the truth.

What we touch, what we hear, what we taste, what we dream are other senses that aren't necessarily denied, but they are ignored. That's why when I play with my grandchildren we play games in which all of the senses are involved. And it's fun; it's fantastic to see how it works with very young children.

Once I was driving in the car with one of my grandchildren. I think he was five, and he asked me, "Do you know what happens when people die?" I said, "Yeah, well, sort of. What do you think happens?" He said, "New people are born." It was such a practical answer that I told him he was absolutely right. . . . and I told him I loved him too. Then he said, "When you love me, don't you feel something warm here?" He touched his chest. Other times, I take my grandchildren and say, "Let's go and see the fairies." The same grandchild said to me that the fairies are only in my mind. I told him that they are still real. You know what he said? He said that they are only real for me, because his fairies are different.

18. Lightning Bolts and Illuminations
by Richard Heinberg, adapted from Willis Harman and Howard Rheingold, Higher Creativity: Liberating the Unconscious for Breakthrough Insights

In this encouraging report on historic moments of illumination, Richard Heinberg asks:"What would a history of creativity look like? It would likely be a story of men and women who managed to tap into an extraordinary reservoir of possibilities. It would focus not so much on outer circumstances as on the inner experiences of people who made a difference."

Here, in their own words, we read the accounts of famous Westerners whose work was inspired by dreams, through focused concentration, and the kind of knowing that "just shows up." Keen observers of their own process, they were aware of tapping into an intensified inner clarity, but each offers a personal explanation of the event.

As it is currently written, history is a collection of tales about people pursuing rational political and economic goals. When something extraordinary happens—the advent of the age of the pyramids in Egypt or the Renaissance in Italy—we look for explanations in prevailing social conditions, wars, pestilence, invasions, migrations, or the introduction of new technologies. Historians typically explore the context in which new ideas occur and the effects of those ideas upon civilization, but they don't bother much with the *source* of such breakthroughs—human creativity.

This kind of history—the history we learn in school—is not so much incorrect as incomplete. What about the elements that are customarily left out of the picture? What about the dreams and visions that inspire bold inventions, radically different scientific paradigms, movements in the arts, or new religions?

Many of us have heard stories of how the young Mozart composed brilliant symphonies entirely in his mind, often while playing billiards or riding in a carriage, and later used pen and paper merely to record the completed work. The stage play and movie *Amadeus* showed how Antonio Salieri, Mozart's older contemporary, worked far more methodically and had as great a knowledge of music, but somehow failed to find the same divine source of inspiration.

We commonly acknowledge the mysterious role that intuitive breakthroughs play in artistic endeavors, such as music, literature, and painting. But what about other fields, such as science, mathematics, and technological invention? The truth is, when we trace the great innovations on which our modern civilization is built, we discover at nearly every juncture the pivotal importance of an experience Emily Dickinson called "a blossom of the brain" and that William Blake described as seeing "the world in a grain of sand, eternity in an hour," of crucial moments in which, as James Joyce put it, "the soul of the commonest object . . . seems to us radiant."

The paradox is astounding: Many of our culture's most important achievements in the arts, science, and technology were made by people who had breakthrough insights in dreams, visions, intuitive flashes, and altered states of consciousness. And yet our society generally discounts such experiences, sometimes even treating them as grounds for a diagnosis of mental illness. Schools teach us to honor the products of genius and drill us in step-by-step problem-solving methods. However, regarding those rare moments of illumination that are the real key to new ways of thinking, there seems to be a conspiracy of silence. Surely it is time we outgrew the cultural taboos that post "off-limits" signs at the wellsprings of creativity.

RENÉ DESCARTES (1596–1650)

It is common these days for progressive thinkers to refer disparagingly to the "Newtonian-Cartesian paradigm" of a clockwork universe, operating according to mechanical laws. Indeed, Descartes, author of the famous—or infamous—phrase, "I think, therefore I am," launched the Western world on a belief system that, for the next three hundred years, would equate consciousness with thought. It is ironic, therefore, that Descartes' own radical new ideas were born in his own subconscious.

As a young man, Descartes had a series of dreams that would change the course of his life. In one of them, he saw the image of a bolt of lightning and a shower of sparks filling his room. In another, he saw himself holding a dictionary and a poem that began with the words, "What path shall I follow in life?" Later that same night, he dreamed that he was awake and interpreting the previous dreams. In his journals, he recorded his interpretation, which included the conviction that it was his destiny to reform human knowledge and unify the sciences: "I begin to understand the foundations of a wonderful discovery. . . . All the sciences are interconnected as by a chain; no one of them can be completely grasped without taking in the whole encyclopedia at once." Descartes's dream-inspired insights led directly to his writing his famous treatise *The*

Discourse on Method, which was originally titled: "Project of a universal science destined to raise our nature to its highest degree of perfection."

ISAAC NEWTON (1642–1727)

Born on Christmas day 1642, the year Galileo died, Newton began where his illustrious predecessor had ended, and went on to establish the basic principles of modern physics. . . .

Newton had extraordinary powers of concentration and was "so happy in his conjectures," according to one of his biographers, "as to seem to know more than he could possibly have any means of proving." While studying as an undergraduate at Cambridge, the young mathematician devoured everything he could find by the pioneers of the scientific revolution. However, it was only when the school was closed, due to the plague, and he was forced to spend a year in virtual isolation at his mother's house, that he came up with the breakthroughs that would eventually lead to his famous *Principia,* published 20 years later, and his development of calculus.

In his memoirs of 1749, William Whiston remarked that in mathematics Newton "could sometimes see almost by intuition, even without demonstration." Even in his work in physics, Newton seems to have used experiments only after the fact, to demonstrate for others principles that he already "knew." Similarly, John Maynard Keynes observed that Newton's "peculiar gift" was:

> the power of holding continuously in his mind a purely mental problem until he had seen straight through it. I fancy his preeminence is due to his muscles of intuition being the strongest and most enduring with which a man has ever been gifted. Anyone who has ever attempted pure scientific or philosophical thought knows how one can hold a problem momentarily in one's mind and apply all one's powers of concentration to piercing through it, and how it will dissolve and escape and you find that what you are surveying is a blank. I believe that Newton could hold a problem in his mind for hours and days and weeks until it surrendered to him its secret. Then being a supreme mathematical technician, he could dress it up, for purposes of exposition, but it was his intuition which was preeminently extraordinary.

FRIEDRICH AUGUST KEKULÉ VON STRADONITZ (1829–1896)

In one of the most famous incidents of dream-inspired scientific breakthroughs, the Flemish chemist Kekulé laid the groundwork for the modern structural theory of organic chemistry. In the mid–nineteenth century, this new science was struggling to describe the molecular structure of organic compounds. Kekulé, who had begun his studies intending to be an architect, spent years wrestling with the structure of benzene; when he finally achieved the correct result, it was called "the most brilliant piece of prediction in the whole history of science." Kekulé himself related the story as follows, in a lecture given to a society of chemists:

> One fine summer evening, I was returning by the last omnibus. . . . I fell into a reverie, and lo! the atoms were gamboling before my eyes. Whenever, hitherto, these diminutive beings had appeared to me, they had always been in motion; but up to that time I had never been able to discern the nature of their motion. Now, however, I saw how, frequently, two smaller atoms united to form a pair, how a larger one embraced two smaller ones, how still larger ones kept hold of three or even four of the smaller, whilst the whole kept whirling in a giddy dance. I saw how the larger ones formed a chain. . . . I spent part of the night putting on paper sketches of these dream forms.

His insight into the "ring" structure of benzene was not complete, however, until years later, when he had the following dream, while dozing before a fire:

> Again the atoms were gamboling before my eyes. This time the smaller groups kept modestly in the background. My mental eye, rendered more acute by repeated visions of this kind, could now distinguish larger structures, of manifold conformation, long rows, sometimes more closely fitted together; all twining and twisting in snakelike motion. But look! What was that? One of the snakes had seized hold of its own tail, and the form whirled mockingly before my eyes. As if by the flash of lightning I awoke.

Kekulé's advice to his fellow scientists: "Let us learn to dream, gentlemen."

THOMAS ALVA EDISON (1847–1931)

Thomas Edison was the inventor of the electric light bulb, the phonograph, motion pictures, and hundreds of other devices that earned him the title of "America's Most Useful Citizen." Indeed, Edison registered a new patent an average of every two weeks of his adult life.

According to one biographer, as a child, "his demands for explanations of what seemed obvious to his elders created the belief that he was less than normally intelligent. As his head was abnormally large, it was thought that he might have a brain disease." As he grew older and became successful, his lack of knowledge of scientific theory made him the target of criticism by highly trained scientists and engineers. Edison's response: "I can always hire mathematicians, but they can't hire me."

Edison is known to have worked on as many as 50 different inventions at one time, first formulating a problem—such as how to make an electric light or how to record sound—then trying one approach after another, until the solution would come in a flash of inspiration. As one biographer described it, Edison would be eating or talking with friends, "when something he saw, a topic of conversation, or an intruding memory, jogged up a technological possibility," which he would jot down in one of the 200-page notebooks he always carried. At the time of his death, Edison had filled 3,400 such notebooks.

According to Edison's secretary, he did most of his work at night, but in general paid little attention to the time of day, eating and sleeping whenever he wished. Concerning his creative process, Edison was matter-of-fact. Upon returning from his first trip to England, he said, "The English are not an inventive people; they don't eat enough pie. To invent, your system must be all out of order, and there is nothing that will do that like the good old-fashioned American pie."

NIKOLA TESLA (1856–1943)

One of the most fertile and inventive minds in history belonged to Nikola Tesla, the Serbian-American originator of alternating-current motors and generators, robotics, and the radio (for which Marconi is often wrongly credited). While other inventors—including Westinghouse and Edison—profited from Tesla's discoveries, it was actually this tall, thin, relatively unknown Yugoslav immigrant who laid the groundwork for the electrical technology that has driven the twentieth century.

From an early age, Tesla had a remarkable capacity for visualizing machines in three dimensions and in remarkable detail. He used this ability to design working models of his inventions in his imagination. Concerning this skill, he wrote:

> It is absolutely immaterial to me whether I run my turbine in thought or test it in my shop. I even note if it is out of balance. There is no difference whatever, the results are the same. In this way I am able to rapidly develop and perfect a con-

ception without touching anything. When I have gone so far as to embody in the invention every possible improvement I can think of and see no fault anywhere, I put into concrete form this final product of my brain. Invariably my device works as I conceived that it should, and the experiment comes out exactly as I planned it. In twenty years there has not been a single exception.

On one occasion, his proposal for a newly designed dynamo was ridiculed by one of his professors. Tesla took up the challenge and "started by first picturing in my mind a direct current machine, running and following the changing flow of the currents in the armature." The solution came unexpectedly when Tesla and a friend were walking in a park, reciting poetry. This youthful flash of insight was to become the basis for the alternating-current electrical system that powers the modern world:

> The idea came like a flash of lightning, and in an instant the truth was revealed. I drew with a stick on the sand the diagrams shown six years later in my address before the American Institute of Electrical Engineers. . . . The images I saw were wonderfully sharp and clear and had the solidity of metal and stone, so much so that I told [my companion]: "See my motor here, watch me reverse it." I cannot begin to describe my emotions. Pygmalion seeing his statue come to life could not have been more deeply moved. . . . For awhile I gave myself up entirely to the intense enjoyment of picturing machines and devising new forms. It was a mental state of happiness about as complete as I have ever known in life. Ideas came in an uninterrupted stream and the only difficulty I had was to hold them fast. . . . I delighted in imagining the motors constantly running, for in this way they presented to the mind's eye a more fascinating sight. In less than two months I evolved virtually all the types of motors and modifications of the system which are now identified with my name.

ALBERT EINSTEIN (1879–1955)

According to Einstein, knowing which questions to ask and how to frame a problem was "often more essential than its solution." As a child, he was a daydreamer and a mediocre student; according to one of his teachers, the boy who would one day revolutionize our picture of the universe was "a lazy dog. He never bothered about mathematics at all."

Einstein often stressed the value of intuition and described his own theories as a "free invention of the imagination," rather than the result of arduous inductive logic. "There are no logical paths to these [natural] laws," he wrote, "only intuition resting on sympathetic understanding of experience can reach them."

Einstein's insights showed how creative breakthroughs are often the result of going beyond logical understanding. His general relativity theory, which he called "the happiest thought of my life," was born when he realized that a person falling from a roof was both at rest and in motion at the same time. Similarly, many of his ideas came to him while he was shaving, and he used his famous "thought experiments" as a way of arriving at solutions to complex problems. For example, his breakthrough insight into the relativity of time was the result of his imagining a person riding on a beam of light. The solution came to him early one morning just as he got out of bed. "Intuitively," he wrote, "it seemed clear to me that, judged by such an observer [i.e., the light beam traveler], everything should follow the same laws as for a stationary observer."

Perhaps even more surprising is the fact that Einstein's creative solutions to mathematical problems did not come to him in words, which we normally associate with "logic." As Einstein explained:

> The words or the language, as they are written or spoken, do not seem to play any role in my mechanism of thought, the physical entities which seem to serve as elements in thought are certain signs and more or less clear images which can be "voluntarily" reproduced and combined. . . . The above-mentioned elements are, in my case, of visual and some of muscular type. Conventional words or other signs have to be sought for laboriously only in a secondary stage.

Part Five

Developing Your Awareness

We experience ourselves and our world differently, according to our focus of attention. No two people undertake a task or enter a relationship from the same perspective, and where we place our attention determines our reality at any given moment. By deliberately shifting focus of attention, we can witness a task or a relationship from different vantage points, each of which has its own logic and validity.

One of the governing laws of physics is that work requires a focus, or an object of attention. Energy follows attention—if I am focused on jogging up a hill in a morning workout, my energy supports that physical activity. But if I stop running to consider my route, my energies are redirected to thought.

Focus of attention is also directly linked to our feelings. Remembering a pleasant event makes us feel good, and so we find ourselves paying more attention to the pleasant aspects of our surroundings. Likewise, shifting focus to an irritating incident rekindles our annoyance, which swiftly reminds us of other annoying matters, and so on.

Yet we rarely consider interrupting the cycle, even when we recognize that mood influences what we pay attention to—and that focus of attention in turn reinforces our feelings. Of course we know that focusing on vacation plans is likely to create positive anticipation, and we also know that anticipating a frightening interaction makes us anxious. We know all that intellectually, but we are so strongly identified with our customary placement of attention that we do not pause to question it.

Attention typically operates on automatic. We go with familiar habits, however aggravating or distracting they may be. Our placement of attention determines "the way the world looks," and that reality is entirely believable. So much so, that we suppose we can pay attention to anything we choose. We think we control where our attention goes, that we can decide to pay attention to whatever captures our interest. The sobering actuality is that placement of attention is largely habitual. Our perceptions are limited by a characteristic way of attending, which highlights certain information, while screening out equally relevant data.

Attention is generally passive, moving unconsciously from thing to thing, drawn by habit, comfort, passing curiosity, and a need to avoid anxiety. But attention can also be made active, directed and voluntary. William James, a founder of American psychology, enumerates the varieties of attention with

which we are all familiar: focused activity, passive wandering, and the dis-
tractedness that comes when we face an unpleasant task. James placed a high
value on the ability to concentrate, locating it at the very root of character and
will. He knew that psychological freedom depends on redirecting attention
from its characteristic habits, but didn't have the technology of meditation to
pursue that objective.

In meditation practice, concentration exercises are attention-active. They
depend on sustained focus—staying with the same object or activity—
instead of being distracted. Whenever attention wanders, it is gently returned
to focus over and over again. But whenever an activity becomes truly interesting, the customary stream of distractions lessens all by itself, as attention
becomes one-pointed, and energy flows into the task.

In contrast to concentration, there are techniques of "open awareness"
where everything is allowed to emerge on the inner screen of consciousness,
without choosing an object. All meditation practice is rooted in different
modes of attention. The practices are traditionally divided between those that
narrow the field of awareness to a single object, and practices in which the
field of awareness is opened.

The first three selections in this part, are by authors who explore the faculty of attention. Krishnamurti favors open awareness, a way of paying attention that is unfamiliar in the West. Daniel Goleman shows us how the mind
"presorts" information in ways that determine what information we retain.
Finally, Michael Novak offers a comprehensive look at the modes of attention
underlying meditation practice, particularly those rooted in concentration.

The last three selections present contemporary techniques that may be used
to confirm our inner knowing. Unlike the objective realm of scientific inquiry,
there are no standard experiments to confirm the rightness of our inner
impressions. How can we recognize the difference between projection and
accurate inner knowing? How do we discern the difference between fantasy
and fact? Like scientists, we must discover a technology to guide our explorations. We must distinguish between habitual impressions and real information, between our wishes and authentic intuition.

These approaches require paying attention in new ways, so as to bypass
thoughts and feelings. Like all good tools they rely on physical feedback.
There's really nothing "new" about listening to bodily cues, or recognizing
when a task feels meaningful, or sensing the pleasure of losing ourselves in
work. But when it comes to acquiring knowledge, our rational minds have
been trained to dismiss the body's feedback.

Good inner tools work for everyone, and, like those described in this section, do not depend on involvement in any special discipline or system of thought. They help us to discriminate between the vague awareness that something might be so, and being certain. The tools work, because they evoke a focus of attention that bypasses emotion, cognition, and mental confusion.

19. *Listening to the Silence by J. Krishnamurti*

In this deceptively simple description, Krishnamurti introduces us to an entirely new way of paying attention. It is different from the absorbed attention that comes into play when reading an engrossing novel, and different from the attention of resistance, as when we fight distractions. This form of attention is without resistance. It is fully comprehending, rather than a dividing of attention between two things.

For Krishnamurti, it is like listening both to the sounds and the silence between the sounds. He suggests that all learning would become easier and have deeper significance, if we paid more attention to how we pay attention.

HAVE YOU EVER paid any attention to the ringing of the temple bells? Now, what do you listen to? To the notes, or to the silence between the notes? If there were no silence, would there be notes? And if you listened to the silence, would not the notes be more penetrating, of a different quality? But you see, we rarely pay real attention to anything; and I think it is important to find out what it means to pay attention. When your teacher is explaining a problem in mathematics, or when you are reading history, or when a friend is talking, telling you a story, or when you are near the river and hear the lapping of the water on the bank, you generally pay very little attention; and if we could find out what it means to pay attention, perhaps learning would then have quite a different significance and become much easier.

When your teacher tells you to pay attention in class, what does he mean? He means that you must not look out of the window, that you must withdraw your attention from everything else and concentrate wholly on what you are supposed to be studying. Or, when you are absorbed in a novel, your whole mind is so concentrated on it that for the moment you have lost interest in everything else. That is another form of attention. So, in the ordinary sense, paying attention is a narrowing-down process, is it not?

Now, I think there is a different kind of attention altogether. The attention which is generally advocated, practised or indulged in is a narrowing-down of the mind to a point, which is a process of exclusion. When you make an effort to pay attention, you are really resisting something—the desire to look out of the window, to see who is coming in, and so on. Part of your energy has already gone in resistance. You build a wall around your mind to make it con-centrate completely on a particular thing, and you call this the disciplining of the mind to pay attention. You try to exclude from the mind every thought but the one on which you want it to be wholly concentrated. That is what most people mean by paying attention. But I think there is a different kind of attention, a state of mind which is not exclusive, which does not shut out anything; and because there is no resistance, the mind is capable of much greater attention. But attention without resistance does not mean the attention of absorption.

The kind of attention which I would like to discuss is entirely different from what we usually mean by attention, and it has immense possibilities because it is not exclusive. When you concentrate on a subject, on a talk, on a conversation, consciously or unconsciously you build a wall of resistance against the intrusion of other thoughts, and so your mind is not wholly there; it is only partially there, however much attention you pay, because part of your mind is resisting any intrusion, any deviation or distraction.

Let us begin the other way round. Do you know what distraction is? You want to pay attention to what you are reading, but your mind is distracted by some noise outside and you look out of the window. When you want to concentrate on something and your mind wanders off, the wandering off is called distraction; then part of your mind resists the so-called distraction and there is a waste of energy in that resistance. Whereas, if you are aware of every movement of the mind from moment to moment then there is no such thing as distraction at any time and the energy of the mind is not wasted in resisting something. So it is important to find out what attention really is.

If you listen both to the sound of the bell and to the silence between its strokes, the whole of that listening is attention. Similarly, when someone is speaking, attention is the giving of your mind not only to the words but also to the silence between the words. If you experiment with this you will find that your mind can pay complete attention without distraction and without resistance. When you discipline your mind by saying, "I must not look out of the window, I must not watch the people coming in, I must pay attention even though I want to do something else," it creates a division which is very destructive because it dissipates the energy of the mind. But if you listen comprehensively so that there is no division and therefore no form of resistance then you will find that the mind can pay complete attention to anything without effort. Do you see it? Am I making myself clear?

Surely, to discipline the mind to pay attention is to bring about its deterioration—which does not mean that the mind must restlessly wander all over the place like a monkey. But, apart from the attention of absorption, these two states are all we know. Either we try to discipline the mind so tightly that it cannot deviate, or we just let it wander from one thing to another. Now, what I am describing is not a compromise between the two; on the contrary, it has nothing to do with either. It is an entirely different approach; it is to be totally aware so that your mind is all the time attentive without being caught in the process of exclusion.

Try what I am saying, and you will see how quickly your mind can learn. You can hear a song or a sound and let the mind be so completely full of it that there is not the effort of learning. After all, if you know how to listen to what your teacher is telling you about some historical fact, if you can listen without any resistance because your mind has space and silence and is therefore not distracted, you will be aware not only of the historical fact but also of the prejudice with which he may be translating it, and of your own inward response.

I will tell you something. You know what space is. There is space in this room. The distance between here and your hostel, between the bridge and your home, between this bank of the river and the other—all that is space. Now, is there also space in your mind? Or is it so crowded that there is no space in it at all? If your mind has space, then in that space there is silence—and from that silence everything else comes, for then you can listen, you can pay attention without resistance. That is why it is very important to have space in the mind. If the mind is not overcrowded, not ceaselessly occupied, then it can listen to that dog barking, to the sound of a train crossing the distant bridge, and also be fully aware of what is being said by a person talking here. Then the mind is a living thing, it is not dead.

20. *The Mechanics of Attention by Daniel Goleman*

In responding to the question, What does it mean to pay attention? Daniel Goleman, science consultant for the New York Times, offers a highly informative but easy-to-read model of how the mind processes information. His model traces the path through which incoming stimuli emerge into awareness, assessing the influence of long-term memory on what we perceive and what we filter out.

Because we are constantly bombarded by an overload of data, the mind automatically filters out all but the most significant information. Out of necessity we learn to run on "autopilot," paying attention mechanically and passively most of the time. This underscores the need to pay attention deliberately and voluntarily, thereby liberating our awareness from robotic activity.

THERE WAS A half-century lapse before experimental psychologists seriously addressed the proposals Freud made in the seventh chapter of *The Interpretation of Dreams* [on how the mind processed information]. From the 1920s on, the ascendancy of behaviorism made what went on within the mind a taboo topic for most psychologists. When the mechanics of mind finally re-entered psychological research, one immediate impetus was most unlikely: the rise of aviation. . . .

Donald Broadbent, a British psychologist, worked with the British Royal Navy in the years after World War II. Because of the explosive growth of aviation in that era, the volume of air traffic besieged controllers. The controllers, Broadbent realized, took in far more information through their eyes and ears than they could deal with. He wondered just how the mind sorted out this barrage.

Broadbent, like Freud, used a flow chart to describe how the mind handles information. His chart showed that people receive more data through the senses than they can handle (see figure 1 on page 140). This information gets to a short-term store—akin to the sensory store—and then flows on to a "selective filter," where most of it is weeded out. This filter somehow blocks all but those messages that merit fuller attention. The passage is seemingly instantaneous. But the few thousandths of a second it takes allow ample time for the mind to sort through the mass of data in sensory storage and filter out irrelevancies before the information passes into conscious awareness.

Broadbent assumed that the mind needs to filter the information that

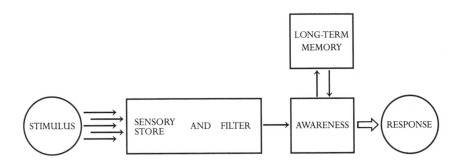

*Figure 1: Broadbent's model of the mind, slightly modified: Sensory stimuli are
analyzed as they reach the sensory store and sorted and filtered
on their way to awareness (or short-term memory).*

impinges on it through the senses because it has only a limited capacity. The
selective filter, he believed, is essential here because of a bottleneck: there is
a sharply limited channel capacity at the next stage of processing, often called
"short-term" or "primary" memory.

Primary memory is the region of perception that falls under the beam of
attention. For our purposes we will call it "awareness." The contents of the
zone of awareness are what we take to be "on our minds" at a given moment;
it is our window onto the stream of consciousness. This zone is quite fragile,
its contents fleeting.

The traffic between awareness and long-term memory is two-way, according to Broadbent's model; what is in long-term memory can be called into
awareness, what is in awareness finds a place in memory. Only information
that reaches awareness, he proposed, will be retained for very long—that is,
we remember only what we first pay attention to. Awareness, then, is the gateway to memory, and a filter controls what enters awareness. But what controls the filter?

For Broadbent, only the gross physical aspects of a message—its loudness
or brightness, say—determined whether it would get through, not its meaning. That view was put to rest soon after he proposed it by experiments on the
"cocktail party effect." At a cocktail party or in a crowded restaurant there is
typically a din of competing conversations, all carried on at high volume within
earshot of the others.

Contrary to Broadbent's prediction, you don't hear simply the loudest
voice. For example, if you are stuck listening to a bore recount the gruesome
details of his last vacation, rocky relationship, or nearly consummated deal, it
is easy to tune him out and tune in on a more interesting conversation

nearby—particularly if you hear your own name mentioned. During the course of these tune-outs and tune-ins, the *sounds* coming to your ears may be identical in volume. What changes is the focus of your *attention*.

This means that information is scanned for *meaning* before it reaches the filter, contradicting Broadbent's assertion that the filter tunes in or out based solely on physical aspects of a message. The filter seems to have some intelligence; it is tuned by the importance to a person of the message.

This has major consequences for how the mind's architecture must be arranged. In order for an intelligent filter—one that reads meaning—to operate during the few moments of sensory storage, the arrangement of the mind's elements must be modified in a critical fashion. If the filter is intelligent, then there must be some circuit that connects the part of the mind that cognizes—that recognizes meanings—with the part that takes in and sorts through initial impressions. A simple, linear model such as Freud and Broadbent proposed would not work.

Meanings are stored in long-term memory. What is required is a *loop* between long-term memory and the earlier stages of information processing. That loop is shown in figure 2. Such a feedback loop allows for the sensory store to sort its contents by drawing on the vast repertoire of experience, on the meanings and understandings built up over a life span, stored in long-term memory. The judgment "salient" or "irrelevant" can be made only on the basis of the knowledge in long-term memory. With access to the mind's lifelong store of experience, preferences, and goals, the filter can sift through the mass of impressions that assail it at each successive moment, and immediately tune in or out what matters.

Indeed, contemporary theorists now assume that information passing

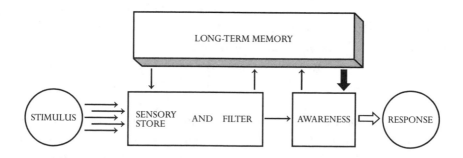

Figure 2: A simplified model of the mind, loosely adapted from Donald Norman: Memory screens perception at the earliest stage of information flow, filtering for salience what is allowed through to awareness.

through the sensory store is subjected to scrutiny and filtered on the basis of its meaning and relevance. "Essentially," sums up Matthew Erdelyi, a cognitive psychologist, "long-term memory itself becomes the filter, deciding what to block from short-term storage (and therefore awareness), thereby determining indirectly what to accept for eventual storage in long-term memory itself."[1]

That means the contents of awareness come to us picked over, sorted through, and pre-packaged. The whole process takes a fraction of a second.

There are compelling reasons for this arrangement in the design of the mind. It is much to our benefit that the raw information that passes from sensory storage to awareness sifts through a smart filter. The region of consciousness would be far too cluttered were it not reached by a vastly reduced information flow. While the information in consciousness seems limited, it also seems to be the case that before getting there, that information—and an even vaster amount left behind, seemingly to evaporate—has gone through a massive amount of analysis.

The more thoroughly information in sensory storage can be sorted out, the more efficiently the next way station—awareness—can operate. If too much gets through, awareness is swamped; as we have seen, one such intrusion is anxiety. It is of critical import that this filter operate at a peak, in order to save us from continuous distraction by a mass of irrelevant information. If the filter were much less thorough we might literally be driven to distraction by distractions, as happens in schizophrenia.

The idea that information passes through an intelligent filter led to what has become the prevailing view of how information flows through the mind. The most commonly pictured flow chart was proposed by Donald Norman in 1968; figure 2 is a simplified version of his model.[2] In this model what enters through the senses gets a thorough, automatic scan by long-term memory—specifically by "semantic" memory, the repository of meanings and knowledge about the world. For example, every bundle of sounds automatically is directed to an "address" in semantic memory that yields its meaning. If you hear the word "grunt," semantic memory recognizes its meaning; if you hear a grunt, semantic memory also recognizes that that sound is not a word.

All this filtering goes on out of awareness. What gets through to awareness is what messages have pertinence to whatever mental activity is current. If you are looking for restaurants, you will notice signs for them and not for gas stations; if you are skimming through the newspaper, you will notice those items that you care about. What gets through enters awareness, and only what is useful occupies that mental space.

Perception, says Norman, is a matter of degree. In scanning incoming information, semantic memory need not go into every detail; it need only sort out what is and is not relevant to the concern of the moment. Irrelevant information is only partly analyzed, if just to the point of recognizing its irrelevancy. What *is* relevant gets fuller processing. For example, if you casually scan a newspaper page and suddenly see your name, it will seem to "leap out" at you. Presumably the words you saw as you skimmed were partly processed and found irrelevant; your name—which is always relevant—rated full processing.

This model of the mind has several important implications. For one, it posits that information is screened by memory at every stage of its processing, and that memory scans information and filters it for salience. All this processing goes on *before* information enters awareness; only a small portion of the information available at a given moment filters through to consciousness.

That is not to say that attention is entirely passive. We can, after all, decide to scan for something, and so awareness can modify how the filter operates. But awareness does so indirectly, through the services of long-term memory: the activity of the filter is never directly evident to awareness. We can, however, bring information into awareness from long-term memory. There is two-way traffic, then, between awareness and long-term memory, but there is only one-way traffic between the filter and awareness. There is a very real sense in which long-term memory—the sum total of experience one has about life—has a more decisive say in the flow of information than we ordinarily realize.

21. The Practice of Attention by Philip Novak

An expert technician of consciousness, Philip Novak asserts that "attention" is an overused term that describes an entire continuum of mental states. He is not concerned about the lower end of the spectrum, where he locates "ordinary attention" and random imaginal wandering. He is interested in developing the upper end of the spectrum, the place of "active" or "concentrative attention." Here we no longer identify with the objects—or contents—of consciousness, but with the empty screen where these contents are born.

Writing within the context of a spiritual tradition, Novak lucidly tackles differences between "active" and "nonreactive"—or choiceless—awareness. Attention exercises are of central significance, says Novak, because they help release human consciousness to realize its full potential.

ATTENTION IS, OF course, a concept that occurs outside the domain of religious practice. It is part of the vocabulary of everyday mental functioning, and even there it seems to be overworked, a single, blunt term for a wide variety of mental states. The temptation to think of it as one thing should be resisted. It is better to think of it as a spectrum that reaches from the virtual absence of attention, as in sheer daydreaming and mechanically determined mental flux, to acutely active alertness. Though contemplative practices themselves vary widely, the quality of attention that they require and at which they aim resides at the upper end of the spectrum. The varieties of contemplative attention, in other words, resemble each other more than any one of them resembles that uneven and intermittent phenomenon of ordinary mental functioning we usually call attention. Some further notion of the relative difference between ordinary kinds of attention and the kinds of attention at which contemplative practices aim must be developed if we are to avoid confusion later on.

Ordinary attention may be described as discursive, intermittent, and passive. It moves incessantly from object to object, its intensity "flickers," often succumbing to mental wandering, and it is reactive, or "passive," in relation to some sequence of external objects or to the autonomous stream of consciousness. Let us take, for example, the act in which the reader is currently engaged. You are following this exposition closely, attempting to understand it. Surely this is attention rather than inattention. The contemplative would agree. But he would suggest that this attention is discursive, and largely passive. In this particular case, my words are doing the discursing for your attention, leading it from place to place. Moreover, it is highly likely that, while reading, your attention will have wandered a surprising number of times, pulled down one associational path or another by autonomous psychic fluctuations. Even if you now turned away from this article and turned inward to work out a chain of reasoning, it is likely that you would do so in a state of predominantly passive attention, for such creative activity largely involves a sorting out of what the automatic activity of the psyche presents.

In ordinary mentation, attention is not a quality of mind that we bring to experience, but something that occurs, rather haphazardly, as our organism becomes momentarily more interested in some inner or outer sequence of phenomena. Ordinary attention comes and goes without our consent; it is not something we *do,* but something that *happens* to us. For most of us most of the time, "attention" is stimulated, conditioned, and led by mobilizations of energy along the habit-pathways within our organism so that when it confronts its object it is always faced, as it were, by a *fait accompli.*

The attention at which contemplative exercises aim, then, may be distinguished not only from sheer inattention but from ordinary discursive attention as well. It is, instead, sustained, non-discursive, active attention which is, in fact, quite extraordinary. For there are many of us who in all our uncountable billions of mental moments and in all their variety, have never known a moment of truly active attention. Such a moment curtails the autonomous activities of ordinary psychological activity. If the reader doubts this, he may perform a simple experiment. Take up a "speak-I-am-listening" attitude of acute attention toward the screen of consciousness, standing close guard, as it were, at the place where the contents of consciousness are born. For as long as one is able to hold this posture of intense active attention, the inner dialogue and the flow of images will be stopped. As Hubert Benoit proposes:

> Our attention, when it functions in the active mode, is pure attention without manifested object. My mobilized energy is not perceptible in itself, but only in the effects of its disintegration, the images. But this disintegration occurs only when my attention operates in the passive mode; active attention forestalls this disintegration.[1]

Anyone who has ever attempted active attention as we have just described it finds, however, that it is difficult to maintain for any extended duration. The ubiquitous admonition in contemplative texts to somehow go beyond images, ideas, and all discursive thought involves one in the seemingly self-defeating task of trying to stop the mind with the mind. And so we find under the guid-ance of a teacher that this admonition against discursive thought is but a cavalry charge subsequently balanced by a far more subtle strategy, a second movement as it were.

Given the fact that the deep-seated habit patterns of the psyche will repeat-edly overpower an inchoate concentrative ability and assuming that the practi-tioner will repeatedly attempt to establish active, concentrative attention, his constant companions in all of this are impartiality, equanimity, and nonreactive acceptance. When concentrated attention falters, one is to be a non-reactive witness to what has arisen. Whatever emerges in the mind is observed and allowed to pass without being elaborated upon or reacted to. Images, thoughts, and feelings arise because of the automatism of deeply embedded psychologi-cal structures, but their lure is not taken. They are not allowed to steal attention and send it floundering down a stream of associations. One establishes and re-establishes concentrated attention, but when it is interrupted one learns to disidentify with the contents of consciousness, to maintain a choiceless, non-reactive awareness, and to quiet the ego with its preferences.

Should this description appear distinctly Asian and raise doubts regarding its relevance to contemplative prayer practices in the monotheisms, consider, by way of balance, this passage from *Your Word Is Fire,* a work on Hasidic prayer:

> Any teaching that places such great emphasis on total concentration in prayer must . . . deal with the question of distraction. What is a person to do when alien thoughts enter his mind and lead him away from prayer? . . . The Ba'al Shem Tov . . . spoke against the attempts of his contemporaries to . . . do battle with dis-tracting thoughts. . . . He taught that each distraction may become a ladder by which one may ascend to a new level of devotion. . . . God [is] present in that moment of distraction! And only he who truly knows that God is present in *all* things, including those thoughts he seeks to flee, can be a leader of prayer.[2]

Though some scholars have drawn a mutually exclusive distinction between "concentrative" and "receptive" forms of attentional practice, the foregoing suggests that this distinction must not be pressed too far.

In any case, this scholarly quibble need not detain us any longer from looking at the more important issue. The question is: How does the regular and long-term practice of attention, in the context of a spiritual tradition, enable the self to extricate itself from compulsive ego-centeredness and from the blind-ness to subtler and more inclusive realities which result therefrom?

Most spiritual traditions contain some notion or other of the false consciousness, or false self, which when overcome, rendered transparent, or otherwise transcended, allows the self-manifesting quality of truth to disclose itself. Let us say, therefore, that the central significance of attentional exercises is to release the human being from bondage to the machinations of that false self.

To better grasp this concept, let us consider that human beings experience a persistent need to preserve and expand their being, and thus each of us, from birth, undertakes what may be called a self-project. Everyone longs to be special, to be a center of importance and value, to possess life's fullness even unto immortality, and everyone spends energy in pursuit of those things that, according to his level of understanding, will fulfill these longings. According to many contemplative traditions, such longing is grounded in a profound truth: ultimately, we share in the undying life of the ultimately real. Unfortunately, however, the ego transcendence that contemplative traditions prescribe is usually rejected in favor of endless vain attempts to expand the ego in the external world through possession, projection, and gratification.

The false self, then, can be understood as a metaphor for psychic automatism, that is, automatic, egocentric, habit-determined patterns of thought, emotive reaction and assessment, and imaginary activity that filter and distort reality and skew behavior, according to the needs of the self-project. Having hardened into relatively permanent psychological "structures," these predispositional patterns may be conceived as constantly feeding on available psychic energy, dissolving it into the endless associational flotsam in the stream of consciousness. Energy that would otherwise be manifested as the delight of open and present-centered awareness is inexorably drawn to these structures and there disintegrates into the image-films and commentaries—the "noise"—that suffuse ordinary consciousness.

What allows the self-aggravating automatism of the false self to function unchecked is, in a word, *identification*. As long as we are unconsciously and automatically identifying with the changing contents of consciousness, we never suspect that our true nature remains hidden from us. If spiritual freedom means anything, however, it means first and foremost a freedom from such automatic identification.

Once automatism and identification are understood to be the sustainers of the false self, we are in a position to understand the psycho-transformative power of concentrated, nonreactive attention. For whether a human being is a Muslim repeating the names of God or a Theravāda Buddhist practicing bare attention, he or she is, to one degree or another, cultivating the disidentification that leads to the de-automatization[3] of the false self.

The mere act of trying to hold the mind to a single point, an act with which higher forms of meditation begin, teaches the beginner in a radically concrete and experiential way that he or she has little or no control over the mental flow. All attentional training starts with this failure. This is the first great step in the work of objectifying the mental flow, that is, of seeing it not as something that "I" am doing but something that is simply happening. Without this realization no progress can be made, for one must first know one is in prison in order to work intelligently to escape. Thus, when the Christian is asked to concentrate his attention solely upon God, when the Muslim attempts to link his attention solely to the names of God, when the Tibetan Buddhist attempts with massive attention to construct elaborate images of Tārā on the screen of consciousness, the first lesson these practitioners learn is that they *cannot* do it. Ordinary mentation is freshly understood to be foreign to the deepest reality of one's being. The more regularly this is seen the clearer it becomes that one is *not* one's thoughts, and the more profoundly one understands the distinction between consciousness as such and the contents of consciousness. Objectification of the contents of consciousness and disidentification with them are natural outcomes.

Contemplative attentional exercises are strategies of starvation. Every moment that available energy is consolidated in concentrative and nonreactive attention is a moment when automatized processes cannot replenish themselves. In the dynamic world of the psyche, there is no stasis: if automatisms do not grow more strongly solidified, they begin to weaken and dissolve. When deprived of the nutriment formerly afforded to them by distracted states of mind, the automatized processes of the mind begin to disintegrate. Contemplative attention practiced over a long period of time may dissolve and uproot even the most recalcitrant pockets of psychological automatism, allowing consciousness to re-collect the ontic freedom and clarity that are its birthright.

De-automatization, then, describes an essential aspect of the process of spiritual liberation, the freeing of oneself from bondage to the false self. It names, furthermore, a gradual, long-term process of transformation, a process within which discrete mystical experiences reach fruition and without which they are destined to fade into ineffectual memories.

However, it should be clear that the function of contemplative work is largely destructive. The accoutrements of a spiritual tradition provide a protective and constructive framework within which this destructive work can proceed. The more seriously the foundations of the false self are undermined by the practice of attention, the fiercer become the storms of protest from within. The "dying" that occurs during contemplative work can cause internal shocks and reactions so profound that only the deep contours of a tradition can absorb them and turn them to creative effect. The support of a tradition hundreds of years old—rich in symbolism, metaphysical and psychological maps, and the accumulated experience of thousands of past wayfarers—and the guidance of an experienced teacher are indispensable. A "new age" movement that wishes to champion contemplative technique but jettison the traditional context in which it was originally lodged seems likely to be either very superficial or very dangerous or both.

Moreover, tradition stresses and a spiritual community supports, in a way that a mere technique cannot, the importance of morality as a *sine qua non* foundation and necessary ongoing accompaniment to the inner work. Without the rectification of external conduct, inner work cannot proceed far. One would be hard pressed to find a single exception to this rule in the great traditions.

Finally, human transformation is effected not solely by isolated bouts of intense attentional training; such training must be linked to ordinary life by an intentionality that makes every aspect of life a part of the spiritual work. The contemplative opus, in other words, is hardly limited to formal periods of attentional practice. Ordinary activity and formal contemplative practice must reinforce each other and between them sustain the continuity of practice that alone can awaken the mind and help it realize the *telos* adumbrated for it in the images and concepts of the tradition to which it belongs.

Attentional exercises are hardly meant to be practiced in isolation. Their effectiveness requires not only long practice but also the support of a community, the guidance of tradition, the tranquillity effected by moral purification, and, finally, the continuity of practice that allows the power of will, indispensable to the transformative work, to be fully born.

22. The Flow Experience *by Mihaly Csikszentmihalyi*

The flow experience is about knowing how to be happy. It is the way that people feel when their consciousness is ordered, and they pursue whatever they are doing for its own sake. As a feeling, flow has been described as playing, as being creative, and even as a religious phenomenon, because those activities typically produce internal enjoyment.

Part of the problem with knowing how to be happy is that the pleasure of flow is mistakenly identified with the activity that produces it. Csikszentmihalyi cites data collected from thousands of people over two decades, revealing eight major components of flow. We are reminded that happiness is sought for its own sake, whereas every other goal—health, beauty, money, or power—is valued because we expect it will make us happy if we achieve it.

THERE IS A common experiential state which is present in various forms of play, and also under certain conditions in other activities which are not normally thought of as play. For lack of a better term, I will refer to this experience as "flow." Flow denotes the wholistic sensation present when we act with total involvement. It is the kind of feeling after which one nostalgically says: "That was fun," or "That was enjoyable." It is the state in which action follows upon action according to an internal logic which seems to need no conscious intervention on our part. We experience it as a unified flowing from one moment to the next, in which we feel in control of our actions, and in which there is little distinction between self and environment: between stimulus and response; or between past, present, and future.

The most typical kind of flow experience is play, and games are the most common forms of play activity. Excellent descriptions of what we here call flow have been given by Murphy (1972) in his book on golf, Herrigel (1953) in regards to Zen archery, Abrahams (1960) on chess, and Unsworth (1969) on rock climbing.

But play is not synonymous with flow. Experiential states undistinguishable from those we have called "flow" and that are reported in play are also reported in a great variety of other contexts. What Maslow (1962, 1965, 1971) has called "peak experiences," and de Charms (1968) has called the "origin" state, share many distinctive features with the process of flow.

The working out of creative ideas also involves analogous experiences. In fact, almost any description of the creative experience (e.g., Dillon, 1972; Getzels & Csikszentmihalyi, 1974; Ghiselin, 1952; Montmasson, 1939) gives experiential accounts which are in important respects analogous with those obtained from people at play.

It is quite obvious that certain states of rapture which are usually labelled "religious" share the characteristics of flow with play and creativity. These include almost any account of collective ritual (e.g., Deren, 1953; Turner, 1969; Worsley, 1968); of the practice of Zen, Yoga, and other forms of meditation (e.g., Eliade, 1969; Herrigel, 1953; Narango & Ornstein, 1971); or of practically any other form of religious experience (e.g., Laski, 1962; Moltman, 1972; Rahner, 1967).

While flow is often experienced in play, in creativity, or in religious ecstasy, it is not always present in these activities, nor is it limited to them. In fact, part of the problem with this phenomenon is that previously what here is called flow has been identified with the behavioral pattern within which it has been experienced. Thus flow has been described as play, as creativity, as religious ecstasy, etc., and its explanation has been sought in these activities which define different behavioral patterns. It is my task to analyze out the experience of flow as a conceptually *independent process* which might or might not underlie these activities.

ELEMENTS OF THE FLOW EXPERIENCE

Merging Action and Awareness

Perhaps the clearest sign of flow is the experience of merging action and awareness. A person in flow does not operate with a dualistic perspective: he is very aware of his actions, but not of the awareness itself. A tennis player pays undivided attention to the ball and the opponent, a chess master focuses on the strategy of the game, most states of religious ecstasy are reached by following complex ritual steps, yet for flow to be maintained, one cannot reflect on the act of awareness itself. The moment awareness is split so as to perceive the activity from "outside," the flow is interrupted.

Therefore, flow is difficult to maintain for any length of time without at least momentary interruptions. Typically, a person can maintain a merged awareness with his or her actions for only short periods interspersed with interludes (from the Latin *inter ludes,* "between plays") in which the flow is broken by the actor's adoption of an outside perspective.

These interruptions occur when questions flash through the actor's mind such as "am I doing well?" or "what am I doing here?" or "should I be doing this?" When one is in a flow episode these questions simply do not come to mind.

Steiner (1972) gives an excellent account of how it feels to get out of the state of flow in chess, and then back into it again:

> The bright arcs of relation that weld the pieces into a phalanx, that make one's defense a poison-tipped porcupine shiver into vague filaments. The chords dissolve. The pawn in one's sweating hand withers to mere wood or plastic. A tunnel of inanity yawns, boring and bottomless. As from another world comes the appalling suggestion . . . that this is, after all, "only a game." If one entertains that annihilating proposition even for an instant, one is done for. (It seemed to flash across Boris Spassky's drawn features for a fraction of a second before the sixty-ninth move of the thirteenth game.) Normally, the opponent makes his move and in that murderous moment addiction comes again. New lines of force light up in the clearing haze, the hunched intellect straightens up and takes in the sweep of the board, cacophony subsides, and the instruments mesh into unison [p. 94].

For action to merge with awareness to such an extent, the activity must be feasible. Flow seems to occur only when persons face tasks that are within their ability to perform. This is why one experiences flow most often in activities which have clearly established rules for action, such as rituals, games, or participatory art forms like the dance.

Here are a few quotes from our interviews with people engaged in flow-producing activities. Their words illustrate more clearly what the merging of action and awareness means in different cases. An outstanding chess-player:

> The game is a struggle, and the concentration is like breathing—you never think of it. The roof could fall in and if it missed you, you would be unaware of it.

A basketball player from a state champion high-school team:

> The only thing that really goes through my mind is winning the game . . . I really don't have to think, though. When I am playing it just comes to me. It's a good feeling. Everything is working out—working smooth.

And one of his team-mates:

> When I get hot in a game . . . Like I said, you don't think about it at all. If you step back and think about why you are so hot all of a sudden you get creamed.

Centering of Attention

The merging of action and awareness is made possible by a centering of attention on a limited stimulus field. To insure that people will concentrate on their actions, potentially intruding stimuli must be kept out of attention. Some writers have called this process a "narrowing of consciousness," a "giving up the past and the future" (Maslow, 1971, pp. 63–65). One respondent, a university science professor who climbs rocks, phrased it as follows:

> When I start on a climb, it is as if my memory input has been cut off. All I can remember is the last thirty seconds, and all I can think ahead is the next five minutes.

The same experience is reported by dancers:

> I get a feeling that I don't get anywhere else . . . I have more confidence in myself than at any other time. Maybe an effort to forget my problems. Dance is like therapy. If I am troubled about something I leave it out the door as I go in (the dance studio).

And by composers—in this case a woman composer of modern music:

> I am really quite oblivious to my surroundings after I really get going. I think that the phone could ring, and the doorbell could ring, or the house burn down, or something like that . . . when I start working I really do shut out the world. Once I stop I can let it back in again.

In games, the rules define what the relevant stimuli are, and exclude everything else as irrelevant. But rules alone are not always enough to get a person involved with the game. Hence the structure of games provides motivational elements which will draw the player into play. Perhaps the simplest of these inducements is competition. The addition of a competitive element to a game usually insures the undivided attention of a player who would not be motivated otherwise. When being "beaten" is one of the possible outcomes of an activity, the actor is pressured to attend to it more closely. Another alternative is to add the possibility of material gains. It is usually easier to sustain flow in simple games, such as poker, when gambling is added to the rules. But the payoff is rarely the goal of a gambler. As Dostoevski (1961) clearly observed about his own compulsion, "The main thing is the play itself, I swear that greed for money has nothing to do with it, although heaven knows I am sorely in need of money." Finally there are play activities which rely on physical danger to produce centering of attention, and hence flow. Such is rock climbing, where one is forced to ignore all distracting stimuli by the knowledge that survival is dependent on complete concentration.

The addition of spurious motivational elements to a flow activity (competition, gain, danger), make it also more vulnerable to intrusions from "outside reality." Playing for money may increase concentration on the game, but paradoxically one can also be more easily distracted from play by the fear of losing. A Samurai swordsman concerned about winning will be beaten by his opponent who is not thus distracted. Ideally, flow is the result of pure involvement, without any consideration about results. In practice, however, most people need some inducement to participate in flow activities, at least at the beginning, before they learn to be sensitive to intrinsic rewards.

Loss of Ego

Most writers who have described experiences similar to what here is called "flow," mention an element variously described as "loss of ego," "self-forgetfulness," "loss of self-consciousness," and even "transcendence of individuality" and "fusion with the world" (Maslow, 1971, p. 65–70).

When an activity involves the person completely with its demands for action, "self-ish" considerations become irrelevant. The concept of self (Mead, 1934) or ego (Freud, 1927) has traditionally been that of an intrapsychic mechanism which mediates between the needs of the organism, and the social demands placed upon it.

A primary function of the self is to integrate one person's actions with that of others, and hence it is a prerequisite for social life (Berger & Luckmann, 1967). Activities which allow flow to occur (i.e., games, rituals, art, etc.), however, usually do not require any negotiation. Since they are based on freely accepted rules, the player does not need to use a self to get along in the activity. As long as all the participants follow the same rules, there is no need to negotiate roles. The participants need no self to bargain with about what should or should not be done. As long as the rules are respected, a flow situation is a social system with no deviance. This is possible only in activities in which reality is simplified to the point that it is understandable, definable, and manageable. Such is typically the case in religious ritual, artistic performances, and in games.

Self-forgetfulness does *not* mean, however, that in flow a person loses touch with his or her own physical reality. In some flow activities, perhaps in most, one becomes more intensely aware of internal processes. This obviously occurs

in yoga and many religious rituals. Climbers report a great increase of kines-
thetic sensations, a sudden awareness of ordinarily unconscious muscular
movements. Chess players are very aware of the working of their own minds
during games. What is usually lost in flow is not the awareness of one's body
or of one's functions, but only the *self-construct,* the intermediary which one
learns to interpose between stimulus and response.

The same experience is reported by people involved in creative activities.
An outstanding composer has this to say about how he feels when he is writing music:

> You yourself are in an ecstatic state to such a point that you feel as though you
> almost don't exist. I've experienced this time and time again. My hand seems
> devoid of myself, and I have nothing to do with what is happening. I just sit there
> watching it in a state of awe and wonderment. And it just flows out by itself.

Or in chess:

> Time passes a hundred times faster. In this sense, it resembles the dream state. A
> whole story can unfold in seconds, it seems. Your body is nonexistent—but actu-
> ally your heart pumps like mad to supply the brain. . . .

Control of Action and Environment

A person in flow is in control of his actions and of the environment. While
involved in the activity, this feeling of control is modified by the "ego-less" state
of the actor. Rather than an active awareness of mastery, it is more a condition
of not being worried by the possibility of lack of control. But later, in thinking back on the experience, a person will usually feel that for the duration of
the flow episode his skills were adequate to meeting environmental demands,
and this reflection might become an important component of a positive self-
concept.

A dancer expresses well this paradoxical feeling of being in control and
being merged with the environment at the same time:

> If I have enough space, I am in control. I feel I can radiate an energy into the atmos-
> phere. It's not always necessary that another human being be there to catch that
> energy. I can dance for walls, I can dance for floors . . . I don't know if it's usually
> a control of the atmosphere. I become one with the atmosphere.

In nonflow states, such a feeling of control is difficult to sustain for any
length of time. There are too many imponderables. Personal relationships,

career obstacles, health problems—not to mention death and taxes—are always to a certain extent beyond control.

Even where the sense of control comes from defeating another person, the player often sees it as a victory over his or her own limitations, rather than over the opponent. A basketball player:

> I feel in control. Sure I've practiced and have a good feeling for the shots I can make . . . I don't feel in control of the other player—even if he's bad and I know where to beat him. It's me and not him that I'm working on.

Flow experiences occur in activities where one can cope, at least theoretically, with all the demands for action. In a chess game, for instance, everything is potentially controllable. A player need never fear that the opponent's move will produce any threats except those allowed by the rules.

The feeling of control and the resulting absence of worry are present even in flow situations where "objectively" the dangers to the actor seem very real. The famous British rock climber, Chris Bonington, describes the experience very well:

> At the start of any big climb I feel afraid, dread the discomfort and danger I shall have to undergo. It's like standing on the edge of a cold swimming-pool trying to nerve yourself to take the plunge; yet once in, it's not nearly as bad as you have feared; *in fact it's enjoyable. . . . Once I start climbing, all my misgivings are forgotten.* The very harshness of the surrounding, the treacherous layer of verglas covering every hold, even the high-pitched whine of falling stones, all help build up tension and excitement that are ingredients of mountaineering [Unsworth, 1969; italics added].

Although the dangers in rock climbing and similar activities are real, they are finite and hence predictable and manageable; a person can work up to mastering them. Practically every climber says that driving a car is more dangerous than the incredible acrobatic feats on the rock; and in a sense it may be true, since in driving, the elements outside one's control are more numerous and dangerous than in climbing. In any case, a sense of control is definitely one of the most important components of the flow experience, whether an "objective" assessment justifies such feeling or not.

Demands for Action and Clear Feedback

Another quality of the experience is that it usually contains coherent, non-contradictory demands for action, and provides clear unambiguous feedback to a person's actions. These components of flow, like the preceding ones, are made possible by limiting awareness to a restricted field of possibilities. In the artificially reduced reality of a flow episode it is clear what is "good" and what is "bad." Goals and means are logically ordered. A person is not expected to do incompatible things, as in real life. He or she knows what the results of various possible actions will be.

But in flow, one does not stop to evaluate the feedback—action and reaction have become so well practiced as to be automatic. The person is too concerned with the experience to reflect on it. Here is the clear account of a basketball player:

> I play my best games almost by accident. I go out and play on the court and I can tell if I'm shooting o.k. or if I'm not—so I know if I'm playing good or like shit—but if I'm having a super game I can't tell until after the game . . . guys make fun of me because I can lose track of the score and I'll ask Russell what the score is and he'll tell me and sometimes it breaks people up—they think "That kid must be real dumb."

In other words, the flow experience differs from awareness in everyday reality because it contains ordered rules which make action and the evaluation of action automatic and hence unproblematic. When contradictory actions are made possible (as for instance when cheating is introduced into a game), the self reappears again to negotiate between the conflicting definitions of what needs to be done, and the flow is interrupted.

Autotelic Nature of Flow

A final characteristic of the flow experience is its "autotelic" nature. In other words, it appears to need no goals or rewards external to itself. Practically every writer who has dealt with play has remarked on the autotelic nature of this activity (e.g., Callois, 1958; Huizinga, 1950; Piaget, 1951, 1965). In the *Gita,* Lord Krishna instructs Arjuna to live his whole life according to this principle: "Let the motive be in the deed, and not in the event. Be not one whose motive for action is the hope of reward" [2.47].

A young poet who is also a seasoned climber, describes the autotelic experience in words that would be difficult to improve on:

The mystique of rock climbing is climbing; you get to the top of the rock glad it's over but really wish it would go forever. The justification of climbing is climbing like the justification of poetry is writing; you don't conquer anything except things in yourself . . . the act of writing justifies poetry. Climbing is the same; recognizing that you are a flow. The purpose of the flow is to keep on flowing, not looking for a peak or utopia but staying in the flow. It is not a moving up but a continuous flowing; you move up only to keep the flow going. There is no possible reason for climbing except the climbing itself; it is a self-communication.

The various elements of the flow experience are inextricably linked together and dependent on each other. By limiting the stimulus field, a flow activity allows people to concentrate their actions and ignore distractions. As a result, they feel in potential control of the environment. Because the flow activity has clear and noncontradictory rules, people performing it can temporarily forget their identity and its problems. The result of all these conditions is that one finds the process intrinsically rewarding.

23. The Focusing Technique: Confirmatory Knowing Through the Body by Ann Weiser Cornell

Focusing is a body-based technique that helps to confirm inner knowing. Author Ann Cornell, a focusing therapist, offers a few simple steps that enable us to attend to "felt-sense" bodily signals that bring fuzzy, preverbal knowledge into conscious awareness.

This "ability to receive and confirm inner knowing" through focusing is a fundamental human ability that most people in Western cultures have lost. Yet all it takes is quiet and the patience to attend to vague physical impressions, until they become defined and meaningful.

Unlike techniques that depend on releasing inhibiting habits and old beliefs, the focusing technique is a way of attending to inner knowing until it blossoms into awareness.

FOCUSING IS A body-oriented process of self-awareness and emotional healing, in which we learn to become aware of the subtle level of knowing that speaks to us through the body.

THE DISCOVERY OF FOCUSING

The Focusing process is based on research into successful personality change done by Eugene Gendlin and his colleagues. They compared successful therapy clients with unsuccessful ones, discovering that success in therapy could be predicted from client behavior in the first few sessions. If at some point in the session the client had an unclear bodily awareness, and slowed down his or her talking in order to refer to this and try to symbolize it, then the psychotherapy would ultimately be successful.

Gendlin named this unclear bodily awareness the "felt sense," and the process of attending to the felt sense, in such a way that meaning emerges, he called Focusing. He developed a method of teaching Focusing, taught it to therapy clients and others, and eventually wrote a book for the general public (1981). By 1997 Gendlin and his colleagues had brought the Focusing process to schools, businesses, hospitals, religious communities, and tens of thousands of individuals throughout the world.

Although Gendlin developed it as a teachable technique, Focusing is not an invention. It is a naturally occurring skill that can be observed in people of all cultures and backgrounds. The ability to receive and confirm inner knowing through Focusing is a human birthright. Unfortunately, Focusing ability is trained out of most people living in industrial and postindustrial societies, which place a premium on logical, intellectual ways of knowing. Most of us must be retrained in order to use Focusing effectively, and even people who have retained their natural Focusing ability can benefit from learning it as a consciously accessible skill.

THE FELT SENSE

The key concept of Focusing is the felt sense: a body sensation that is meaningful. Examples include a jittery feeling in the stomach as you stand up to speak, or a heaviness in the heart as you think of a distant loved one.

A felt sense is usually experienced in the middle of the body: abdomen, stomach, chest, throat—although felt senses also occur in other parts of the body. A person may get a felt sense of "this relationship," or "that creative project," or "the part of me that has a hard time with public speaking," and so on.

Felt senses are different from emotions, although they are likely to contain emotions. If emotions are like primary colors, felt senses are like subtle blends of colors. The emotion might be "fear," but the felt sense of the fear would be more like: "jumpy, almost excited," or "frozen like a rabbit in the headlights," or "clutching in my throat, won't let go." There is a uniqueness to a felt sense, a quality of "here is how it is right now, for me."

Felt senses are often (but not always) elusive, vague, temporary, subtle, and hard to describe. One of the most difficult aspects of learning Focusing, for most people, is the shift of attention from experiences that are definite, clear, and unmistakable (like headaches) to experiences that are, as Gendlin puts it, "indefinable, global, puzzling, odd, uneasy, fuzzy."

FEELING "TOO MUCH" OR "TOO LITTLE"

People typically come to learn Focusing from two ends of a feeling spectrum. On the one hand, we have people who are troubled by feeling "too much." Their stomachs tighten each time they assert themselves. They have a constricted throat for hours after a difficult phone call. Such people have no doubt that their emotional life has an impact on their bodies—in fact, they often wish it didn't! To them, Focusing offers a way to have a friendlier, more positive relationship with feeling experience. They learn to acknowledge their bodily felt senses without becoming overwhelmed by them. Further, they make the almost miraculous discovery that when these felt senses are listened to and "heard," they lighten, soften, relax, and often release completely.

The other type of person who comes to learn Focusing is someone who feels "too little." This person has thoroughly learned the lesson of our culture: that the body is devoid of meaning and should be ignored whenever possible. When he or she puts awareness in the body, it feels blank, like nothing is there. This is the person who simply cannot answer when asked, "How do you feel?" For this person, learning Focusing means learning how to feel (rather than ignore) the body's meaningful reactions.

THE FOCUSING PROCESS

In its "long form," Focusing is done either individually and silently, as in meditation, or speaking out loud to a Focusing partner or guide. A typical Focusing session takes from ten to sixty minutes. The person who is Focusing usually keeps eyes closed as he or she attends inwardly. In its "short form," Focusing can happen in a few moments, at a stoplight while driving, for example, or during a phone call.

Although every Focusing session is different, I have identified typical stages, for teaching purposes. These stages are described with key phrases that the focuser says inwardly.

"I'm sensing into my body." The focuser begins the process by bringing awareness to the body. First, awareness can be brought to the outer area of the body: hands, feet, the contact of the body with the chair. This serves as a grounding in body awareness. Next the focuser brings awareness into the middle area of the body: throat, chest, stomach, abdomen. These areas are sensed from within.

"What wants my awareness now?" or *"How am I feeling about that issue?"* Once awareness is in the body, the focuser may discover that there is a felt sense already there. ("Yes, there's a tightness in my stomach; I've been feeling it all day.") The other possibility is that the middle of the body may be feeling fairly clear and open, but a felt sense can come if invited. The focuser gives the invitation by saying something like, "What wants my awareness now?" or "How am I feeling about (some particular) issue?" The focuser gives the invitation

inwardly, in the inner area of the body, and waits. The felt sense usually forms within about sixty seconds.

"I'm saying hello to what's here." When the focuser becomes aware of something, he/she greets it, by saying, "Hello. I know you're there." This is a powerful and important move that marks the beginning of the inner relationship.

"I'm finding the best way to describe it." Now the focuser describes the felt sense, using a word, or words, or an image, or a sound or a gesture. The focuser is finding a symbol that will fit or match the feel of the felt sense. This is usually quite simple, for example: "tight," "heavy," "squeezing," "angry pressing," "a knot," and so on.

"I'm checking back with my body." Any words, sentences, images, or ideas that come *from* the felt sense need to be offered *back* to the felt sense for confirmation. When the focuser finds a word to describe the felt sense (e.g., "tightness"), he/she then offers that word back to the felt sense to make sure it is right (accurate, fitting). Later in the session, when whole sentences emerge from the felt sense (e.g., "This part of me is afraid of feeling good"), these too are offered back to the sense in the spirit of "Did I understand you correctly?" Anything emerging in the process is checked back with the sense to see if it feels right. This impels the forward movement of the process, and helps the focuser stay grounded in the body.

"Is it OK to just be with this right now?" Inheritors of Western industrial culture, especially Americans, are very oriented toward *doing,* toward *making something happen.* So it can be a very powerful inner attitude to *just be.* This is a process of being with something without agenda, spending time with it, keeping it company—and no more.

"I'm sitting with it, with interested curiosity." Now the focuser spends time with the felt sense with an attitude of friendly, respectful curiosity. The quality of inner attention in this stage can be difficult to achieve at first. It involves an attitude of openness, of "not-knowing," of receptivity. Most people are more used to talking to themselves ("Come on now, get it together!") than to listening to themselves. Even experienced focusers may find that patience is called for. Fortunately, if some inner aspect interferes with the attitude needed for this step, it itself can be treated as a felt sense to be focused on. ("Let me just *be with* this impatience I'm feeling.")

"I'm sensing how it feels from its point of view." The focuser shifts empathically from his or her own point of view to sensing the felt sense's point of view. This is like sitting with a friend who doesn't feel like talking. You can still be curious about the friend and empathize with how she or he is feeling. The felt sense rarely "talks," yet the focuser can sense its mood.

Sensing from the felt sense's point of view is essentially the difference between "It feels uncomfortable" (my point of view) to "It feels scared" (its point of view).

"*I'm asking . . .*" The focuser has become an empathic listener to his or her own inner felt sense. By this time, the focuser may be receiving more and more intricate levels of meaning. This is the part of the session that is hardest to describe, because it is so variable. But if not much seems to be happening, the focuser may want to invite meaning by asking gentle, open-ended questions, like, "I'm asking it if it has an emotional quality," or "I'm asking it what gets it so scared" (if "scared" is the emotion).

"*I'm letting it know I hear it.*" The meaningful communication from the felt sense is received and acknowledged. This often results in a felt shift of relief, release, warmth, or other pleasurable feelings.

"*I'm saying I'll be back.*" "*I'm thanking my body and the parts that have been with me.*" As a way of ending the session, the focuser tells the felt sense that he or she will return to it at another time for further "conversation" and takes time to thank and appreciate the body.

CONFIRMATORY KNOWING

The knowing that comes through Focusing is often surprising, and operates from its own logic rather than following in a linear fashion from something previously known. Its signal can be an intensification or a releasing. It can also be a sense of flow, fresh air, opening, expansion, or the like. Tears are a strong confirmation: tears that have nothing to do with sadness, but rather with the rightness of the knowing—"truth tears." In contrast, the body's way of saying "No" is a feeling of something being "off," an uneasiness, a wrongness, limitation, or contraction, or backing away.

THE WISDOM OF THE BODY

Many people now understand that our bodies "know" what good health is, and can show us the way to optimum physical health if we so desire. But to see the scope of the body's wisdom as exclusively physical is to take too narrow a view.

Our bodies are wise in ways hardly ever acknowledged by our culture. Our bodies carry knowledge about how we are living our lives, about what we need to be more fully ourselves, about what we value and believe, about what has hurt us emotionally and how to heal it. Our bodies know which people around us bring out the best in us, and which do not. Our bodies know the right next step to bring us to more fulfilling and rewarding lives.

Learning Focusing means returning to a kind of nonanalytic knowing that connects us to our wholeness. We build a better relationship with our emotional life. Trust in our own process deepens. Focusing becomes an inner "compass" that points the way more and more reliably the more it is used.

24. Creative Knowing by Betty Edwards

Betty Edwards is the originator of a phenomenally popular technique known as drawing from the right side of the brain, and has been responsible for introducing thousands of people to this method for accessing inner knowing.

Interestingly, the tool of knowing is not the mind, but the hand. "That which I have not drawn, I have not seen," is the way art teacher Frederic Frank expressed it. In this selection, Edwards explores the unique mode of attention that artists must learn so that the eye can tell the hand what to draw. Only when the drawing is done does the artist truly "see" what has already been accomplished.

I HAVE LONG admired an ambiguous statement credited to philosopher Michael Polanyi: "We know more than we know we know." This dark saying is in contrast to Emanuel Kant's self-confident proclamation in his *Critique of Pure Reason:* "All our knowledge begins with sense, proceeds thence to understanding, and ends with reason, beyond which nothing higher can be discovered in the human mind for elaborating the matter of intuition and subjecting it to the highest unity of thought." Ludwig Wittgenstein, in his *Tractatus Logica-Philosophicus,* added another dimension to a description of knowing: Wittgenstein said, "In order to know an object, I must know not its external but all its internal qualities." Early on, however, the American transcendentalist Ralph Waldo Emerson, in an essay on the French philosopher Montaigne, had gloomily dashed hopes of knowing with a flat statement: "Knowledge is the knowing that we can not know."

These quotations are only a brief sampling of centuries of human pondering on what it means to *know* something. We seem to agree that there are multiple ways of knowing, but what it is that we know and how we know that we know are questions still pending.

Drawing, my field of interest, brings up some interesting aspects of knowing. Drawing a perceived object or person gives rise to an unusual sensation of *comprehending* that object or person. From my own experience and from hearing of others' experiences, this way of knowing by means of drawing is very different from more ordinary ways of knowing objects or persons.

Often, in drawing, one has a strange sense that some curtain has been drawn back, enabling one to see more clearly—as one artist put it, "I *see,* at last!" A surprising aspect of this sensation is an overwhelming sense that the object or person is (unexpectedly) beautiful. This response occurs not just with objects that one would judge beautiful anyway, say a perfect rose or a lovely young person or a marvelous landscape. It occurs in drawing a battered old shoe or the lined face of a very old person or a crumpled-up piece of paper. Seeing in this way is so pleasurable, so uplifting of the spirit (for want of better words) I feel quite sure that it accounts for much of the joy of drawing.

I think that the recurring experience I have just described conforms to what is commonly termed these days "the aesthetic experience." The phrase comes from the Greek word *aesthetikos,* meaning "of sense perception." The term "aesthetics," however, is a relatively recent derivation, meant to designate the branch of philosophy that deals with the nature of beauty. Aestheticians develop theories of beauty and criteria for judgment of the beautiful in both art and nature. They ponder difficult questions—for example, must beauty be inherent in the object or can beauty be in the eye of the beholder and therefore dependent on the viewer's taste and knowledge?

While aesthetics as a recognized branch of philosophy did not come into existence until the nineteenth century, speculation concerning the nature of beauty runs through all cultures. In Western thought, the Greeks laid the foundation for our familiar triad of fundamental values—the good, the true, and the beautiful. Many issues, however, remain unresolved. For example, heated controversy still surrounds the issue of the objectivity versus the subjectivity of beauty.

The term "aesthetics" also signifies the description and explanation of artistic works and aesthetic response. Aestheticians draw on other sciences, such as psychology, sociology, ethnology, or history, and mainly use language as the means of description. Herein lies the greatest problem. Can the aesthetic experience be replicated or even described in words? And if not—that is, if the experience is untranslatable—can we say that we (nonverbally) "know" what that experience is? Do we, in Polanyi's words, know more than we know we know?

An English painter and lecturer at the University of London, Michael Stephan, has proposed a bold new approach to this problem in a book titled *A Transformational Theory of Aesthetics* (Routledge, 1990). Stephan starts with an assumption that all human cognition is best defined as *ways of knowing.* He points out that we can tell the difference between ways of knowing music and ways of knowing literature and ways of knowing works of art. Therefore, he states, it seems possible that these different ways of knowing are not necessarily compatible or intertranslatable.

This question of translatability in the field of the visual arts has been a burning issue for centuries. Can the art historian, art theoretician, or art critic, whose stock in trade is the manipulation of words, translate the work of the artist, whose stock in trade is the manipulation of visual images? Stephan questions to what extent language can plausibly explicate a visual image. Does a drawing or painting translate into words? And if not, why do the art theoreticians continue to try? In fact, he continues, if the whole purpose of making art is to elicit a unique, nonlinguistic way of knowing, what causes us to feel compelled to describe in words that other, visual, untranslatable way of knowing?

Even artists are often not immune to the compulsion to *talk about* their work, and even E. H. Gombrich, eminent art theorist who conceded that the phrase "aesthetic experience" constitutes "a notorious difficulty," finally resorted to metaphor and analogy—another difficult and controversial branch of verbal cognition—to better explain the artist's vision and his (Gombrich's) response to works of art. In a tightly ordered and carefully built theory, Stephan works his way through this labyrinth to propose that, in his words, "It is therefore not so much a case of a picture being worth a thousand words, or a thousand words being worth a picture—rather, it is a case of it being questionable, on evolutionary and neuropsychological grounds, to expect any amount of words to explicate a picture or vice versa."

Stephan hypothesizes that our (right hemisphere) perception of a work of art—often, but not necessarily, of a representational or "realistic" image—causes a compellingly pleasurable affective or *feeling* response, and that this feeling is what is commonly termed the aesthetic experience. Although generally conceded to be, as Gombrich put it, notoriously difficult to explicate, the experience prompts, even compels, a linguistic discourse as the left hemisphere attempts to explain both the pleasurable feeling emanating from the "silent" hemisphere and what it is about the visual image that caused the feeling. Because the *feeling* is nontranslatable, the language system apparently scans the image to find whatever it has words for: factual data (artist's name, title and date of the work, medium, size), cultural context, stylistic and color characteristics, provenance, previously known judgments of quality, and the artist's apparent use of principles such as balance, repetition, rhythm.

What remains untranslated, however, is the very core of the matter, the aesthetic experience itself, and aestheticians must resort, as Gombrich resorted, to metaphor and analogies. Art historian and aesthetician Sir Kenneth Clark, for example, once exclaimed, "When I see that foot (of the half-reclining nude "Olympia" by the nineteenth-century painter Edouard Manet) I could jump for joy!" And I recall once asking an art historian how he could tell, on viewing a painting by an unknown artist, whether it was really good, he replied, "If my hands sweat, it's good."

If Michael Stephan is right in his theory—which seems completely plausible to me—it follows that the *act* of drawing or painting perhaps is even more nondiscursive than merely viewing artworks created by another person. For me, the act of drawing almost shuts down language. In doing demonstration drawings, for example, my wish is to explain to my students what I am seeing and drawing. My students tell me that I sound as though I am speaking "from a long way off" and they find it quite amusing that I lose half of every other sentence, unable to continue talking despite my wish to explain the process.

Moreover, I am aware that my perceptions are radically different during the act of drawing. For example, I recall being asked to draw a portrait of a man with whom I had shared an office for a full semester. I had barely started the drawing when the thought struck me that I had never really *seen* this person before. That is to say, I had "seen" him verbally (name, position, conversational characteristics, etc.) but not visually (a certain shape to the nose, the shape of the head, and particular configuration of the mouth, etc.). This experience calls to mind a statement by art teacher and writer Frederic Frank, who wrote, "That which I have not drawn I have not seen."

Furthermore, personal experience has shown me that the simple act of sketching a person or a scene embeds a whole array of explicit memories connected with the sketch—memories that can be recalled with extraordinary vividness. Turning the pages of my sketchbook, I can call up the time of day, the particular light, sounds, smells, colors for each scene. Ordinary memories do not have this almost eidetic quality, and it has often occurred to me that much of human life (including my own) is spent "revving" along on a very narrow band of consciousness.

In my experience, these moments of awareness seem beyond reach in most of ordinary life. Perhaps for many of us, eidetic memories are created mainly at moments of extreme emotion. For my generation, such a shared moment was the shooting of President John Kennedy. It became a cliché that all persons could vividly recall exactly what they were doing at the moment of hearing that shocking news. I have heard many people try to describe that experience, and I myself have tried, but, again, the words do not seem sufficient to the task.

If we accept as fact that this intense way of knowing lies just under our verbally conscious existence, and if we also accept Michael Stephan's theory of the nontranslatability of the aesthetic experience, it seems to me that we might do well to try to better know that other part of our existence by giving up on linguistic explanation, accepting the nontranslatability of the aesthetic experience, and focusing on the experiences themselves.

The *how* of that knowing will surely be an individual choice. For me, drawing is a chosen path. Through drawing, I feel that perhaps I can part the curtain one more time and catch a fragment of another kind of knowing. I'm sure that enticement is what keeps me at it. Others find different paths. Yet I believe a certain mystery will forever adhere to the aesthetic experience. So much of our nonverbal life is deeply puzzling and is likely to remain so, despite our wish to explicate it. Perhaps a first step toward understanding is to cease—for a moment, at least—talking about it.

Part Six

Highways to Higher Consciousness

The Sacred Wisdom of Mind, Body, and Heart

*T*he twin roots of consciousness are traditionally called "being" and "knowing." They are as inextricably connected as roots that support a single tree, but as a working definition, ontology—the study of being—refers to a wide spectrum of different qualities of consciousness, whereas knowing—also called epistemology—refers to the particular viewpoint and intuitive intelligence inherent in each quality.

To make a highly complex topic more accessible, we might see the lives of the saints, who appear in every spiritual tradition, as embodying different qualities of higher being, such as love, courage and hope. And since each saint found their way from the duality of ordinary consciousness to the nondual wisdom of higher being, their activities and writings serve as instructional guides to those who want to know the way as well.

Every genuine tradition acknowledges the full spectrum of consciousness, but as a practical matter emphasizes certain qualities of knowing over others. The word "visualization," for example, doesn't come up in the practices of Zen, yet visionary consciousness is a mainstay for intuitive training within a different cultural framework. Likewise the nondual somatic qualities of knowing, such as at-oneness with people and the environment, is traditionally approached through practices associated with Zen, rather than concentrating on inner imagery.

Intuitive practices work their magic by shaping different routes to inner knowing, and just as the outer sense allows us to see, hear, and orient to the physical environment, intuition also has its organs of perception. The three primary "organs," or centers of subtle knowing, are experienced as being in the head where dreams appear at night, in the abdomen where breath and attention join, and in the area of the heart. There is also a fourth form of intuition, called "direct knowing," that does not rely on any intermediary cues. Direct knowing is the fruit of intuitive practice, and is approached by way of developing the three organs of subtle perception.

All spiritual traditions acknowledge the three locations, but for training purposes, each brings a particular emphasis about the centers to its teachings. In Part VI, three prominent authors focus their ideas about intuition and how it might be developed. To circumvent the problem of describing a state of mind that cannot be grasped by analysis or thought, each in their own way defines intuition by what it is not.

In one of my all-time favorites, Arthur Deikman locates hunches, accurate promptings, and psychic impressions, as lower-order indicators of spiritual knowing. Frances Vaughan joins him in categorizing lower-order impressions as mental, emotional, and body-based intuition. She contrasts these impressions with "direct" or mystical knowing that does not depend on intermediary cues. Finally, Philip Goldberg takes scientism to task, arguing for the primary role of intuition in decision-making and problem-solving.

The three highways to intuition, defined by the mental, body-based, and emotional centers, should be distinguished from the ordinary functions of sensation, feeling, and cognitive thought. What is meant by "mind" for example, is not the cognitive mind, but the spiritual definition of mind, as a repository of everything knowable.

Gurdjieff, a teacher of great personal accomplishment, favored a teaching approach aimed at balancing the activity of all three centers, rather than emphasizing one over the others. I happen to prefer a three-centered training method, because it captures the personal aptitudes that different types of people bring to the work. Some have strong sensory intuition, others experience vivid inner imagery, while still others are prone to knowing of the heart.

The centers are obviously interconnected, each supporting the others, just as the systems of the physical body perform their specialized functions. In fact, from the perspective of the centers, every spiritual system does encourage stability of mental concentration, a sustained flow of refined, quiet energy from the belly center, and receptivity of heart. Whether the focus is mantra, visualization, prayer, breath observation, repetition, or any other spiritual object of attention, every practice clears an opening for spiritual energies to manifest through all three inner organs of perception.

The authors in Part VI discuss traditional practices of body, heart, and mind. Jack Kornfield, a source figure in bringing Buddhism to the West, introduces the practice of mindfulness, a basic way of paying attention required for every spiritual practice. Charles Tart, best known for his work in altered states of consciousness, distinguishes between perception and interpretation, applying this distinction to Gurdjieff's basic practices of self-observation and self-remembering. Finally, Joseph Goldstein, a distinguished teacher in the Vipassana tradition, identifies the typical hindrances of mind and suggests a way to deal with them.

The Japanese term Hara refers to the body's subtle organ of perception. Located about two inches below the navel, where energy and awareness unite during meditation, Hara functions as a "power pack," directly linking human awareness with the intelligence of the life force. The cultural understanding of Hara is that physical vitality is inseparably connected with the intelligent vitality of nature, whether we know it or not.

By dropping our placement of attention to Hara as much as possible, the whole self is experienced as a single entity, without sense of separation between body and mind, or thought and action, or self and others. The practices that develop this inner organ of perception are of two kinds, sitting and moving. Zen is well known to Westerners as a classic sitting practice in which abdominal breath is the focus of awareness. Anchored in physical posture, breath, and inwardly directed attention, the belly's subtle organ of perception is also expressed through the moving practices of martial arts, archery, flower arrangement, and swordsmanship.

The most-traveled highway to inner knowing is probably through the emotions. The Ba'al Shem Tov, who founded Hasidic mysticism saw love as the true path to wisdom, and the Christian monastic who ceaselessly works at expanding Caritas or caring, is following this route. The Sufi poet Rumi wrote: "The astrolabe of the mysteries is love."

Once again, distinctions should be drawn between the hopes and fears of ordinary emotionality and the heart as an organ of subtle perception. In being emotionally drawn to a person, a place, a thought, or a thing, we clearly see ourselves as separate from the object that captures our attention. Emotional bonding is rooted in our own history, social conditioning, and a host of other factors. Yet all this expression is entirely subjective, as no two people have the same feelings about themselves, others, or the environment.

But when nonduality is evoked, the heart responds to qualities of higher being. Compassion and love are frequently referred to as attributes of a sentient heart, so are gratitude, empathy, hope and joy, humility and generosity. We are reminded on a daily basis that the human heart reflects the objects of its attention, because we feel sad when surrounded by sorrow, uplifted when other people are joyous, and maddened when our situation goes sour. If all of that is true, then we are also affected when a loving person walks through the door, for whether we know it or not, our feelings register their quality of being.

Heart-based practice requires discriminating between ordinary emotional identification, and more subtle perceptions that emerge when emotions are still. Knowing of the heart is categorically different from bridging the gap between ourselves and others by imagining what they feel. However altruistic and deeply felt, the close identification of imagining "about" does not occur in the same state of consciousness as the experience of nondual inseparability.

The heart can also be seen as a crossroad of consciousness, where energy rising from the belly center unites with the concentrated focus of the mind. Here the activity of the subtle centers join forces to develop a complete inner body, filled with new potentials of being and knowing. From the perspective of the subtle centers, the path of the mind offers refined understanding of ourselves and each other. The belly center supplies energetic support for the turn inward, and when the center of the heart matures, the apparent separation between ourselves and the world becomes transparent.

25. Intuition by Arthur Deikman

In this classic work, psychiatrist Arthur Deikman leads us directly to the contin-
uum of consciousness by categorizing hunches and gut reactions as instances of
lower-order intuition. Higher intuition, he contends, is a direct knowing of non-
dual realities that extends perception beyond the boundaries of time and place.
Defined by what it is not, intuition is not psychological insight, not unconscious
reasoning or inference, and not what Jung called the intuitive function. Defined
in this way, intuition is not *a fallible psychological structure mediated by the*
unconscious.

Moving up the continuum toward higher consciousness, Deikman lucidly points
to the true use of intuition as a vehicle of clarification of the self, of the ongoing
flow of events, and of key purposes that are hidden from ordinary perception.

THE WORD *INTUITION* has its roots in the Latin *intueri:* to look at or toward, to
contemplate. A typical dictionary definition of the word reads, "the act or faculty of knowing without the use of rational processes: immediate cognition."[1]
The term *intuition* has been used to describe any process of acquiring knowledge that differs from conscious thought and bypasses the senses and memory.
Thus, hunches, sudden solutions to problems, "feeling" the right choice in a
dilemma, scientific creativity, the axioms of geometry, and receiving the inef-
fable "knowledge" that mysticism seeks, have all been termed *intuition.* Accordingly, many different explanations of intuition have been offered, and the
true meaning of the term as used in the mystical tradition has been clouded.

The basic concept of intuition is ancient. Throughout history, human beings
have had the experience of knowing more than what was given them by their
senses. They have attributed such unexplained knowledge either to divine intervention, as in the case of prophecy, or to a special quasi-magical ability possessed by only a few individuals, such as clairvoyants or great scientists. This
"gift" was long considered to be the property of gods or spirits, not the heritage
of ordinary men and women. Few people considered the possibility that such
sporadic instances of intuition might be lower-order manifestations of a capacity that could be developed until it became a reliable channel of knowing.

The existence of such a channel, operating outside the intellect and sensory
pathways, seems impossible to Western science, because there is no place in
its cosmology or psychology for any means of knowing other than rationality

or sensation. We cannot imagine any other process at work. Indeed, because we have achieved vast control and understanding of the physical and biological domains we have not been motivated to challenge scientific rationalism or to look for other avenues of knowledge. After all, what else is there? The answer to that question is intuition.

For thousands of years, thinkers have attempted to grapple with the issue of our knowing more than we should and have used the term *intuition* in different ways, each reflecting particular theories of knowledge based on the assumptions of specific cultures. A brief historical overview of the concept of intuition will reveal the origins of the multiple meanings now attached to the term and the implications of those meanings for one's view of human consciousness.

In Plato's *Meno,* Socrates declares:

> The soul, then, as being immortal, and having been born again many times, and having seen all things that exist, whether in this world or in the world below, has knowledge of them all; and it is no wonder that she would be able to call to remembrance all that she ever knew . . . for all inquiry and all learning is but recollection. [2]

Remembrance has been called intuition because it does not result from the use of the intellect or the senses; rather, it is a recollection: we already know and therefore *recognize* the truth. Strictly speaking, Plato's concept is not precisely the same as the intuition of mystical science, which is a perception at a higher level than that of geometric truth or the "good" of popular consensus. Furthermore, mystical intuition is developed; it is not given. However, Plato may have intended this description to serve as a teaching device for communicating a similar concept, since in other passages, especially in the cave metaphor of *The Republic,* he indicates the need to free oneself from preoccupation with the world of appearances in order to see clearly. The prisoners in the cave cannot immediately confront the sun but must progress by degrees to that capacity:

> . . . the natural power to learn lives in the soul and is like an eye which might not be turned from the dark to the light without turning round of the whole body. The instrument of knowledge has to be turned around to the things of being, till the soul is able, by degrees, to support the light of true being and can look at the brightest. [3]

Thus, by a power higher than the senses or ordinary reason, human beings can perceive a certain and permanent truth—provided their attention is no longer fixed upon the shadows.

Plato's vision finds a striking parallel in the legends of the Hopi people, whose cultural roots go back as far as those of the Greeks. The Hopi tradition speaks of a fall from grace in which human beings experience themselves as progressively more separate from earth, animals, and other humans. The return to grace is through reunion. The cause of the fall is ascribed to people's forgetting their true nature and purpose. According to the Hopis, a psycho-physical vibratory center responsive to the Great Spirit exists in the top of the head to serve as a guide—it "sees" what other senses do not. Persons with "the door open" have not forgotten their relationship to the divine and continue to praise it. They are saved in each epoch because they can hear the instructions of the Spirit.[4]

Why do the Hopi myths parallel Plato? Although Plato has been interpreted in different ways, from the perspective of mystical science he teaches that basic truth is arrived at intuitively, not logically. His dialogues are not intended to "prove" anything; rather, they communicate a perception similar to that of the mystics, which is not the property or creation of any one culture or epoch. For both Greeks and Hopis, the deep perception of the human situation was similar. The special "insight" mentioned in their teachings is gained neither through the senses nor through reason; it is intuitive and transcends culture and time.

Spinoza's definition of intuition is closest of all the philosophers' to that of mystical science. Writing in the seventeenth century, Spinoza distinguished between knowledge derived from the sense perception and careful reasoning about observed phenomena ("opinion" and "reason") and the highest stage of human knowledge, in which the whole of the universe is comprehended as a unified interconnected system. This highest knowledge he termed intuition, something that grows out of empirical and scientific knowledge but rises above them. In essence, it is knowledge of God. To Spinoza, God exists in different "manifestations," all of which are part of the same unified system operating in harmony. Rationality provides a broader scope for intuition but it cannot show us what intuition can.[5]

Kant proposed that space and time, as commonly conceived, are, like the fundamental axioms of geometry, absolutely true and exist as "categorical imperatives," prior to logical thought or sensation. He regarded these concepts as the products of "pure intuition."[6]

Unfortunately for Kant's philosophy, modern mathematics and physics have demonstrated that the fundamental axioms of geometry, thought for centuries to be irrefutable, are only relatively true, depending entirely on the frame of reference employed. Ordinary concepts of space and time are found to be matters of habit based on early learning. In a similar vein, Richard Von Mises cites Gonseth: "The . . . rules of logic and common sense are nothing else than an abstract schema drawn from the world of concrete objects."[7]

Less abstractly, Von Senden's studies of the congenitally blind who later acquire sight . . . indicate why "space" can be a fallible concept: it is learned, not given. Reports suggest that human beings develop the experience of space through practice in looking at objects. The "intuition" of space is most likely a posteriori, not a priori. According to mystics, intuitive truth is usually of a higher order than what can be expressed in simple object world concepts, such as geometric axioms. Thus, Kant's "intuition" is closer to what contemporary philosophers call "implicit inference" than to intuition as defined by the mystics. The thinking process used to arrive at the concepts Kant calls intuitive goes on outside awareness but is not different from conscious thought or learning.

Two hundred and fifty years after Kant, at the beginning of the twentieth century, Henri Bergson emphasized the importance of employing intuition rather than relying exclusively on the intellect or "analysis":

> . . . philosophers agree in making a deep distinction between two ways of knowing a thing. The first implies going all around it, the second entering into it. The first depends on the viewpoint chosen and the symbols employed, while the second is taken from no viewpoint and rests on no symbols. Of the first kind of knowledge, we shall say that it stops at the relative; of the second that, wherever possible, it attains the absolute . . . an absolute can only be given in an intuition, while all the rest has to do with analysis. We call intuition here the sympathy by which one is transported into the interior of an object in order to coincide with what there is unique and consequently inexpressible in it.[8]

Bergson's point of view is quite close to that of mystical science in his emphasis on intuition as direct (absolute) knowing.

In modern times, however, the "intuitionism" of the philosophers, whatever its form, has been largely replaced by logical positivism, which assumes that all knowledge comes from reasoning about sensory information. Any knowledge labeled "intuitive" is believed to originate from the reasoning processes outside awareness. The "intuitor" is unaware of the steps or the inferences he or she actually employs and thus mistakenly believes a nonsensory and nonrational process has taken place. This reduces intuition to unconscious inference, an interpretation that dominates current philosophy, psychiatric thinking, and almost all contemporary psychological theory and research.

In fact, modern psychiatry has never paid much attention to intuition in the classical sense of that term. In 1932, in his *New Introductory Lectures,* Freud declared with confidence that ". . . no new source of knowledge or methods of research have come into being. Intuition, and divination would be such, if they existed; but they may safely be reckoned as illusions, the fulfillment of wishful impulses."[9] This view persists among contemporary psychoanalysts, who classify intuition as either empathy (a process of emotional identification), imagination, or creativity ("regression in the service of ego").[10,11]

Some people think Carl Jung was attuned to the mystical. It is easy to assume that he used *intuition* to refer to the same process as the one that concerns mystical science, but this is not so. Rather, he used *intuition* to refer to a basic personality capacity: "But intuition, as I conceive it, is one of the basic functions of the psyche; namely, *perception of the possibilities inherent in a situation.*"[12] Jung considered intuition to be an unconscious process whose primary function "is simply to transmit images, or perceptions or relations between things, which could not be transmitted by other functions, or only in a very roundabout way."[13] Thus, intuition perceives the relationship of entities. However, Jung's position was closer to Freud's than to mysticism's, for his "intuition" is another function, like thinking, sensation, and feeling, that can be right or wrong—it is not direct knowing.[14]

Similarly, contemporary psychoanalytic theory and the general literature of psychiatry do not recognize intuition as being qualitatively different from functions with which we are familiar.

Jerome Bruner expressed the view of the majority of psychologists that intuitive discoveries are the result of free combinations of the elements of a problem:

> Intuition implies the art of grasping the meaning or significance or structure of a problem without explicit reliance on the analytic apparatus of one's craft . . . It is founded on a kind of combinatorial playfulness.[15]

Such a view comes largely from restricting the investigation of intuition to the type of isolated "problem" that lends itself to controlled psychological experiment. Unfortunately, Bruner applies the conclusions derived from this limited domain to a much broader field of human experience, as if the two were identical. As a result, the term he uses to denote the capacity to solve a geometric puzzle is the same as that for the capacity to perceive the meaning of life, and he jams both together into the same mechanical box.

In fairness to Bruner, he recognized that intuition was not just a matter of running through all the possible permutations of the elements of a problem like a super computer, and that discernment or choice is exercised among those few combinations that are useful:

> To create consists precisely in not making useless combinations and in making those which are useful and which are only a small minority. Invention is discernment, choice. If not a brute algorithm, then it must be a heuristic that guides us to a fruitful combination. What is the heuristic?[16]

That Bruner cannot specify.

In reviewing the history of the concept of intuition, we can see that intuition was first considered to be a special kind of contact with ultimate reality. The view later shifted to intuition as a perception of rather limited basic truths in the same category as principles of deductive logic, mathematical axioms, the idea of causality, and the like. Finally, the dominant view today is that intuition is merely unconscious inference. The concept of a special capacity for suprasensory, direct knowing is rejected, as is the concept of truth itself. Westcott summarizes the current notion:

> Truth is to be understood as either a set of conventions or a set of probability statements, both subject to change. Immediate evidence (intuition) is seen as a result of insufficient analysis or inferential processes.[17]

In this latter view, the consequences of intuition have no more intrinsic value than those of reason and sensation.[18]

THE ANALOGY IN SCIENTIFIC DISCOVERY

The basic problem for philosophers, psychologists, and everyone else is that they cannot be convinced of the reality of something they have not experienced. So those who define intuition as implicit inference are probably referring, correctly, to that type of "intuition" with which they are familiar. Certain forms of problem solving, "hunches," and "feelings" undoubtedly fall within the purview of Freud's or Bruner's view and also constitute the "implicit inference" of logical positivists. However, the intuition that Plato, Spinoza, Bergson, and the mystics refer to is an experience different from the lesser events ordinarily labeled "intuition." In contrast to "hunches," mystics say, their "sight" clarifies the nature of the self, the meaning of the flow of events, and the purpose of life. At the same time, mystical intuition can be applied to the domains of physical science and psychology—as evidenced by the *Maha yana* sutras and the writings of Lao Tse, Dogen, El Ghazali, and Shabastari. The unanimity of mystics' descriptions of intuited reality indicates that their experience is not idiosyncratic but universal, and the parallel between their descriptions and the discoveries of modern physics supports the validity of the universal view. Indeed, a Westerner can gain some appreciation of the reality of mystical intuition through the study of parallels between mystical insights of centuries ago and the view of reality currently being constructed by physicists. Such comparisons have been made by LeShan,[19] Capra,[20] and Zukav.[21]

It is ironic that academic psychology, which has tried to model itself after the physical sciences, dismisses intuition except as unconscious reasoning or inference, while physical scientists are much readier to acknowledge intuition as a process that is fundamentally different from, and superior to, reason, in discovering truth. Wigner, a Nobel physicist, commented:

> The discovery of the laws of nature requires first and foremost intuition, conceiving of pictures and a great many subconscious processes. The use and also the confirmation of these laws is another matter . . . logic comes after intuition.[22]

And Gauss, the famous mathematician, was, in the common view, describing the dilemma that arises from this reversal of the scientific method when he said, "I have had my solutions for a long time, but I do not yet know how I am to arrive at them."[23]

The most extensive and detailed survey of the process of scientific discovery was made by Michael Polanyi, who studied scientists' own descriptions of how they arrived at their "breakthroughs" to a new view of reality. Like Wigner, he found that logic, data, and reasoning came last—they first used another channel of knowing. There was no word for that channel in ordinary vocabulary, so Polanyi used an analogy to convey its nature:

> And we know that the scientist produces problems, has hunches, and, elated by these anticipations, pursues the quest that should fulfill these anticipations. This quest is guided throughout by feelings of a deepening coherence and these feelings

have a fair chance of proving right. We may recognize here the powers of a dynamic intuition. The mechanism of this power can be illuminated by an analogy.

Physics speaks of potential energy that is released when a weight slides down a slope. Our search for deeper coherence is guided by a potentiality. We feel the slope toward deeper insight as we feel the direction in which a heavy weight is pulled along a steep incline. It is this dynamic intuition which guides the pursuit of discovery.[24]

Mystics view such experiences of direct, intuitive knowing as a foretaste of the development of intuitive consciousness, made possible by means of their science.

26. *Mental, Emotional, and Body-Based Intuition by Frances Vaughan*

Transpersonal psychotherapist Frances Vaughan describes the initial stages of intuitive knowing as perceived through mental, emotional, and somatic signals. She advises greater sensitivity to personal signals as a way to differentiate between vague promptings and authentic guidance. This is a good treatment of the early stages of intuitive awakening during which ordinary feedback, such as physical tension or emotional unsteadiness, is typically confused with emerging intuitive indicators.

Vaughan also describes the direct knowing associated with mystical experience. At this level of development, the knower's awareness is infused with wisdom that does not rely on intermediary cues. Here, the signals that support lower-order intuition become distractions that vanish as awareness becomes fully united with an object of attention.

Levels of Intuitive Awareness

The broad range of intuitive human experiences falls into four distinct levels of awareness: physical, emotional, mental, and spiritual.[1] Although any given experience may have elements of more than one level, experiences are usually easy to categorize according to the level at which they are consciously perceived. For example, mystical experiences are intuitive experiences at the spiritual level, and as such they do not depend on sensory, emotional, or mental cues for their validity. Intuition at the physical level is associated with bodily sensations, at the emotional level with feelings, and at the mental level with images and ideas.

Physical Level

The intuitive experiences defined as inspirational or psychic frequently depend on physical and emotional cues that bring them to conscious awareness. At the physical level a strong body response may be experienced in a situation where there is no reason to think that anything unusual is going on. The kind of jungle awareness which enables primitive people to sense danger when there are no sensory cues of its presence, is a highly developed form of intuition at the physical level. It differs from instinct in that instinct remains unconscious, while intuition becomes fully conscious, although a person may act on it without stopping to justify or rationalize it. The person simply knows something he or she needs to know without knowing how he or she knows it.

For people living in an urban environment this type of awareness is no less useful. Though it may not always be particularly dramatic, it can also be a matter of life and death. When you are in a situation that is uncomfortable for you, you may notice such bodily symptoms as tension, headaches, or stomachaches. If you stop to pay attention to these cues, you may find that you are indeed in a situation which is unhealthy and which is creating undue stress on the organism. If, for example, you always get a stomachache when you attend staff meetings at work, you should probably consider what needs to be changed in the situation to reduce the stress, even if this means a change in jobs. If you pay attention to physical symptoms which on the surface seem inexplicable, you may very well find out a lot about what your needs are. The cues of intuition on a physical level are not, however, always easy to perceive. Unfortunately, one often fails to acknowledge messages from the body until they become painful. If you are attuned to your body, you will notice your body responding differently to different people and different situations even without a stomachache or a headache. At times you may feel open, warm, and responsive, and at other times you may feel that you want to close up and withdraw. Learning to trust your bodily responses is part of learning to trust your intuition.

Bodily responses are a source of information about both yourself and your environment. Ann Dreyfuss, a Reichian therapist in San Francisco and professor of psychology at the California State College at Sonoma, reminds us that the body is one's access to the world. "It is possible," says Dr. Dreyfuss, "to be out of touch with oneself, unaware of one's body and in conflict with one's bodily process. Such disharmony distorts one's view of the world, one's perceptions and conceptions. A basic way of working toward personal enrichment involves increasing congruence between body and awareness . . . Whatever dimension of the outer world one considers, it is through the body that one experiences it, and it is through the body that one distorts it to make it comprehensible."[2]

Noticing physical symptoms of stress can often allow you to take care of your physical and emotional needs before they reach a painful or destructive level. Intuitive insight into your personal needs cannot only prevent serious disorders, but can also give you a direct indication of immediate needs. The desire to close up and withdraw, for example, may be an indication that the situation is not appropriate for you to open up in, or it may indicate an inner need for stillness and solitude. Or, if it is a habitual response, it may be related to some underlying fear which is preventing you from expanding your life and exploring new possibilities. If this is the case, you may want to change the pattern, and the first step is to become aware of what is happening to you. When you become aware of your body responses, you can choose whether or not you wish to act on them. Sometimes you may experience tension in response to a particular situation and choose to leave. Other times you may experience tension and choose to remain and confront the difficulty. Either way, being conscious of body responses is an essential part of a holistic intuitive awareness of yourself in relation to your environment. . . .

EMOTIONAL LEVEL

On the emotional level, as on the physical level, awakening intuition is inseparable from developing self-awareness. On this level intuition comes into consciousness through feelings. Sensitivity to other people's "vibes" or "vibrations of energy," instances of immediate liking or disliking with no apparent justification, or a vague sense that one is inexplicably supposed to do something, can be instances of intuition operating on this level.

When you learn to tune in to your feelings, they can become just as clear as bodily sensations in giving you information about a particular situation, be it a matter of changing jobs, finding a partner, or merely deciding what to do on a free weekend. How you feel about yourself, your relationships, and everything you do is related to how willing you are to take emotional intuitive cues into account when you are making choices. The better you know yourself, the more you can trust your intuition when it attracts you to someone you would like to know better, or warns you not to get involved. Occurrences of love at first sight, although they can be explained away as projection, may also be strongly intuitive. A woman in one of my classes described meeting her husband in a group five years ago. She said she knew the minute she saw him that he was *it* for her, despite the fact that "He didn't look like much," and she did not feel a strong physical attraction for him at first. Less romantic, but nonetheless meaningful instances of intuition at the emotional level occur every day.

What is commonly called "woman's intuition" is intuition on the emotional level. There is no evidence that men and women are inherently different in their intuitive capacities, but the popular belief that women are more intuitive than men is related to the fact that women in our society are not taught to repress feelings as much as men. Little boys are taught early not to cry and not to be emotional. Little girls may escape some of the rigorous training in rational intellectual development, which is stressed for boys wanting to be successful in a highly competitive society. Boys, however, are just as capable as girls when it comes to developing the intuitive functions of the right hemisphere of the brain.

Judith Hall, Assistant Professor of Psychology at Johns Hopkins University, Baltimore, reports that research in the area of sensitivity to nonverbal communication indicates that women tend to be more attentive to visual cues such as facial expression, body gestures, tone of voice, and the way people look at each other or touch each other. Females do score higher than males in tests designed to measure accuracy of interpretation of nonverbal communication. There is, however, no data to support the belief that these differences are inherent. On the contrary, one study cited by Dr. Hall showed that more traditional males scored lower at nonverbal judging than more liberal males, and more traditional females scored higher than more liberal females. The differences reported by Dr. Hall are not large, and she points out that these findings suggest that eliminating strong gender roles could make male and female scores converge.[3]

Although this type of perceptual awareness contributes to one's understanding of other people, it should not be confused with developing awareness of one's own internal feeling states. Intuition cannot be reduced to observation of behavior, body language, and other visual cues. It is a holistic awareness which includes both internal and external sensitivity, and which sometimes transcends sensory input altogether.

At the emotional level, women and men who are aware of their feelings and who follow them tend to be comfortable with their diffuse intuitive understanding, except when called upon to give a logical, rational justification for actions based on intuitive feelings. Demands for explanations, either from oneself or from another, are usually met with inadequate rationalizations that fail to satisfy anybody. Rarely is someone willing to say simply that he or she chose to do something simply because it felt right. Nevertheless, people in all kinds of occupations and lifestyles do act on the basis of intuitive feelings, and feel that their decisions are better for it.

Expanding awareness of the emotional level of intuition is often associated with an increase in synchronicity and psychic experiences. For example, you might feel like calling someone with whom you have not spoken in some time for no particular reason. If you act on the feeling, you may discover that the person you called had been trying to get in touch with you, or that it was timely for you to call just then. You may discover later a reason for your intuitive feeling, or you may not. However, the more you act on your feelings and take the risk of checking out the validity of your intuition, the more reliable it can become.

Sometimes intuition on this level will tell you something about your interpersonal relations that you would rather not know, and in these instances it may seem easier to repress it than to act on it. You might, for instance, meet someone you think you would like to befriend, although you have a feeling that this will not happen. When I was in graduate school a friend of mine had told me how much he wanted to get to know one of our professors whom he greatly admired. One night he dreamed that he was talking to him, but the professor did not say much, and refused to take off his overcoat. As my friend reflected on what the dream was telling him, he realized that he had felt intuitively that this man had wanted to keep his distance ever since they met. Repeated attempts to get better acquainted were of no avail. He later regretted the time and effort expended, for he had "known" all along that it would be fruitless. . . .

MENTAL LEVEL

Intuition on the mental level often comes into awareness through images, or what is called "inner vision." Patterns of order may be perceived where everything at first appears chaotic, or patterns of change may be apprehended intuitively long before the verification process of careful observation is completed. In the West, the intuitive flashes which follow the exhaustive use of logic and reason tend to be more highly valued than other types of intuition, since they are associated with the kind of discovery and invention involved in technological progress.

Intuition on the mental level is operative in the formulation of new theories and hypotheses in any field, for this type of intuition implies an ability to reach accurate conclusions on the basis of limited information. Although all intuition is mental in the sense that it is a function of the mind, intuition on the mental level refers particularly to those aspects of intuition related to thinking. Thus intuition on this level is often associated with problem solving, mathematics, and scientific inquiry.

Malcolm Westcott reviews the writing of mathematicians, with particular reference to Poincaré. Poincaré writes about the importance of intuition in his own work, and asserts that both intuitive and analytical activity are crucial to the advance of mathematics as well as the empirical sciences.[4] Jacques Hadamard confirms these views and adds the observations of other mathematicians. Hadamard quotes Einstein as follows: "The words or the language, as they are written or spoken, do not seem to play any role in my mechanism of thought. The psychical entities which seem to serve as elements in thought are certain signs and more or less clear images which can be 'voluntarily' reproduced and combined."[5] Einstein believed that objective physical reality can only be grasped by an intuitive leap, not directly empirically or logically.[6] He further asserts that the axiomatic basis of theoretical physics cannot be an inference from experience, but is a free invention of the human mind.[7] Writing on "The Structure of Creativity in Physics," Siegfried Muller-Markus supports this contention and concludes: "An idea like Planck's quantum of action was not logically entailed by experiment, nor could it be derived from previous theories. Planck conceived it out of his own self."[8]

The role of intuition in creativity and problem solving has also been recognized by individuals concerned with business management. Successful businessmen are typically intuitive on a mental level. Research indicates that successful executives tend to score far above average on ESP tests.[9] The ability to know intuitively what will succeed in any type of business certainly contributes to the success which is often attributed to luck. Henry Mintzberg suggests that managers should have well-developed right-hemispheric processes. It is important for managers to "see the big picture," says Mintzberg, and this implies a relational, holistic use of information (i.e., synthesis rather than analysis of data). He also points out the dearth of literature on this subject: ". . . despite an extensive literature on analytical decision making, virtually nothing is written about decision making under pressure. These activities remain outside the realm of management science, inside the realm of intuition and experience." Mintzberg supports the hypothesis that the important policy-level processes required to manage an organization rely to a considerable extent on the faculties identified with the brain's right hemisphere, and suggests that while policy makers conceive strategy in holistic terms, the rest of the bureaucratic hierarchy implements the policy in a linear sequence. Mintzberg points out that all intuitive thinking must be translated into linear order if it is to be articulated and put to use, and that truly outstanding managers are the ones who couple effective right-hemispheric processes with effective processes of the left.[10]

Although lateralization of brain functions may be overemphasized,[11] the basic point that intuitive thinking plays a vital part in decision making is supported by other authors in the field. Ostrander, Schroeder, Dean and Mihalasky maintain that people who have highly developed intuition are more successful. ESP seems to be particularly useful in decision making, economic forecasting, and personnel selection.[12]

Intuition in business is often referred to as a "gut feeling," yet a person whose intuition may be well-developed on a mental level is not necessarily one who is equally well-developed on an emotional level. Carson Jeffries, a physicist who attended one of my seminars at the University of California in Berkeley, told me that he valued his intuition and used it in his research, but felt out of touch with it in interpersonal relationships. For him intuition was working on the mental level, but not on the emotional level. After becoming aware of this he was able to expand the range of his intuitive ability to encompass more of his experience.

You do not have to be a scientist or a business executive to appreciate the value of intuition at the mental level. The sudden recognition of a pattern in your life, the "aha!" experience in psychotherapy when unconscious processes are suddenly illuminated, or the "eureka" of a new discovery, are ways in which anyone can experience this type of intuition. Such insights are often accompanied by mental imagery, but not necessarily. Pattern recognition is not always visual. It may be auditory to a musician, or simply a flash of understanding in which events or ideas seem to fall into place.

Melvin Calvin, Nobel Laureate in Chemistry in 1961, for example, describes his most exciting moment in research like this:

> One day I was waiting in my car while my wife was on an errand. I had had for some months some basic information from the laboratory which was incompatible with everything which, up until then, I knew about the photosynthetic process. I was waiting, sitting at the wheel, most likely parked in the red zone, when the recognition of the missing compound occurred. It occurred just like that—quite suddenly—and suddenly, also, in a matter of seconds, the cyclic character of the path of carbon became apparent to me, not in the detail which ultimately was elucidated, but the original recognition of phosphoglyceric acid, and how it got there, and how the acceptor might be regenerated, all occurred in a matter of 30 seconds. . . .[13]

SPIRITUAL INTUITION

Spiritual intuition is associated with mystical experience, and at this level intuition is "pure." Pure, spiritual intuition is distinguished from other forms by its independence from sensations, feelings, and thoughts. In a discussion of intuition in spiritual psychosynthesis, Assagioli considers intuition as an independent psychological function which is "synthetic" in that it apprehends the totality of a given situation or psychological reality. Assagioli says: "Only intuition gives true psychological understanding both of oneself and others."[14] In its purest manifestation, Assagioli maintains, intuition is devoid of feeling, and as a normal function of the human psyche, it can be activated simply by eliminating the various obstacles to its unfolding. At this level intuition does not depend on sensing, feeling, or thinking. It is not associated with the body, the emotions, or pattern perception relating to specific problems or situations. Paradoxically, the cues on which intuition depends on other levels are regarded as interference on this level. However, an awareness of how intuition functions on other levels helps to dispel the misconception that intuition as a way of knowing is an all-or-nothing proposition. Degrees of intuitive awareness may also be affected by such factors as time, place, mood, attitude, state of consciousness, and many other variables.

In Spinoza's terms, spiritual intuition is knowledge of God. James Bugenthal equates this knowledge with man's experience of his own being and says: "Man knows God in his deepest intuitions about his own nature."[15] Dr. Bugenthal describes the inward vision through which man discovers his nature as a creative process that does more than observe what is already at hand, bringing into being fresh possibilities.

Among those fresh possibilities is the potential for transcending duality and personal separateness. The capacity for transcending duality is not particularly unusual. Abraham Maslow, in his study of self-actualizing persons in the 1960s, found that, "While this transcendence of dichotomy can be seen as a usual thing in self-actualizing persons, it can also be seen in most of the rest of us in our most acute moments of integration within the self and between self and the world. In the highest love between man and woman, or parent and child, as the person reaches the ultimates of strength, self-esteem, or individuality, so also does he simultaneously merge with the other, lose self-consciousness and more or less transcend the self and selfishness. The same can happen in the creative moment, in the profound aesthetic experience, in the insight experience . . . and others which I have generalized as peak experiences."[16]

Spiritual intuition as a holistic perception of reality transcends rational, dualistic ways of knowing and gives the individual a direct transpersonal experience of the underlying oneness of life. Describing the difference between dual (rational, conceptual) and non-dual (intuitive, holistic) modes of knowing, Ken Wilbur writes: "If we are to know Reality in its fullness and wholeness, if we are to stop eluding and escaping ourselves in the very act of trying to find ourselves, if we are to enter the concrete actuality of the territory and cease being confused by the maps that invariably own their owners, then we will have to relinquish the dualistic-symbolic mode of knowing that rends the fabric of Reality in the very attempt to grasp it. In a word, we will have to move from the dimness of twilight [dualistic] knowledge to the brilliance of daybreak [intuitive] knowledge—*if we are to know Reality, it is to the second mode of knowing that we must eventually turn.* Enough it is now to know that we possess this daybreak knowledge; more than enough it will be when at last we succeed in fully awakening it."[17]

In yoga spiritual intuition is called soul guidance,[18] and is said to emerge spontaneously when the mind is quiet. In writing about the teachings of Sri Aurobindo, Satprem describes the intuitive mind as follows: "The intuitive mind differs from the illumined mind by its clear transparency— . . . all is so rapid, flashing—terrible rapidities of the clearing of consciousness." Although intuitive knowledge may be translated or interpreted according to personal preoccupations, it is "always, essentially, a shock of identity, a meeting—one knows because one recognizes. Sri Aurobindo used to say that intuition is *a memory of the Truth.*"[19]

The practice of meditation prepares the mind for the experience of spiritual intuition, by clearing away the obstacles which ordinarily interfere with its becoming conscious. Learning to recognize pure awareness or consciousness as the context of all experience, distinct from the contents of consciousness, is one way of understanding this level of intuition.

In order to make a subjective distinction between your own consciousness and its contents you can try the following experiment: Write down everything you are conscious of at this moment. Do this for several minutes. When you have done this, notice what you left out. At any given moment you are conscious of only a fraction of what is going on in your mind. Consciousness is selective, and the normal range of awareness is extremely narrow in the ordinary waking state. When consciousness begins to observe itself, however, it begins to expand. You may notice that while you are reading this you are simultaneously aware of your surroundings, what time it is (approximately), whether you are feeling hungry or thirsty, and you may also be wondering when your friend will call and how you are going to make arrangements for what you want to do tomorrow. You may also be reviewing an unsatisfactory conversation you had with someone earlier in the day. Can you observe your own stream of consciousness in a manner that is satisfactory to you? Or are there so many streams running simultaneously in all directions that you cannot observe them all? Learning to empty the mind in order to experience consciousness devoid of contents is one of the objectives of meditation. By observing your thoughts, feelings, and sensations without interfering with them, you may begin to experience that quiet state in which spiritual intuition unfolds.

Activating spiritual intuition means focusing on the transpersonal rather than the personal realms of intuition. At this level it is consciousness as context, rather than the content of consciousness, which comes into awareness. Other forms of intuition focused on sensation, feeling, and thinking become obstacles to pure awareness, empty of content. If you become too engrossed with the powers that intuition can make available to you at other levels, you may fail to recognize your potential for developing spiritual intuition. Yet this dimension of intuition is the basic ground from which all other forms of intuition are derived.

27. The Intuitive Edge by Philip Goldberg

Philip Goldberg sees intuition as a close companion to intellect in all practical matters. Focusing on the rigorous logic of scientific investigation, he shows us the fallacy of neglecting the intuitive factor in problem-solving. Rather than disregarding experimental evidence, he calls for education of the intuitive talents required for original solutions.

On a practical level, many intuitions can be verified for their accuracy, even if they appear infrequently, or only when the conditions are right. Taking the approach that intuition can be trained, Goldberg shows how key points in any scientific discovery require both deductive reasoning and intuitive leaps of understanding.

The really valuable thing is intuition.
—Albert Einstein

UNTIL RECENTLY INTUITION has been treated like an employee who, forced to retire, keeps going to work because he is indispensable. Attitudes about him vary: some people don't know he exists, some downgrade his contributions as trivial, some revere him privately while trying to keep his presence a secret. A growing minority are exuberant supporters who feel that credit is long overdue and that such a valuable asset can function even better when recognized and encouraged. This book is in the latter category, part of the corrective effort to bring intuition out into the open, to demystify it, to see what it is, how it works, and what can be done to cultivate its full potential.

In recent years, the subject has emerged from obscurity. Intuition is increasingly recognized as a natural mental faculty, a key element in discovery, problem solving, and decision making, a generator of creative ideas, a forecaster, a revealer of truth. An important ingredient in what we call genius, it is also a subtle guide to daily living. Those people who always seem to be in the right place at the right time, and for whom good things happen with uncanny frequency, are not just lucky; they have an intuitive sense of what to choose and how to act. We are also coming to realize that intuition is not just a chance phenomenon or a mysterious gift, like jumping ability or perfect pitch. While individual capacities vary, we are all intuitive, and we can all be *more* intuitive, just as we can all learn to jump higher and sing on key.

The emergence of intuition is part of a more global shift in values that has been chronicled by numerous sharp-eyed observers. The passionate pursuit of both individual growth and a better world, begun in earnest in the 1960s, has led to a reevaluation of conventional beliefs, among them the way we use our minds and the way we approach knowledge. Our decisions and actions spring from what we know. Therefore, if collective problems remain intractable and the gap between individual desires and fulfillment remains vast, it is only natural that we start to wonder if there isn't a better way to go about knowing.

Contributing to the new attitude is a resurgence of respect for the world within. The behaviorist school of psychology, which dominated the field during most of this century, had declared irrelevant the deeper realms of mind and spirit. To believers in orthodox religions and Freudian psychotherapy, those areas seethed with dark urges and repressed instincts that, depending on the point of view, should either be kept under cover, liberated, or therapeutically neutralized. These assumptions are giving way to a more positive, often sublime vision. The growth of cognitive research, theoretical advances in humanistic and transpersonal psychologies, provocative brain studies, the remarkable acceptance of Eastern philosophies and disciplines—such developments have led large numbers of people to believe that there is untapped power and wisdom within us. They sense there is a part of ourselves that—although obscured by bad habits and ignorance—understands who we are and what we need and is programmed to move us toward the realization of our highest potential. There is a growing conviction that perhaps we ought to trust the hunches, vague feelings, premonitions, and inarticulate signals we usually ignore.

These trends are characteristic of a basic contemporary pattern: the desire to eliminate obstacles that keep us from being what we really are. Where intuition is concerned, the obstacles are rooted in long-standing epistemological assumptions, which are perpetuated in the institutions that teach us how to use our minds. A brief look at those premises will help us understand why we have not been encouraged to use and develop our intuitive capacities.

THE LEGACY OF SCIENTISM

For over three centuries the prevailing model for gaining knowledge in the Western world has been what we loosely call science, that robust and precocious offspring of such giants as Galileo, Descartes, and Newton. Let's use the word *scientism* to refer to the ideology, as opposed to the practice, of science, since the two are rather different. According to scientism, the right way to approach knowledge is with a rigorous interchange of reason and systematically acquired experience.

This philosophy developed as a hybrid of rationalism and empiricism. Empiricism holds, essentially, that the experience of the senses is the only reliable basis for knowing; rationalism contends that reasoning is the prime avenue to truth. In science, empirical information and reason are supposed to work in tandem, each acting as a check on the other's shortcomings. Since experience can be deceptive, information is scrutinized with rigorous logic; since reason is not entirely flawless, tentative conclusions—hypotheses—are put to the empirical test with controlled experiments subject to repeated verification. For this game plan to work, the data should be quantifiable and the players should be objective, thus keeping biases, emotions, and opinions from contaminating the findings.

Ancients such as Plato and modern philosophers such as Spinoza, Nietzsche, and, at the turn of the century, Henri Bergson pointed beyond reason and sense data to higher, intuitive forms of knowing. So, too, have mystics, romantics, poets, and visionaries in all cultures. There have been "intuitionist" schools in mathematics and ethics, and psychologists such as Gordon Allport, Abraham Maslow, Carl Jung, and Jerome Bruner have all acknowledged the importance of intuition. For the most part, however, intuition has been only a peripheral concern in the West, where the revered mode of knowing has been rational empiricism, thanks largely to the astonishing success of science.

Nothing said on behalf of intuition . . . should be taken as a deprecation of either science or rational thought. In wresting authority from faltering religious institutions, they freed us from the tyranny of dogma and arbitrary ideas. Insistence on evidence and rigorous verification, the heart and soul of scientism, enables us—collectively and over time—to sort out the true from the false. In a secular, pluralistic society, such standards are imperative. And science has given us a way to precisely analyze and shape the material world, providing us with unprecedented affluence, comfort, and health.

Like most rebellions, however, the scientific revolution created some new problems. Flushed with success, the juggernaut of science gobbled up terrain formerly held by philosophy, metaphysics, theology, and cultural tradition. We sought to apply the methods that worked so well in the material realm to answer questions about the psyche, the spirit, and society. Through experimentation and the application of reason—which was elevated to the pinnacle of the mind—it was assumed we would come to know the secrets of the universe and learn how to live. To accomplish this, we set out to perfect the objective tools of knowing; we invented devices and procedures that extended the range of our senses and made more rigorous our logic and our calculations. Over time, our organizations and educational institutions made scientism the *sine qua non* of knowing, the model for how to think.

This ideological bias is reflected in our vocabulary; words that suggest truthfulness stem from the rational-empirical tradition. We use the word *logical,* even when the rules of logic have not been applied, to indicate that a statement seems correct. So highly regarded is reason that we use the word *reasonable* to refer to anything we consider appropriate—for example, "Twenty dollars is a reasonable price to pay for a theater ticket." We also have the noun form of reason, which is what you are asked to provide in order to justify a proposition. People demand *reasons;* they seldom say, "Give me one good feeling why you think John is wrong" or "What are your intuitions for claiming that jogging will cure insomnia?"

The word *rational*—which, strictly speaking, suggests the use of reason and logic—has come to be synonymous with sanity, while *irrational* connotes madness. *Sensible* and *making sense,* along with their antonym *nonsense,* link soundness and truth with the sense organs, as if adequate meaning came through those channels alone—the classic conviction of empiricism. *Objective* has come to imply fairness, honesty, and precision, suggesting that the only way to gain untainted knowledge is to remain detached and treat whatever you study as if it were a material object. As for the word *scientific,* that is the ultimate pedigree for any claim whatsoever.

Fortunately, the language also contains some reservations about the rational-empirical ideal. Thanks to Freud, we have the word *rationalize,* a pejorative term referring to the way we justify bad guesses, mistakes, and neurotic behavior with faulty reasoning. We also use the term *sense* in an effort to legitimize knowledge that can't be attributed to the customary five senses, as when we say "I sense danger in this room" or "I have a sense of what that poem is about." But, despite these few colloquial exceptions, we generally act as if sense perceptions and rational thought are the only ways to know anything. This strikes many people as illogical, unreasonable, and maybe even nonsensical.

The unfortunate aspect of this tendency is not the veneration of rationality or the insistence on experimental evidence, but the discrediting of intuition. The whole thrust of scientism has been to minimize the influence of the knower. It protects knowledge from the vagaries of subjectivity with a system of checks and balances that are as essential as their equivalent in democracies. But if the system becomes imbalanced, the power of a particular branch can become so diluted as to lose its real effectiveness.

The institutions that teach us how to use our minds, as well as the organizations in which we use them, are so skewed toward the rational-empirical ideal that intuition is seldom discussed, much less honored or encouraged. From grade school to graduate school, and in most of our work settings, we are taught to emulate the idealized model of scientism in our thinking, problem solving, and decision making. As a result, intuition is subject to various forms of censure and constraint. What psychologist Blythe Clinchy said of early education applies throughout our culture: "We may convince our students that this mode of thought is an irrelevant or indecent way of approaching formal subject matter. We do not actually stamp out intuition; rather, I think, we drive it underground."

There are twin ironies in this situation. First, the model we seek to emulate is something of a fiction, erroneous in some of its assumptions and inappropriate in many of its applications. Second, like the employee in our opening metaphor, intuition is a vital—although restricted—contributor to the very institutions that tried to retire it.

DO AS IT DOES, NOT AS IT SAYS

Real day-to-day science and real day-to-day problem solving are to their formal descriptions what a jam session is to sheet music. For one thing, the detached objectivity that scientism prizes is an impossible ideal. Psychological research tells us that even ordinary sense perception is an interpretive act, influenced by expectations, beliefs, and values. For example, the same coin is perceived as larger in size by poor children than by their more affluent counterparts.

We also know from science itself that the long-standing theoretical separation of observer and observed, object and subject, can no longer be assumed. As Werner Heisenberg noted when he formulated the uncertainty principle, which proved that on the subatomic level the act of observation influences what is being observed: "Even in science, the object of research is no longer nature itself but man's investigation of nature." Furthermore, every discipline is rooted in a set of assumptions and beliefs—what philosopher Thomas Kuhn called a *paradigm*—and, like all of us, individual scientists have convictions, attachments, and passions that influence their work. Indeed, without them scientists could never muster the courage and tenacity to discover anything worthwhile.

The real objectivity of science pertains to the macrocosm, the collective enterprise where hunches, beliefs, and intuitive convictions confront one another in the public arena and are rigorously evaluated. What survives we call objective, scientific knowledge. The knower will always be subjective and will always use his intuition. We have tried to minimize the imperfections of subjectivity; what we have not done is try to elevate the knower's subjective ability to know.

When given the opportunity, intuition has done wonders. If reason and empirical observation steer the course of discovery and the passion for truth supplies the fuel, it is intuition that provides the spark. (Although we are discussing science, the same comments apply to creative decision making and problem solving in any field.) Abraham Maslow distinguished two types of scientists, each essential to the overall endeavor. One type he compared to tiny marine animals who build up a coral reef; they patiently pile up fact after fact, repeat experiments, and cautiously modify theories. The other breed, whom Maslow called the "eagles of science," make the soaring leaps and imaginative flights that lead to revolutions in thought. Intuition is what gives wing to the eagles.

[There are] many . . . anecdotes [that] demonstrate this point, and an army of quotations could be culled from the pantheon of science and mathematics to support it. Here are just two. First, Einstein on the discovery of natural laws: "There are no logical paths to these laws, only intuition resting on sympathetic understanding of experience can reach them." Second, John Maynard Keynes on Isaac Newton: "It was his intuition which was preeminently extraordinary. So happy in his conjectures that he seemed to know more than he could have possibly any hope of proving. The proofs were . . . dressed up afterwards; they were not the instrument of discovery."

Keynes's point is an essential one: formal proofs are instruments of verification and communication. The final descriptions of research are what the public sees and what we learn about in school. But they are the end products, the logical, orderly presentations compiled after all the sloppy work has been done, all the false starts and dead ends corrected, all the vague hunches and gut feelings sorted out. What we see is an idealized road map, constructed retrospectively, like a traveler's outline of a cross-country journey that excludes the side trips, the backtracking, the mistakes, and the spontaneous changes of direction.

We are led to believe that the finished product depicts the actual process. Then we are advised to emulate it in our thinking. Hence our schooling centers on recalling facts and following standardized methods for solving problems whose beginning and end points are clearly defined. Imagination and the vague intuitive notions that prefigure discovery are devalued or ignored. In classrooms they are even considered to be mere guessing, particularly when the student is unable immediately to produce a logical defense. We are asked to do what science says, not what it does, which is both unfortunate and ironic. As psychologist Jerome Bruner wrote in *The Process of Education:* "The warm praise that scientists lavish on those of their colleagues who earn the label 'intuitive' is major evidence that intuition is a valuable commodity in science and one we should endeavor to foster in our students."

If great ideas actually did follow inexorably from piling up facts through reason and experimentation, as the orthodox model suggests, then all it would take to walk away with history's prizes would be to show up in the right place at the right time, like the millionth customer to enter a supermarket. Nothing but chance would distinguish the geniuses we venerate, the ones who looked at the same facts everyone else had looked at and thought what no one else had ever thought. But, as the philosopher of science Karl Popper says, "There is no such thing as a logical method of having new ideas, or a logical reconstruction of this process. . . . Every discovery contains an 'irrational element' or a creative intuition."

The very essence of breakthroughs is that they defy conventional assumptions. They go beyond anything we have any logical or factual reason to accept. The general relativity theory, for example, was born when Einstein had what he called "the happiest thought of my life." He realized that a person falling from a roof was both at rest and in motion at the same time. What could be more illogical? Years later, when the theory was proven, it started to seem logical because our assumptions about space and time had been transformed, thanks to Einstein's intuition.

28. Mindfulness Training by Jack Kornfield

Regardless of its level of complexity, every practice relies on steadiness of concentration. Jack Kornfield, psychologist and meditation teacher, describes the practice that forms a cornerstone of every meditation system.

Whereas Western psychology has many excellent tools for reducing human suffering, it has few awareness techniques for enhancing well-being. Using the metaphor of training a puppy to behave, Kornfield shows us how to redirect attention away from painful thoughts by using a focal object.

*Concentration is never a matter of force or coercion. You
simply pick up the puppy again and return to reconnect
with the here and now.*

A STORY IS told of the Buddha when he was wandering in India shortly after his enlightenment. He was encountered by several men who recognized something quite extraordinary about this handsome prince now robed as a monk. Stopping to inquire, they asked, "Are you a god?" "No," he answered. "Well, are you a deva or an angel?" "No," he replied. "Well, are you some kind of wizard or magician?" "No." "Are you a man?" "No." They were perplexed. Finally they asked, "Then what are you?" He replied simply, "I am awake." The word *Buddha* means to awaken. How to awaken is all he taught.

Meditation can be thought of as the art of awakening. Through the mastering of this art we can learn new ways to approach our difficulties and bring wisdom and joy alive in our life. Through developing meditation's tools and practices, we can awaken the best of our spiritual, human capacities. The key to this art is the steadiness of our attention. When the fullness of our attention is cultivated together with a grateful and tender heart, our spiritual life will naturally grow. . . .

Some healing of mind and body must take place for many of us before we can sit quietly and concentrate. Yet even to begin our healing, to begin understanding ourselves, we must have some basic level of attention. To deepen our practice further, we must choose a way to develop our attention systematically and give ourselves to it quite fully. Otherwise we will drift like a boat without a rudder. To learn to concentrate we must choose a prayer or meditation and follow this path with commitment and steadiness, a willingness to work with our practice day after day, no matter what arises. This is not easy for most people. They would like their spiritual life to show immediate and cosmic results. But what great art is ever learned quickly? Any deep training opens in direct proportion to how much we give ourselves to it.

Consider the other arts. Music, for example. How long would it take to learn to play the piano well? Suppose we take months or years of lessons once a week, practicing diligently every day. Initially, almost everyone struggles to learn which fingers go for which notes and how to read basic lines of music. After some weeks or months, we could play simple tunes, and perhaps after a year or two we could play a chosen type of music. However, to master the art so that we could play music well, alone or in a group, or join a band or an orchestra, we would have to give ourselves to this discipline over and over, time and again. If we wanted to learn computer programming, oil painting, tennis, architecture, any of the thousand arts, we would have to give ourselves to it fully and wholeheartedly over a long period of time—a training, an apprenticeship, a cultivation.

Nothing less is required in the spiritual arts. Perhaps even more is asked. Yet through this mastery we master ourselves and our lives. We learn the most human art, how to connect with our truest self.

Trungpa Rinpoche called spiritual practice manual labor. It is a labor of love in which we bring a wholehearted attention to our own situation over and over again. In all sorts of weather, we steady and deepen our prayer, meditation, and discipline, learning how to see with honesty and compassion, how to let go, how to love more deeply.

However, this is not how we begin. Suppose we begin with a period of solitude in the midst of our daily life. What happens when we actually try to meditate? The most frequent first experience—whether in prayer or chanting, meditation or visualization—is that we encounter the disconnected and scattered mind. Buddhist psychology likens the untrained mind to a crazed monkey that dashes from thought to memory, from sight to sound, from plan to regret without ceasing. If we were able to sit quietly for an hour and fully observe all the places our mind went, what a script would be revealed.

When we first undertake the art of meditation, it is indeed frustrating. Inevitably, as our mind wanders and our body feels the tension it has accumulated and the speed to which it is addicted, we often see how little inner discipline, patience, or compassion we actually have. It doesn't take much time with a spiritual task to see how scattered and unsteady our attention remains even when we try to direct and focus it. While we usually think of it as "our mind," if we look honestly, we see that the mind follows its own nature, conditions, and laws. Seeing this, we also see that we must gradually discover a wise relationship to the mind that connects it to the body and heart, and steadies and calms our inner life.

The essence of this connecting is the bringing back of our attention again and again to the practice we have chosen. Prayer, meditation, repeating sacred phrases, or visualization gives us a systematic way to focus and steady our concentration. All the traditional realms and states of consciousness described in mystical and spiritual literature worldwide are arrived at through the art of concentration. These arts of concentration, of returning to the task at hand, also bring the clarity, strength of mind, peacefulness, and profound connectedness that we seek. This steadiness and connection in turn gives rise to even deeper levels of understanding and insight.

Whether a practice calls for visualization, question, prayer, sacred words, or simple meditation on feelings or breath, it always involves the steadying and conscious return, again and again, to some focus. As we learn to do this with a deeper and fuller attention, it is like learning to steady a canoe in waters that have waves. Repeating our meditation, we relax and sink into the moment, deeply connecting with what is present. We let ourselves settle into a spiritual ground; we train ourselves to come back to this moment. This is a patient process. St. Francis de Sales said, "What we need is a cup of understanding, a barrel of love, and an ocean of patience."

For some, this task of coming back a thousand or ten thousand times in meditation may seem boring or even of questionable importance. But how many times have we gone away from the reality of our life?—perhaps a million or ten million times! If we wish to awaken, we have to find our way back here with our full being, our full attention.

St. Francis de Sales continued by saying:

> Bring yourself back to the point quite gently. And even if you do nothing during the whole of your hour but bring your heart back a thousand times, though it went away every time you brought it back, your hour would be very well employed.

In this way, meditation is very much like training a puppy. You put the puppy down and say, "Stay." Does the puppy listen? It gets up and it runs away. You sit the puppy back down again. "Stay." And the puppy runs away over and over again. Sometimes the puppy jumps up, runs over, and pees in the corner or makes some other mess. Our minds are much the same as the puppy, only they create even bigger messes. In training the mind, or the puppy, we have to start over and over again.

When you undertake a spiritual discipline, frustration comes with the territory. Nothing in our culture or our schooling has taught us to steady and calm our attention. One psychologist has called us a society of attentional spastics. Finding it difficult to concentrate, many people respond by forcing their attention on their breath or mantra or prayer with tense irritation and self-judgment, or worse. Is this the way you would train a puppy? Does it really help to beat it? Concentration is never a matter of force or coercion. You simply pick up the puppy again and return to reconnect with the here and now.

29. *Sitting and Walking Meditation by Jack Kornfield*

Mindfulness practice relaxes the thoughts and feelings of ordinary consciousness, allowing deeper wisdom to emerge. States such as peace, joy, and nonattachment become apparent when distraction lessens, and the mind becomes receptive. Using the breath as a focus of attention, Jack Kornfield outlines two mindfulness practices that can be done on a daily basis.

SITTING MEDITATION

First select a suitable space for your regular meditation. It can be wherever you can sit easily with minimal disturbance: a corner of your bedroom or any other quiet spot in your home. Place a meditation cushion or chair there for your use. Arrange what is around so that you are reminded of your meditative purpose, so that it feels like a sacred and peaceful space. You may wish to make a simple altar with a flower or sacred image, or place your favorite spiritual books there for a few moments of inspiring reading. Let yourself enjoy creating this space for yourself.

Then select a regular time for practice that suits your schedule and temperament. If you are a morning person, experiment with a sitting before breakfast. If evening fits your temperament or schedule better, try that first. Begin with sitting ten or twenty minutes at a time. Later you can sit longer or more frequently. Daily meditation can become like bathing or toothbrushing. It can bring a regular cleansing and calming to your heart and mind.

Find a posture on the chair or cushion in which you can easily sit erect without being rigid. Let your body be firmly planted on the earth, your hands resting easily, your heart soft, your eyes closed gently. At first feel your body and consciously soften any obvious tension. Let go of any habitual thoughts or plans. Bring your attention to feel the sensations of your breathing. Take a few deep breaths to sense where you can feel the breath most easily, as coolness or tingling in the nostrils or throat, as movement of the chest, or rise and fall of the belly. Then let your breath be natural. Feel the sensations of your natural breathing very carefully, relaxing into each breath as you feel it, noticing how the soft sensations of breathing come and go with the changing breath.

After a few breaths your mind will probably wander. When you notice this, no matter how long or short a time you have been away, simply come back to the next breath. Before you return, you can mindfully acknowledge where you have gone with a soft word in the back of your mind, such as "thinking," "wandering," "hearing," "itching." After softly and silently naming to yourself where your attention has been, gently and directly return to feel the next breath. Later on in your meditation you will be able to work with the places your mind wanders to, but for initial training, one word of acknowledgement and a simple return to the breath is best.

As you sit, let the breath change rhythms naturally, allowing it to be short, long, fast, slow, rough, or easy. Calm yourself by relaxing into the breath. When your breath becomes soft, let your attention become gentle and careful, as soft as the breath itself.

Like training a puppy, gently bring yourself back a thousand times. Over weeks and months of this practice you will gradually learn to calm and center yourself using the breath. There will be many cycles in this process, stormy days alternating with clear days. Just stay with it. As you do, listening deeply, you will find the breath helping to connect and quiet your whole body and mind.

Working with the breath is an excellent foundation. After developing some calm and skills, and connecting with your breath, you can then extend your range of meditation to include healing and awareness of all the levels of your body and mind. You will discover how awareness of your breath can serve as a steady basis for all you do.

WALKING MEDITATION

Like breathing meditation, walking meditation is a simple and universal practice for developing calm, connectedness, and awareness. It can be practiced regularly, before or after sitting meditation or any time on its own, such as after a busy day at work or on a lazy Sunday morning. The art of walking meditation is to learn to be aware as you walk, to use the natural movement of walking to cultivate mindfulness and wakeful presence.

Select a quiet place where you can walk comfortably back and forth, indoors or out, about ten to thirty paces in length. Begin by standing at one end of this "walking path," with your feet firmly planted on the ground. Let your hands rest easily, wherever they are comfortable. Close your eyes for a moment, center yourself, and feel your body standing on the earth. Feel the pressure on the bottoms of your feet and the other natural sensations of standing. Then open your eyes and let yourself be present and alert.

Begin to walk slowly. Let yourself walk with a sense of ease and dignity. Pay attention to your body. With each step feel the sensations of lifting your foot and leg off of the earth. Be aware as you place each foot on the earth. Relax and let your walking be easy and natural. Feel each step mindfully as you walk. When you reach the end of your path, pause for a moment. Center yourself, carefully turn around, pause again so that you can be aware of the first step as you walk back. You can experiment with the speed, walking at whatever pace keeps you most present.

Continue to walk back and forth for ten or twenty minutes or longer. As with the breath in sitting, your mind will wander away many, many times. As soon as you notice this, acknowledge where it went softly: "wandering," "thinking," "hearing," "planning." Then return to feel the next step. Like training the puppy, you will need to come back a thousand times. Whether you have been away for one second or for ten minutes, simply acknowledge where you have been and then come back to being alive here and now with the next step you take.

After some practice with walking meditation, you will learn to use it to calm and collect yourself and to live more wakefully in your body. You can then extend your walking practice in an informal way when you go shopping, whenever you walk down the street or walk to or from your car. You can learn to enjoy walking for its own sake instead of the usual planning and thinking and, in this simple way, begin to be truly present, to bring your body, heart, and mind together as you move through your life.

30. *Mindfulness Practice for the Whole Spectrum of Life by Charles T. Tart*

It's easy to intellectually grasp the advantages of being more mindful of one's life, and to experience those advantages during meditation retreats. But bringing an attentive mind home after the retreat is more difficult. Tart looks at the causes of pervasive mindlessness from a psychological, and from a more traditionally spiritual perspective. He describes how knowing derived from immediate experience becomes distorted as mind interprets the experience, and recommends Gurdjieff's practices of self-observation and self-remembering to cut through interpretation.

WHAT IS "KNOWING?"

We know how complicated and uncertain the answer can be. How do I really know if I am living my life in harmony with the universe, for example? In some cases the answer seems simple and clear. Right this instant, for example, I feel the keys of my word processor underneath my fingers as they move, and I easily say that I "know" what these keys feel like.

I wrote the above statement from inspiration, while typing rapidly. If I stop for a few seconds, however, and pay more focused attention to the sensations in my fingertips, my "knowing" becomes richer, more specific, more centrally focused in my consciousness than when much of my mind was devoted to composing the first few sentences about knowing. By deliberately moving my fingers about on the keys, new qualities of sensation are generated, especially a vibratory quality as I slide them horizontally over the keys.

I had to stop myself short on the last sentence, as I was about to write ". . . a vibratory quality . . . resulting from the friction of my finger tips against the keys, producing alternating periods of suddenly slipping freely over the key and then sticking, thus generating the vibration." If I had not practiced various disciplines for observing my experience more closely, I would probably not have stopped myself, not realized that I was moving from the domain of *immediate experience* to one of *interpretation of experience*. The almost totally automatized nature of such interpretation, and its confusion with primary experience, is a fantastic human ability—and the cause of much of the suffering we readers of this book experience. This is a simple, spontaneous example, slipping from knowing a simple sensation to the automatic interpretation and explanation of that sensation, but one that demonstrates a key problem in understanding how we "know," and in "knowing" more effectively. *My interpretations of reality are not reality!* Yet they are commonly taken as reality. For those who prefer scientific language, we might say that we constantly mistake our *theories* for our actual *data*.

This discussion focuses on this vital obstacle to clearer knowing, the confusion of basic experience and its cognitive and emotional interpretation.

Our understanding, our knowledge of reality—who we are, what we are like, what we want, what we don't want, what the world and others are like—constantly affects the way we perceive our world, how we interpret it, and how we act in it, and, thus, many of the consequences of our actions. *This is true whether we know it or not.* And most of the time we don't have the slightest inkling of this truth—we naively think we know who we are, perceive things as they are, and act "naturally." We are unwitting philosophers, living a philosophy of "naive realism"—we implicitly believe that things (including ourselves) are essentially what they seem to be, and that we perceive them clearly.

In sharp contrast to this is an idea normally associated with Eastern religions, the idea that we live in illusion. *Maya* is the Hindu term for this idea, *samsara* the Buddhist one. Living in illusion is commonly misunderstood as a belief that the world is not real, but, while some of the many schools of Hinduism and Buddhism might believe this, this misses the central point. That we live in samsara is a psychological statement of great practical importance: the world *as we experience it* is not real because we have highly distorted perceptions of and cognitive and intellectual reactions to both the external world and our own internal processes. It is as if we are intoxicated on some powerful drug that distorts perceptions and produces hallucinations and delusions, but since we have been on this drug all our lives, we don't have the slightest idea that what we take as "normal" and "real" is a product of intoxication.

I find it ironic that while samsara is an Eastern idea that seems strange to us "realistic" Westerners, our own sciences of psychology, psychiatry, and neurology have actually given us a much more detailed knowledge of specific ways our nervous systems and minds distort our perceptions than the East has had. There is no space to review this detailed knowledge here, and I have dealt with it at length elsewhere (Tart, 1986; 1994), but here it may be distilled down to several basic propositions that serve the purpose of this discussion of ways to improve the quality of our knowing.

1. We have a basic capacity to be aware, to experience, to "know." This is our fundamental, irreducible starting point.

2. This basic awareness is, under normal circumstances, intimately mixed with and shaped by physical and information-processing capacities of our body, brain, and nervous system (BBNS), such that we know very little about what basic awareness might be like if it were not compounded with our BBNS.

3. In addition to this shaping of awareness by its intimate interaction with the BBNS, the way we use our basic awareness has been subjected to enormous pressures, conditionings, and shapings in the course of growing up, such that our ordinary, "normal" state of consciousness is not "natural," but a semi-arbitrary and distorted construction, an active *simulation* of self and world rather than a straightforward perception of it. As this semi-arbitrary simulation of self and world is heavily influenced by the particular culture we have been raised in, I characterize ordinary consciousness with a technical term I introduced (Tart, 1975), "consensus consciousness."

4. A primary property of this world simulation process is, as our opening example illustrated, the automatic interpretation and elaboration of perceptions, reactions, and experience in general. We seldom even think to distinguish basic awareness/experience from its automatized interpretation, so we indeed experientially live in samsara, in an ongoing internal drama, a personal/cultural myth, rather than simply in basic reality. Our consequent external actions, in accordance with our personal myth, have consequences in the world and on others.

5. However, since acting in reality while being (at least partly) out of touch with it inevitably leads to inappropriate actions and consequences, living in samsara is, as the Eastern concepts have it, a state of unsatisfactoriness and suffering. No amount of "improvement" of the specifics of samsara—more entertaining movies, for example, or tastier food, or finding the perfect mate—can cure the suffering inherent in it. Awakening from one's illusions, learning to know basic reality unconfused with interpretation, is necessary, if not sufficient, to provide a stable and reliable basis for real happiness.

In consensus consciousness, our attention is unstable, captured by the desires and aversions of the moment, driven by the conditioned aspects of our mind, or our "false personality," as Gurdjieff called it. In order to escape from this "drunken party," we must (1) learn how to focus and control our attention instead of letting it be captured, and then we must (2) use it to observe our experience more clearly than ordinarily happens so that we can gain insight into our selves and our world.

CONCENTRATIVE MEDITATION

With stabilized, nondistracted awareness you have the option of looking at something—external perception or internal experience—in a prolonged and focused enough way to see beyond the fleeting surface, and so potentially know it in a deeper sense. You can pay sustained attention to one speaker, as it were, instead of constantly being pulled on to the dance floor at the drunken party. Even more basically, by paying sustained attention to one thing the primary aim of concentrative meditation is attained, namely, a calming and stilling of the normally restless mind.

DEEPER KNOWING: INSIGHT MEDITATION

Given some skill in focusing clearly on something, and the consequent related quieting of mental processes and distractions, by maintaining steady awareness of the object of focus, deeper qualities of the object and/or the mental processes you bring to your practice begin to reveal themselves. *Vipassana* is the Buddhist term for this practice, generally translated as "insight" meditation.

The term insight meditation can be somewhat misleading to Westerners, though, as it leads us to expect insights of a psychological sort: "Now I know why I did so and so!" Such psychological insights can arise in insight meditation and sometimes be of great importance, but what usually happens is more basic and, in the long run, more important: you get clearer and deeper direct knowledge of the fundamentals of your moment-by-moment experience while learning to not be confused by and sucked up into the secondary interpretations of experience that our world simulation process, our samsaric, consensus consciousness, usually produces. To return to our opening example, you feel the vibratory sensation as you run your hands over the keyboard without confusing it with the interpretation/explanation of alternating periods of sticking and sliding. In terms of our drunken party analogy, you begin to sober up and see what's actually happening more clearly.

It's not that there is something wrong with interpreting and explaining the world: I earlier described it as a great human talent, and it is. *Thinking/inter-*

preting and feeling is not the problem: it is the automatized, driven hyperthinking and hyperemoting that cuts us off from knowledge of our real nature and produces samsaric suffering.

Typically, insight meditation practice involves sitting still for a fixed period and focusing on observing, without interference, a range of changing meditation objects, such as the moment-by-moment flow of sounds you hear or of body sensation.

But what's so wonderful about noticing a body sensation more clearly and not confusing it with your thoughts about it? Why would anyone want to spend years learning to get better at doing this? I've often had this kind of thought, particularly in the middle of long meditation sessions. "So, I'm clearly aware of the pain in my butt from sitting so long, so what? I'm here to find God, not my butt!"

During an insight meditation practice, this kind of thought and feeling is, like all thoughts and feelings, a distraction from my goal of focusing on the flow of bodily sensation, so, if I remember my goal, I gently let go of the thought and feeling and come back to following, paying attention to, the dominant body sensation of the moment. Outside of formal practice, though, it's a good question. What do I really want from this and related practices?

I want to know my world and self as clearly as possible, moment by changing moment, in as clear and truthful a way as possible, given my human nature. As a samsaric being, my hopes, fears, and ignorance are constantly and automatically generating a simulation of reality that is usually a badly distorted representation of what I am actually experiencing of world and self at each moment. By learning the skill of paying sustained and clear attention to more basic aspects of my experience, such as the flow of bodily sensations, I ground myself more deeply in basic experience and learn to distinguish it from automatized interpretation. I *feel* as if I am in deeper touch with the reality of my being and find that the calm and clarity generated both produce immediate happiness and have some carry-over into my daily life, such that I am less "drunk" in everyday life and I function more intelligently and effectively through not confusing basic perceptions and my interpretations.

DIRECT MINDFULNESS PRACTICE IN LIFE

But *how* do you become more mindful in the midst of this drunken party we call ordinary life? This is an important question for most of us, as we aren't interested in spending the bulk of our day in formal meditation, nor would our lives allow us this luxury.

I have found the teachings and methods of G. I. Gurdjieff of most value in bringing mindfulness to everyday life, and believe that a combination of Gurdjieff's self-remembering practice in life and formal meditation periods is highly effective for many people.

Gurdjieff focused on two related techniques, *self-observation* and *self-remembering*. Self-observation involves adopting a basic attitude that knowing exactly what you *are* doing and experiencing, moment by moment, is much more important than your thoughts and beliefs about what you *should* be doing and experiencing or what you would *like* to be doing and experiencing. One takes a basically scientific attitude toward oneself and tries to collect more and more precise and unbiased observations about experience. Although one is focused toward general observation, this could manifest as specific questions, such as: "How exactly am I moving my body in this situation? What does my voice sound like? What emotion, if any, am I feeling?" and so on. When you have a detailed set of relatively unbiased observations about what you are like in your life, the possibility of real change is created.

Self-remembering combines a self-observational attitude with a specific focusing and splitting of attention such that one keeps track of bodily sensation simultaneously with major sensory impressions of vision and hearing. The methods are presented in detail in Ouspensky (1949; 1981), Nicoll (1984), Speeth (1986), and Tart (1986; 1994).

As a scientist, I have long admired the discipline in basic science that data is primary, theory secondary (Tart, 1972). That is, we love to explain things, but explanation must constantly be subjected to the restraint of observation: do my beloved theories really account for the actual data? The mindfulness approaches in the spiritual traditions have always appealed to me because they are consistent with a scientific approach to life. The Buddha himself told his followers to not believe anything just because it was intellectually appealing, venerable, or widely believed, but to test everything against their own experience (Buddha, 1989). I believe I am a better scientist as a result of developing some degree of mindfulness, as well as a better person.

The ultimate development of the spiritual life involves love and compassion just as much as knowledge and wisdom, of course, and while mindfulness approaches do not say much directly about love and compassion, their practical effect is to remove numerous psychological obstacles to their eventual flowering. I hope this all-too-brief outline of mindfulness practices will resonate sufficiently with some readers that you will be inspired to begin testing it against your own immediate experience.

31. The Hindrances by Joseph Goldstein

The hindrances are mental factors that consistently recur. They are a major source of suffering that initially seem automatic and unstoppable. In this description, Joseph Goldstein, meditation teacher in the Vipassana tradition, describes the hindrances as enemies to be conquered. In all instances, awareness is the primary weapon in the battle between a recurring hindrance and inner freedom.

Nowhere is the function of inner knowing more important than in the deceptively simple matter of recognizing and naming a hindrance as it appears. The task is to know when patterns like anger or doubt or desire first arise and to move to mindfulness before the hindrance takes hold.

IMAGINE YOURSELVES IN the middle of a battlefield, single-handedly facing a thousand enemies. Though surrounded on all sides, you somehow manage to conquer them. Imagine yourself on this battlefield a thousand different times, and each time you overcome the enemies around you. The Buddha has said that this is an easier task than the conquering of oneself. It is not a trivial thing we have set about doing. The most difficult of all possible tasks is to come to understand one's own mind. But it is not impossible. There have been many beings who have conquered these thousand enemies a thousand times, and they have given us advice and guidance.

The first big help is to recognize who the enemies are. Unrecognized, they remain powerful forces in the mind; in the light of recognition, they become much easier to deal with. There are five powerful enemies in the battlefield of the mind and learning to recognize them is essential in penetrating to deeper levels of understanding.

The first of these enemies, or hindrances, is sense desire: lusting after sense pleasure, grasping at sense objects. It keeps the mind looking outward, searching after this object or that, in an agitated and unbalanced way. It is in the very nature of sense desires that they can never be satisfied. There is no end to the seeking. We enjoy a pleasurable object, it arises and disappears, as do all phenomena, and we are left with the same unsatiated desire for more gratification. Until we deal with that kind of grasping in the mind we remain always unfulfilled, always seeking a new pleasure, a new delight. It can be desires for beautiful sights, beautiful sounds, tastes or smells, pleasant sensations in the body, or fascinating ideas. Attachment to these objects strengthens the greed factor; and it is precisely greed in the mind, this clinging and grasping, which keeps us bound on the wheel of samsara, the wheel of life and death. Until we deal successfully with the hindrance of sense desire, we stay bound by the forces of attachment and possessiveness.

The second enemy is hatred; anger, ill will, aversion, annoyance, irritation, are all expressions of the condemning mind. It is the mind which strikes against the object and wants to get rid of it. It is a very turbulent and violent state. In English we use two expressions which clearly indicate the effect of these two enemies, sense desire and ill will. We say a person is "burning with desire," or a person is "burning up," to mean he or she is very angry. The mind in these states is literally burning: a great deal of suffering.

The third enemy is sloth and torpor, which means laziness of mind, slug-gishness. A mind that is filled with sloth and torpor wants just to go to sleep. There is an animal called a slug which has always represented to me this qual-ity of sloth and torpor: it barely inches along, rather unergetically. Unless we overcome that kind of drowsiness and sluggishness of mind, nothing gets done, nothing is seen clearly, our mind remains heavy and dull.

The fourth hindrance is restlessness. A mind that is in a state of worry, regret and agitation is unable to stay concentrated. It is always jumping from one object to another, without any mindfulness. This unsettledness of mind prevents the arising of deep insight.

The fifth of the great enemies is doubt, and in some ways it is the most dif-ficult of all. Until we see through it, doubt incapacitates the mind, blocking our effort for clarity. Doubt arises about what one is doing and about one's ability to do it. Perhaps since you've been here the thought has come, "What am I doing here? Why did I come? I can't do it, it's too hard." This is the doubt-ing mind, a very big obstacle on the path.

All of these hindrances—desire, anger, sloth and torpor, restlessness, doubt—are mental factors. They are not self, just impersonal factors func-tioning in their own way. A simile is given to illustrate the effect of these dif-ferent obstructions in the mind. Imagine a pond of clear water. Sense desire is like the water becoming colored with pretty dyes. We become entranced with the beauty and intricacy of the color and so do not penetrate to the depths. Anger, ill will, aversion, is like boiling water. Water that is boiling is very turbulent. You can't see through to the bottom. This kind of turbulence in the mind, the violent reaction of hatred and aversion, is a great obstacle to understanding. Sloth and torpor is like the pond of water covered with algae, very dense. One cannot possibly penetrate to the bottom because you can't see through the algae. It is a very heavy mind. Restlessness and worry are like a pond when wind-swept. The surface of the water is agitated by strong winds. When influenced by restlessness and worry, insight becomes impossible because the mind is not centered or calm. Doubt is like the water when muddied; wisdom is obscured by murkiness and cloudiness.

There are specific ways to deal with these enemies as they confront us on the path. The first is to recognize them, to see them clearly in each moment. If sense desire arises, to know immediately that there is desire in the mind, or if there is anger, or sloth, or restlessness, or doubt, to recognize immediately the particular obstacle that has arisen. That very recognition is the most powerful, most effective way of overcoming them. Recognition leads to mindfulness. And mindfulness means not clinging, not condemning, not identifying with the object. All the hindrances are impermanent mental factors. They arise and they pass away, like clouds in the sky. If we are mindful of them when they arise and don't react or identify with them, they pass through the mind, without creating any disturbance. Mindfulness is the most effective way of dealing with them.

32. Hara—The Belly Center
by Karlfried Graf Von Dürckheim

There are many exponents of the inner life, but those capable of drawing others into their own profound experience are relatively rare. Von Dürckheim had that magnetism, and was one of the first Westerners to combine psychotherapy with Eastern awareness practices. He became the primary exponent of Japanese Zen in Europe, founding a longstanding school that influenced his generation. His book Hara *and his other works have become classic texts in bridging psychological insight with body-based spiritual practice.*

WHOEVER GIVES A lecture to a Japanese audience for the first time may meet with an experience as unexpected as it is unpleasant. The audience, it seems, gradually goes to sleep. This was what happened to me. It was bewildering. The more urgently I talked, the more desperately I tried to save the situation, the more my listeners closed their eyes until finally, so it seemed to me, half the room was blissfully asleep. But when without the least emphasis I uttered the word *Tenno,* Emperor, all were suddenly wide awake as if struck by lightning and gazed at me with wide open and not in the least sleepy eyes. They had not slept after all. Turned in on themselves, they had been attentive in their own way and I had overlooked the fact that although their eyes were closed they had been sitting erect and controlled.

Every stranger in Japan is struck at first by the sight of people apparently asleep and submerged in themselves. In trams and trains everywhere one sees men and women, even young people, girls and students sitting with closed or half closed eyes but erect and completely still. When they open their eyes they do not look in the least sleepy, on the contrary, their glance seems to arise from deep below, completely tranquil and present, from which the world with its turbulent diversity seems to rebound. It is a look which shows that the individual is completely collected and unperturbed, awake but not over-responsive, controlled yet not rigid.

A Japanese sitting on a chair or a bench looks very often as though he were resting in himself rather than on the furniture. The way in which a Japanese sits down on a chair shows the degree of his Westernization. Crossing the legs and so throwing the small of the back out of line and compressing the abdomen is entirely un-Japanese and so is any leaning or lolling position which would eliminate the supporting strength of the back. The Japanese, to whichever class he may belong, holds himself erect and "in form" even when sitting. That this custom is weakening today through the increasing influence of the West is doubtless true—but this is a deviation from the traditional essentially Japanese form which alone concerns us here.

The foregoing examples show two things. The Japanese way of sitting is connected with an inner as well as an outer attitude. The Japanese rests upright and composed within himself. This combination of uprightness and resting within oneself is typical. The whole person is, as it were, gathered inward.

Another striking example of significant posture is the one that a Japanese assumes in front of the camera. The European is often surprised at how much the posture of important public men, such as high ranking army officers or newly elected Cabinet members, differs from that of Europeans when being photographed. Whereas the latter take great pains to stand "at ease" or "with nonchalance" or "with dignity," shoulders drawn up and chest thrust forward, the Japanese stand quite differently, often, to our eyes, with deliberate ungainliness—unassumingly front face with loose hung shoulders and arms but still upright and firm, the legs slightly apart. Never does the Japanese stand with his weight on the one leg while the other "idles." Anyone standing in this way, without centre, without axis, inspires little confidence in a Japanese.

I remember a large reception, the guests European and Japanese, stood around after dinner drinking coffee and smoking. A Japanese friend of mine who knew of my interest in the ways of his country joined me and said, "Do you see that the Europeans standing here could be easily toppled over if one were suddenly to give them a little push from behind? But none of the Japanese would lose their balance even if they were given a much harder push."

How is this stability achieved? The bodily centre of gravity is not drawn upward but held firmly in the middle, in the region of the navel. And that is the point. The belly is not pulled in but free—and yet slightly tensed. The shoulder region instead of being tense is relaxed but the trunk is firm. The upright bearing is not a pulling upwards but is the manifestation of an axis which stands firmly on a reliable base and which by its own strength maintains its uprightness. Whether a person is corpulent or thin is immaterial.

Upright, firm and collected—these are the three marks of that posture which is typical of the Japanese who knows how to stand, and taken altogether, show the presence of Hara.

This Hara as the basis of posture is no less noticeable in women than in men. Only that the posture of women as observed in the street by the foreigner, where at first he mainly encounters them, is different in some ways—the look

of being self-enclosed, of deep inner collectedness is so emphasized as to suggest self-absorption. The Japanese woman emphasizes an attitude which is
completely opposed to that of the pre-potent, more expanding attitude of the
Western woman. "As far as possible, not to be in evidence. To move, taking up
as little space as possible. To be as though one were not there at all!" As a result
of such an inner disposition the women keep their arms pressed close to their
sides, never swinging, heads slightly bent, shoulders dropped and a little
pulled in, and when walking they trip along with knees scarcely separated,
toes turned in and taking very small steps. The stronger the influence of tradition on the Japanese woman the more grotesque appears to her the walk of
the European or American. What strikes us as especially free and at ease seems
to the Japanese woman unfeminine and insolent, quasi-masculine, immodest
and above all naïve—for all this expresses an inner attitude of self-assurance
which takes life altogether too much for granted.

Man in his self-assurance holds too strongly to what he believes is his by his
own efforts. Not only does he not hesitate to attract attention to himself but
he even emphasizes his "persona." This means that he lacks the wise restraint
suitable both in social life and towards those greater forces which are present
everywhere and which may suddenly fall on him and attack him. Vis-à-vis these
forces man is better prepared either to ward them off or deliberately to let
them in, if the deep-centredness of the soul-body posture at least counter-
balances the outward thrust and striving of the mind or, better still, slightly
preponderates over it. When circumstances oblige a Japanese to show himself
in public, for instance, when "the man at the top" has to put himself forward
because his office requires him to do so, or when the Headmaster of a school
has to go on the platform and deliver the speech of the day, one can observe
the most astonishing movements of withdrawal such a man makes when he
steps down from the platform—movements which have only one intention,
that is, to demonstrate that he knows that "one must make a personal withdrawal in the same degree as one's function required one to put oneself forward." Hence the embarrassment, sense of shame even which a Japanese
gathering feels for a European making a speech, for example if in any way he
"shows off." Such behaviour, so often repeated by our Western representatives
in Japan, alienates sympathy far more than we suspect. For avoiding all postures emphasizing the ego the Japanese has one sure remedy—his firm Hara.

The sitting-still of the Japanese, especially of the Japanese woman, this completely motionless and yet inwardly alert sitting still, has baffled many a foreigner. Most Westerners have their first opportunity of observing at close
range the ways of Japanese women in the tea houses where the serving girls

and the geishas are called in to grace an evening. What is most impressive is very often their way of sitting still—knees together, resting on their heels, withdrawn into themselves and yet completely free and relaxed. If with a swift and supple motion they rise from this position to do something such as pouring out the rice wine, they return immediately and without loss of poise to the quiet sitting posture, upright and attentive, completely there, yet not there at all, and just wait until the next thing has to be done. In the same way in her own home the mistress of the house sits by modestly while the men talk, but so also sits the ballad singer, and the singing geisha, and so sits the male choir in the Kabuki, the classical theatre, and so the Samurai—so they all sit and so they stand like symbols of life, collected and ready for anything. And as they sit and stand so also do they walk and dance and wrestle and fence, fundamentally motionless. For every movement is as though anchored in an immovable centre from which all motion flows and from which it receives its force, direction and measure. The immovable centre lies in Hara.

Just as we see in the Buddha effigies the emphasis on the centre of gravity in the lower body we find it again in the representations of mythological figures and of sages. We find it in the pictures of the great leaders, of the popular gods of good luck and in the many illustrations of Boddhidharma, the blue-eyed monk who brought Zen Buddhism to China and became famous for his imperturbable "sitting." His image is still given to children as a tumbler doll with a round, lead-weighted belly which always brings him back to his upright position no matter how often he is knocked down.

It follows as a matter of course that an understanding of the importance of the body-soul centre has influenced the Japanese ideal of beauty. It is characteristic that their "beauty" should be different from ours. In our ideal we see beauty in the symmetry and perfect form of the body. We look for perfection and harmony of the whole and its parts. It is undoubtedly true that this ideal was originally determined by the idea of the unity of body and soul. Today, however, the popular concept of beauty as compared with this ideal has become largely superficial and externalized, and the culture of the body informed by the spirit has been replaced by a cult of the well proportioned body accentuating the erotic in the woman and the virile and masculine in the man. The more discriminating man on the other hand caring less for this merely physical beauty finds it in the expression of the soul beside which the beauty of the outward form has but little importance. Thus the Western ideal of beauty alternates in a typical way between the opposite poles of body and soul. This dichotomy plays no part in the mind of the Japanese. He regards as beautiful the figure which represents a being well grounded in his basic centre.

For this and no other reason he values a certain emphasis on the belly, and the reserved bearing which is evidence of its firmness. It is not surprising therefore that a bridegroom, if he is too thin, tries to acquire a little belly in order to please his bride and also that the strong belly (provided it emphasizes the right centre of gravity—not to be confused with the blown-out stomach) is considered attractive and not repulsive as in the West. Indeed the idols of the people, the *sumo* masters (*sumo* is Japanese wrestling) often have enormous bellies and yet, despite their weight, incredible nimbleness, a cat-like agility and elasticity. The seat of their strength is in their belly, not merely physical strength as is revealed in their often immensely developed muscles but also of a supernatural strength. They demonstrate in a spectacular way what made them masters quite apart from their technical skill—they really demonstrate Hara.

If a man has Hara he no longer needs any physical strength at all, he wins through a quite different kind of strength. I had the opportunity to watch an impressive example of this during the last elimination round of a *sumo* championship.

Breathlessly awaited by thousands of spectators, two masters entered the ring at the Koguki-Kan in Tokyo. With great dignity each one in turn steps out of his corner, casts consecrated rice into the ring, goes with legs wide apart into a full knee bend, then stamps mightily first with one foot then with the other. After a ceremonious bow they approach each other, squat down with hands on the ground and gaze at each other eye to eye. Then both wrestlers spring up from this position—but not before both have inwardly assented to the start of the contest. If one of them while they have been eyeing each other closes his eyelids it means "I am not yet ready." And as the contest can begin only when each one is "in form" this is a signal for them both to stand up, separate, and again squat facing each other until both are finally fully ready. The umpire who has watched everything closely gives the sign and off they go. Both wrestlers leap into the air and the crowd is prepared to see a mighty battle.

But what happens? One, after a short struggle, simply raises his hand, on which the hand of the other lies flat, and, as if he were dealing with a puppet he pushes his opponent almost without touching him and without the use of any visible effort, slowly and softly out of the ring. He wins in the true sense, without fighting. The defeated wrestler falls backwards over the ropes and the multitude goes mad with excitement while everything that is not nailed down is hurled into the air and rains down upon the victor from all sides in tribute to his prowess. That was Hara, demonstrated by a master. And as such it was applauded by the crowd.

This example shows very clearly that in Hara there is a supernatural force which makes possible extraordinary natural achievement in the world. And as Hara is ever present to the Japanese as the sign of a matured inwardness he also knows about it as a mysterious power which can produce super-normal results. From childhood the Japanese is taught the power of Hara. *Hara, Hara,* the father calls to the growing boy when he seems to fail in a task or when physical pain saps his morale and threatens to over-power him or when he loses his head with excitement. This Hara, Hara, however, implies and produces something different from our "pull yourself together." With Hara one remains balanced both in action and in endurance. All this is such a natural, basic and general knowledge for the Japanese that it is not at all easy for him if you ask him about his secret treasure to raise it to consciousness, let alone to explain it.

33. *The Intuitive Body by Wendy Palmer*

In the martial arts, those endowed with sufficient speed, agility, and daring occasionally become living examples of body-based intuition. Such people visibly embody Hara's connection to the power and flow of the life force by demonstrating the ability to blend awareness with attackers, to show evidence of 360-degree perception, and to move through multiple-man attacks. They present a living picture of Hara's intuitive role, but they seldom articulate their inner experience.

More recently, second and third generation American teachers who took their belts in the traditional manner have, like Palmer, developed a vocabulary of energy and attention, opening the teachings of Hara to a wider audience. Palmer is a fourth-degree blackbelt in aikido, who teaches both by demonstration and by describing the energetic foundation of her skill.

WHAT ARE THE components that create or enhance stability in something? What makes a tree, a house, a tent, or a car stable? What do we do to keep something from falling over or collapsing? There are, of course, many possibilities, but one key principle is to strengthen the base—the foundation or root system. Sometimes it is a matter of widening the base, sometimes we deepen the base, and sometimes reinforcing the base is helpful.

Human beings are much more dynamic than houses or cars. Like a plant, whose root system must be nourished to insure the growth and productivity of its limbs, we must engage in constant and subtle maintenance to keep our centering or energetic base strong, well-toned, and vibrant. We can use our attention to achieve more stability and enhance our sense of contact with our base.

Learning to direct our attention empowers us. When our attention is focused and unified, our capacity to function becomes heightened. In fact, phenomenal events can occur. We have all heard the stories of grandmothers who pick up cars to rescue babies or of young boys who lift tractors off their trapped fathers. Energy is like light. When it is diffused it has a pleasant feeling. When energy is focused, it is like a laser, the strongest tool known to us. We have the capacity both to diffuse and to concentrate our energy.

ENERGY FOLLOWS ATTENTION

Energy tends to go where there is the most excitement, most clarity, most intensity. Energy follows attention. Wherever we focus our attention, our energy follows. By focusing our attention, we can stabilize ourselves. There are times in our lives when we feel inspired and know what we want. At other times, we are confused and scattered. During those insecure times, we can arbitrarily choose some quality to steady ourselves and shift our attention. . . .

An experience of a beginning student illustrates how energy follows attention:

> When I first started taking Wendy's class, I was training for a rowing competition. I am a power versus endurance athlete, and I was very focused on my lack of stamina. While rowing, I often heard an inner voice hysterically chanting, "I don't have any stamina." I would offer this negative mantra as a self-appraisal when discussing my rowing with others.
>
> Walking home from work one day, I was thinking about my lack of stamina and it hit me: "Energy follows attention!" Then I asked, "What am I doing to myself?" As of that day, I began to ask, "What would it be like if I had more endurance?" Because I was so physically engaged while rowing, I would register a sensation in my body in response to the question.
>
> As my training progressed, I evoked additional qualities while rowing. Asking "What would it be like if I had more power?" liberated untapped reserves. The most important gain, however, was knowing that I could break free from the panic that could suddenly consume me on the water.
>
> —Kevin

EMBELLISHING OUR CENTERING PRACTICE

Energy follows attention: whatever we put our attention on develops and grows. Our neuroses can be quite versatile and distract us in many ways. They can be in vivid technicolor images, or they can be associated with and evoked by certain sounds and smells. Our neuroses tell stories about us being the best or the worst. They can tell us we are right and the other person is wrong or the reverse, that someone is right and we are wrong. The "if only" style of neurosis tells stories about what we might have done. Our neuroses often have an obsessive quality, like a needle stuck in a groove of a record, repeating the same line over and over again.

Focusing our attention and staying with our centering practice is difficult when we have all those wild scenarios going on internally. This difficulty is just the reality of our practice. It is as if we are in a room with a gigantic, technicolor movie screen controlled by our neuroses and below the screen is a tiny black-and-white television showing our centering practice. Both are competing for our attention. It is hard to watch that little television when the large, bright screen can so easily distract us. Part of the challenge, then, is to embellish our centering practice in any way that makes it interesting enough to hold our attention.

A SPIRAL-BREATH MEDITATION

I begin by imagining that the bottoms of my feet are open, and that energy from the earth can be received through them. As I inhale, I imagine that I am drawing energy from mother earth. The in-breath moves in a counterclockwise direction. When I exhale, the breath is clockwise, moving back into the earth. The inhale is associated with cleansing or purifying. The exhale is associated with strengthening or empowering.

I use nine areas in my body to focus my breath. At each area, I take between one and five complete breaths to cleanse and strengthen that particular area. The number of breaths depends upon my sense of the strength or health of the particular area as well as my ability to focus. If I am feeling scattered, I use three to five breaths to help gather my attention in a particular area. When I lose my concentration in any area, I start that area again or do extra breaths to bring my awareness back into focus.

I begin the spiral-breath meditation with an inhale, drawing the breath through the bottoms of my feet and taking a counterclockwise turn at the ankles. I think of this part of the breath as cleansing the ankle joints. When I exhale, I focus my breath turning back through the ankles again, this time in a clockwise direction. I move to the knee joints, and imagine my breath spiraling there. With each in-breath, I imagine that it is cleansing and purifying my knees. With each out-breath, I imagine it strengthening and empowering my knees. My attention moves to the floor of my pelvis and genital area as I repeat the same process: the inhale cleanses, the exhale strengthens. The next point is the *hara* or abdomen, where I repeat the process drawing the breath from the earth and spiraling it around my belly. After that I move to the solar plexus and continue the breathing pattern. From the solar plexus, I move up to the heart, then to the neck, then to the center of my head, behind my eyes. Finally, I draw the breath to the very top of my head and it spirals towards heaven. The exhale comes down from above, spiraling through my body and strengthening my whole being.

Having completed this part, I relax and allow my breath to flow naturally. Even though I am relaxed, I still retain an awareness of the purifying inhale moving counterclockwise and the strengthening exhale moving clockwise.

After being with my breath in this relaxed way for awhile, I sit as if I am about to hear or feel or see something: the "not-knowing" state. If I see, hear, or feel something, I note it and return to the state of openness. I find this state helpful for suspending any agenda I might have in regards to the next moment.

When I feel it is the time for ending the meditation, I reorient to my breath. I inhale spiraling up, cleansing, and exhale spiraling down, strengthening. I check the perimeter of my field in all directions: in front, behind, to the left and right, above and below. Then I shift my attention to the sensations of heaviness or lightness. I spend a moment evoking my quality. At this point, I open my eyes and I get up and move around. Sometimes the feeling or experience of the meditation will stay with me, other times it falls away.

With regular practice, our centered experiences will increase and become a vital functioning part of ourselves. These experiences can balance us while helping us to tolerate and accept the aspects of ourselves that make us uncomfortable. Meditation practice gives us ground from which we can openly face and work with ourselves. It is ritual in the sense that we bring ourselves to it with intention. We repeat the practice in order to gather and strengthen the energy pattern. It is both sacred and ordinary—we practice in an ordinary manner the sacred concentration of being in the moment.

TAKE YOUR TIME

The universe is dynamic; its energy is always pushing on us. As soon as we are able to manage one aspect of our lives, another challenge is offered as an opportunity to grow. Rather than hoping to remain stable once and for all, our goal is to stabilize momentarily. To clarify this, O Sensei[1] said, "It is not that I don't get off center. I correct so fast that no one can see me." The idea is to become skilled at coming back, not holding on. The benefit comes from developing our ability to return. The more we practice returning to center, the more we can center in everyday situations.

When we are unified and able to experience ourselves as powerful, it is sometimes frightening. Feeling powerful may become an identity crisis. There is a tendency to sabotage ourselves and move back to our old pattern because it is familiar. As appealing as the idea of unification seems, being able to tolerate and embody the actual experience is a long-term, whole-life practice.

I encourage [patience] with this kind of practice and training. There is nothing instantaneous about it. The insights might be instant, but there is a difference between having an insight and living an insight. If insight were enough, then all the people who take hallucinogenic drugs or write books on personal development would be happy, together, and enlightened. They are not. Having insight does not lead to an embodied experience. In fact, it can be incredibly painful to gain an insight and then have our body react in a different way. We need to recognize that conscious embodiment is a long-term process that is integrated into our daily lives.

34. *Perceptions of the Heart by Sylvia Boorstein*

In a contemporary storytelling form, psychotherapist Sylvia Boorstein illustrates compassion and generosity as perceptions of the heart. She draws on the power of real-life illustrations to convey the fact that nondual consciousness is near at hand rather than being distant and exotic.

COMPASSION IS THE natural response of the heart unclouded by the specious view that we are separate from one another. Traditional texts describe it as "the quivering of the heart" in response to realizing someone else's pain. I think we feel it as our own emotional system vibrating in synchrony with someone else's. It requires a quiet state of mind. Quivering is subtle.

I boarded an early morning flight once, in Laramie, Wyoming, after teaching a three-day, mostly silent workshop for thirty people. I had worked hard to stay attentive to everyone's experience, and I felt relaxed and content because I thought I had done a good job.

An elderly man and woman took seats next to mine, and as soon as we were airborne, the flight attendant served breakfast.

"We ordered a kosher breakfast," the old man advised the attendant.

"I'll check," she replied, and returned with apologies. "Apparently they have forgotten to put your meals on board. May I give you a regular breakfast and have you see if you can eat any part of it?" she offered.

"No, I'm sorry," the man said. "We can't do that."

I began to weep and was surprised. The situation wasn't critical, and the flight was a short one. Probably I was particularly touched by the fact that the couple reminded me of my grandparents, and I understood their dilemma. From an outsider's view, their situation was an odd peculiarity. From their perspective, it was a nonnegotiable disappointment. Because my mind was quiet, I could feel their pain.

Every pain is important pain to whomever is feeling it. When I was a child, people sometimes said to children who didn't eat their dinner, "Think of the starving children in Europe." I'm grateful no one said that to me. I was, by nature, a nervous eater, and adding guilt and embarrassment to my already uncomfortable state would have increased my distress. People who made that remark probably forgot that, although being hungry is painful, eating when you aren't hungry is also painful. Pain is pain. Ranking it is extra.

We evaluate pain by passing it through our value systems, which are, after all, only opinions. "This is important pain," or "This is trivial pain." When I feel remote from someone's pain, it's always because I've made a judgment about it. Perhaps I think that person's situation is so terrible it must be unbearable, and I am trying to protect myself by denying it. We did it at the movies, when we were young, covering our eyes in the horrifying scenes, saying, "Let me know when this bad part is over." I still sometimes do it, reflexively, in movies when the scene is too grim.

Sometimes I feel remote from someone's pain because I am alarmed by that person's judgment. "How can you be fretting about *this?*" I think to myself. "What you really should be worried about is this other, much more worrisome thing." It's ridiculous to decide what "should" grieve someone else. Everyone's attachments are unique. I have been embarrassed to admit the degree of pain I have felt over attachments that I know, by other people's standards, are trivial. Even without outside criticism, I judge myself harshly. "What a selfish person you are!" I scold myself. "The world is in terrible shape, and you are agonizing about this nonsense?"

Pain is hard to acknowledge directly because there is so much of it. Perhaps our collective alarm that the Buddha was right about life being suffering causes us, sometimes, to try to minimize pain. "Things *could* be worse," well-meaning people say to friends in distress, hoping perspective will be soothing. "At least you have your health." "At least you have your career." "At least you're not in Blank (any country at war)." Or the ultimate spiritual comparison, "In the sphere of the cosmos, what does this matter?" All these are adult variations of "Children are starving in Europe." They add humiliation to preexisting pain and make it worse.

Of course, it *is* true that in the sphere of the cosmos our current heart pain is minute, inconsequential. In that same sphere-of-the-cosmos perspective, everything is *equally* inconsequential. This does not fit our emotional reality. Some people and some issues feel especially significant to us. Also, we don't live in the sphere of the cosmos. We live here.

Remembering the sphere-of-the-cosmos point of view, *remembering* earthrise from the moon, *remembering* the interconnectedness of all beings—all these remembrances make it possible to look more directly at pain. Perhaps it's the necessary perspective for seeing pain clearly, for being able to stand it. Remembering our own special affinities, our own kinship feelings, our own heartbreaks in our personal stories, which seem so real and important, keeps us *in* this world, not *out* of it, caring deeply and acting kindly.

Generosity as a Natural Act

I am blown away by generosity that is completely unselfconscious. It is the most concrete example of the Buddha's idea of "nonseparate self." Of course our bodies are, in the physical sense, separate from other bodies, popping into and out of this world at different times and different locations. But the essence of consciousness that enlivens all those bodies is singular. With that awareness, fear vanishes and sharing is a totally natural act.

A woman much younger than I am was dressing next to me in the locker room at the gym. We were talking about the benefits of regular exercise for staying fit and trim, and she added, "I just had some surgery a few months ago, and my doctors are amazed at how fast I've gotten my strength back."

"What kind of surgery did you have?" I asked.

"I gave my sister a kidney. She's a diabetic, and she needed it."

She said it with the same matter-of-fact tone that might have accompanied, "I had an extra bike I wasn't using. . . ." She was completely casual about it. It was just what needed to be done.

I've been thinking for many years about one particular story about the Buddha. In one of his previous incarnations, he was walking along the edge of a cliff and heard cries coming from below. Upon looking over the edge, he saw starving tiger cubs with a mother tiger too weak to feed them. The Buddha-in-progress leaped immediately to his death to provide nourishment for the cubs.

The story was told as a generosity story. It worried me because I couldn't imagine that kind of spontaneous selflessness.

Now I can. I have five grandchildren. For them, I would not hesitate a minute about a cliff decision. I'm not even especially proud of that because it's not a big deal. *Not* doing it would be impossible. What would be a big deal for me is the next step, which is to remember always that everyone's grandchildren are mine. Anyone's grandchildren are *everyone's* grandchildren.

You don't need to have children or grandchildren to have this realization. This is the truth of nonseparate self, and it reveals itself when the attention is focused. I see it happen when a disaster occurs. A plane crashes in the Potomac, and passers-by leap into the ice-filled river just because people are in it—not people they know, just people in need. There is a fire in the World Trade Center building, and people carry a co-worker in a wheelchair down sixty-seven flights of stairs, at great risk to themselves. No one thinks, "I'll do heroism," or "I'll do generosity." We realize, when the attention is sharp, that we are all part of each other, and we become caregivers. Perhaps *generosity* is the word we use as long as we think there are donors and recipients. When sharing is a natural and spontaneous act, we probably call it *compassion*.

I used to think if I began seeing all beings as my kin, it would be a big burden. The opposite is true. When someone I know is doing something admirable I don't feel *I* need to be doing it. She is doing it on my behalf, or *as* me, relieving me of that particular task. Mary and Chodren are being nuns for me, Alex is teaching for me in remote places, Itzhak Perlman is me playing the violin, and Joe Montana is me, too. So is his mother.

35. *A Practice of Compassion by Pema Chödrön*

To Pema Chödrön, compassion can be cultivated through the Buddhist lojong *teachings, a series of slogans formulated to exchange oneself for others. The "exchange" is a technique for giving and receiving compassion; it provides immediate practical benefit even when taken out of its original setting and placed in the context of contemporary psychological ideas. This teaching is one of the jewels of sacred tradition, continuously polished by generations of devotional practitioners.*

WITH THE SLOGAN "Three objects, three poisons, and three seeds of virtue" we begin to enter into . . . the teachings on how to awaken compassion. We have so far been attempting to establish that the ground of all of our experience is very spacious, not as solid as we tend to make it. We don't have to make such a big deal about ourselves, our enemies, our lovers, and the whole show. This emphasis on gentleness is the pith instruction on how to reconnect with openness and freshness in our lives, how to liberate ourselves from the small world of ego. We'll keep coming back to this sense of freshness and open space and not making such a big deal, because we are now about to get into the really messy stuff.

In the Buddhist teachings, the messy stuff is called *klesha,* which means poison. Boiling it all down to the simplest possible formula, there are three main poisons: passion, aggression, and ignorance. We could talk about these in different ways—for example, craving, aversion, and couldn't care less. Addictions of all kinds come under the category of craving, which is wanting, wanting, wanting—feeling that we have to have some kind of resolution. Aversion encompasses violence, rage, hatred, and negativity of all kinds, as well as garden-variety irritation. And ignorance? Nowadays, it's usually called denial.

The pith instruction of all the Buddhist teachings and most explicitly of the lojong[1] teachings is, whatever you do, don't try to make these unwanted feelings go away. That's an unusual thought; it's not our habitual tendency to let these feelings hang around. Our habitual tendency is definitely to try to make those things go away.

People and situations in our lives are always triggering our passion, aggression, and ignorance. A good old innocent cup of coffee triggers some people's craving; they are addicted to it; it represents comfort and all the good things in life. If they can't get it, their life is a wreck. Other people have an elaborate story line about why it's bad for you, and they have aversion and a support group. Plenty of other people couldn't care less about a cup of coffee; it doesn't mean much at all to them.

And then there's good old Mortimer, that person who is sitting next to you in the meditation hall, or perhaps someone who works in your office. Some people are lusting when they see Mortimer. He looks wonderful to them. A lot of their discursive thought is taken up with what they'd like to do with Mortimer. A certain number of people hate him. They haven't even talked to him yet, but the minute they saw him, they felt loathing. Some of us haven't noticed him, and we may never notice him. In fact, a few years from now he'll tell us he was here, and we'll be surprised.

So there are three things, which in the slogan are called three objects. One object is what we find pleasant, another is what we find unpleasant, and a third is what we're neutral about. If it's pleasant, it triggers craving; if it's unpleasant, it triggers aversion; if it's neutral, it triggers ignorance. Craving, aversion, and ignorance are the three poisons.

Our experience would write the formula as "Three objects, three poisons, and lots of misery" or "Three objects, three poisons, and three seeds of confusion, bewilderment, and pain," because the more the poisons arise and the bigger they get in our life, the more they drive us crazy. They keep us from seeing the world as it is; they make us blind, deaf, and dumb. The world doesn't speak for itself because we're so caught up in our story line that instead of feeling that there's a lot of space in which we could lead our life, . . . we're robbing ourselves, robbing ourselves from letting the world speak for itself. You just keep speaking to yourself, so nothing speaks to you.

The three poisons are always trapping you in one way or another, imprisoning you and making your world really small. When you feel craving, you could be sitting on the edge of the Grand Canyon, but all you can see is this piece of chocolate cake that you're craving. With aversion, you're sitting on the edge of the Grand Canyon, and all you can hear is the angry words you said to someone ten years ago. With ignorance, you're sitting on the edge of the Grand Canyon with a paper bag over your head. Each of the three poisons has the power to capture you so completely that you don't even perceive what's in front of you.

This "Three objects, three poisons, and three seeds of virtue" is really a peculiar idea. It turns the conventional formula on its head in an unpredictable, nonhabitual way. It points to how the three poisons can be three seeds [for stepping] out of this limited world of ego fixation, how to step out of the world of tunnel vision. And the slogan is just an introduction to how this notion works. . . .

There's nothing really wrong with passion or aggression or ignorance, except that we take it so personally and therefore waste all that juicy stuff. The peacock eats poison and that's what makes the colors of its tail so brilliant. That's the traditional image for this practice, that the poison becomes the source of great beauty and joy; poison becomes medicine.

Whatever you do, don't try to make the poisons go away, because if you're trying to make them go away, you're losing your wealth, along with your neurosis. All this messy stuff is your richness, but saying this once is not going to convince you. If nothing else, however, it could cause you to wonder about these teachings and begin to be curious whether they could possibly be true, which might inspire you to try them for yourself.

The main point is that when Mortimer walks by and triggers your craving or your aversion or your ignorance or your jealousy or your arrogance or your feeling of worthlessness—when Mortimer walks by and a feeling arises—that could be like a little bell going off in your head or a lightbulb going on: here's an opportunity to awaken your heart. Here's an opportunity to ripen bodhichitta,[2] to reconnect with the sense of the soft spot, because as a result of these poisons the shields usually come up. We react to the poisons by armoring our hearts.

When the poisons arise, we counter them with two main tactics. Step one: Mortimer walks by. Step two: klesha arises. (It's hard to separate the first two steps.) Step three: we either *act out* or *repress,* which is to say we either physically or mentally attack Mortimer or talk to ourself about what a jerk he is or how we're going to get even with him, or else we repress those feelings.

Acting out and repressing are the main ways that we shield our hearts, the main ways that we never really connect with our vulnerability, our compassion, our sense of the open, fresh dimension of our being. By acting out or repressing we invite suffering, bewilderment, or confusion to intensify.

Drive all blames into Mortimer. Someone once heard the slogan "Drive all blames into one"[3] and thought it was "Drive all blames into Juan." Whether you call him or her Juan or Juanita or Mortimer, the usual tactic is either to act out or repress. If Mortimer or Juan or Juanita walks by and craving arises, you try to get together by flirting or making advances. If aversion arises, you try to get revenge. You don't stay with the raw feelings. You don't hold your seat. You take it a step further and act out.

Repressing could actually come under the category of ignorance. When you see Juan or Juanita or Mortimer, you just shut down. Maybe you don't even want to touch what they remind you of, so you just shut down. There's another common form of repression, which has to do with guilt: Juan walks by; aversion arises; you act out, and then you feel guilty about it. You think you're a bad person to be hating Juan, and so you repress it.

What we're working with in our basic . . . practice . . . is the middle ground between acting out and repressing. We're discovering how to hold our seat and feel completely what's underneath all that story line of wanting, not wanting, and so forth.

In terms of "Three objects, three poisons, and three seeds of virtue," when these poisons arise, the instruction is to drop the story line, which means— instead of acting out or repressing—use the situation as an opportunity to feel your heart, to feel the wound. Use it as an opportunity to touch that soft spot. Underneath all that craving or aversion or jealousy or feeling wretched about yourself, underneath all that hopelessness and despair and depression, there's something extremely soft, which is called bodhichitta.

When these things arise, train gradually and very gently without making it into a big deal. Begin to get the hang of feeling what's underneath the story line. Feel the wounded heart that's underneath the addiction, self-loathing, or anger. If someone comes along and shoots an arrow into your heart, it's fruitless to stand there and yell at the person. It would be much better to turn your attention to the fact that there's an arrow in your heart and to relate to that wound.

When we do that, the three poisons become three seeds of how to make friends with ourselves. They give us the chance to work on patience and kindness, the chance not to give up on ourselves and not to act out or repress. They give us the chance to change our habits completely. This is what helps both ourselves and others. This is instruction on how to turn unwanted circumstances into the path of enlightenment. By following it, we can transform all that messy stuff that we usually push away into the path of awakening: reconnecting with our soft heart, our clarity, and our ability to open further. . . .

How do we help? How do we create a saner world or a saner domestic situation or job situation, wherever we may be? How do we work with our actions and our speech and our minds in a way that opens up the space rather than closes it down? In other words, how do we create space for other people and ourselves to connect with our own wisdom? How do we create a space where we can find out how to become more a part of this world we are living in and less separate and isolated and afraid? How do we do that?

It all starts with loving-kindness for oneself, which in turn becomes loving-kindness for others. As the barriers come down around our own hearts, we are less afraid of other people. We are more able to hear what is being said, see what is in front of our eyes, and work in accord with what happens rather than struggle against it. The lojong teachings say that the way to help, the way to act compassionately, is to exchange oneself for other. When you can put yourself in someone else's shoes, then you know what is needed, and what would speak to the heart.

I recently received a letter from a friend in which she dumped all over me and told me off. My first reaction was to be hurt and my second reaction was to get mad, and then I began to compose this letter in my mind, this very dharmic letter that I was going to write back to her using all the teachings and all the lojong logic to tell her off. Because of the style of our relationship, she would have been intimidated by a dharmic letter, but it wouldn't have helped anything. It would have further forced us into these roles of being two separate people, each of us believing in our roles more and more seriously, that I was the one who knew it all and she was the poor student. But on that day when I had spent so much energy composing this letter, just by a turn of circumstance, something happened to me that caused me to feel tremendous loneliness. I felt sad and vulnerable. In that state of mind, I suddenly knew where my friend's letter had come from—loneliness and feeling left out. It was her attempt to communicate.

Sometimes when you're feeling miserable, you challenge people to see if they will still like you when you show them how ugly you can get. Because of how I myself was feeling I knew that what she needed was not for somebody to dump back on her. So I wrote a very different letter from what I had planned, an extremely honest one that said, "You know, you can dump on me all you like and put all of your stuff out there, but I'm not going to give up on you." It wasn't a wishy-washy letter that avoided the issue that there had been a confrontation and that I had been hurt by it. On the other hand, it wasn't a letter in which I went to the other extreme and lashed out. For the first time, I felt I had experienced what it meant to exchange oneself for other. When you've been there you know what it feels like, and therefore you can give something that you know will open up the space and cause things to keep flowing. You can give something that will help someone else connect with their own insight and courage and gentleness, rather than further polarize the situation.

"Drive all blames into one" is a pivotal slogan because usually driving blames into *other* comes from the fact that we've been hurt and therefore want to hurt back. It's that kind of logic. Therefore the exchange—putting ourselves in someone else's shoes—doesn't come from theory, in which you try to imagine what someone else is feeling. It comes from becoming so familiar and so openhearted and so honest about who you are and what you do that you begin to understand humanness altogether and you can speak appropriately to the situation.

The basic ground of compassionate action is the importance of working *with* rather than struggling *against,* and what I mean by that is working with your own unwanted, unacceptable stuff, so that when the unacceptable and un-wanted appears out *there,* you relate to it based on having worked with loving-kindness for yourself. Then there is no condescension. This nondualistic approach is true to the heart because it's based on our kinship with each other. We know what to say, because we have experienced closing down, shutting off, being angry, hurt, rebellious, and so forth, and have made a relationship with those things in ourselves.

This is not about problem resolution. This is a more open-ended and coura-geous approach. It has to do with not knowing what will happen. It has noth-ing to do with wanting to get ground under your feet. It's about keeping your heart and your mind open to whatever arises, without hope of fruition. Problem solving is based first on thinking there is a problem and second on thinking there is a solution. The concepts of problem and solution can keep us stuck in thinking that there is an enemy and a saint or a right way and a wrong way.

36. The Cloud of Unknowing by William Johnston

Of the many qualities of inner knowing, love is for some the only aspect of consciousness worth knowing about. This is the belief of the anonymous author of the medieval Christian document The Cloud of Unknowing, *an enduring classic of contemplative heart-based practice.*

How the work of contemplation shall be done; of its excellence over all other works.

THIS IS WHAT you are to do: lift your heart up to the Lord, with a gentle stirring of love desiring him for his own sake and not for his gifts. Center all your attention and desire on him and let this be the sole concern of your mind and heart. Do all in your power to forget everything else, keeping your thoughts and desires free from involvement with any of God's creatures or their affairs whether in general or in particular. Perhaps this will seem like an irresponsible attitude, but I tell you, let them all be; pay no attention to them.

What I am describing here is the contemplative work of the spirit. It is this which gives God the greatest delight. For when you fix your love on him, forgetting all else, the saints and angels rejoice and hasten to assist you in every way—though the devils will rage and ceaselessly conspire to thwart you. Your fellow men are marvelously enriched by this work of yours, even if you may not fully understand how; the souls in purgatory are touched, for their suffering is eased by the effects of this work: and, of course, your own spirit is purified and strengthened by this contemplative work more than by all others put together.[1] Yet for all this, when God's grace arouses you to enthusiasm, it becomes the lightest sort of work there is and one most willingly done. Without his grace, however, it is very difficult and almost, I should say, quite beyond you.

And so diligently persevere until you feel joy in it. For in the beginning it is usual to feel nothing but a kind of darkness about your mind, or as it were, *a cloud of unknowing.* You will seem to know nothing and to feel nothing except a naked intent toward God in the depths of your being. Try as you might, this darkness and this cloud will remain between you and your God.[2] You will feel frustrated, for your mind will be unable to grasp him, and your heart will not relish the delight of his love. But learn to be at home in this darkness. Return to it as often as you can, letting your spirit cry out to him whom you love. For if, in this life, you hope to feel and see God as he is in himself it must be within this darkness and this cloud.[3] But if you strive to fix your love on him forgetting all else, which is the work of contemplation I have urged you to begin, I am confident that God in his goodness will bring you to a deep experience of himself.[4]

Of the simplicity of contemplation; that it may not be
acquired through knowledge or imagination.

I have described a little of what is involved in the contemplative work but now I shall discuss it further, insofar as I understand it, so that you may proceed securely and without misconceptions.

This work is not time-consuming even though some people believe otherwise. Actually it is the shortest you can imagine; as brief as an atom,[5] which, as the philosophers say, is the smallest division of time. The atom is a moment so short and integral that the mind can scarcely conceive it. Nevertheless it is vastly important, for of this minute measure of time it is written: "You will be held responsible for all the time given you." This is entirely just because your principal spiritual faculty, the will, needs only this brief fraction of a moment to move toward the object of its desire.

If you were now restored by grace to the integrity man possessed before sin you would be complete master of these impulses. None would ever go astray, but would fly to the one sole good, the goal of all desire, God himself. For God created us in his image and likeness, making us like himself, and in the Incarnation he emptied himself of his divinity becoming a man like us. It is God, and he alone, who can fully satisfy the hunger and longing of our spirit which transformed by his redeeming grace is enabled to embrace him by love. He whom neither men nor angels can grasp by knowledge can be embraced by love. For the intellect of both men and angels is too small to comprehend God as he is in himself.[6]

Try to understand this point. Rational creatures such as men and angels possess two principal faculties, a knowing power and a loving power. No one can fully comprehend the uncreated God with his knowledge;[7] but each one, in a different way,[8] can grasp him fully through love. Truly this is the unending miracle of love: that one loving person, through his love, can embrace God, whose being fills and transcends the entire creation. And this marvelous work of love goes on forever, for he whom we love is eternal. Whoever has the grace to appreciate the truth of what I am saying, let him take my words to heart, for to experience this love is the joy of eternal life while to lose it is eternal torment.

He who with the help of God's grace becomes aware of the will's constant movements and learns to direct them toward God will never fail to taste something of heaven's joy even in this life and, certainly in the next, he will savor it fully.[9] Now do you see why I rouse you to this spiritual work? You would have taken to it naturally had man not sinned, for man was created to love and everything else was created to make love possible.[10] Nevertheless, by the work of contemplative love man will be healed.[11] Failing in this work he sinks deeper into sin further and further from God, but by persevering in it he gradually rises from sin and grows in divine intimacy.

Therefore, be attentive to time and the way you spend it. Nothing is more precious. This is evident when you recall that in one tiny moment heaven may be gained or lost. God, the master of time, never gives the future. He gives only the present, moment by moment, for this is the law of the created order, and God will not contradict himself in his creation. Time is for man, not man for time. God, the Lord of nature, will never anticipate man's choices which follow one after another in time. Man will not be able to excuse himself at the last judgment, saying to God: "You overwhelmed me with the future when I was only capable of living in the present."

But now I see that you are discouraged and are saying to yourself: "What am I to do? If all he says is true, how shall I justify my past? I am twenty-four years old and until this moment I have scarcely noticed time at all. What is worse, I could not repair the past even if I wanted to, for according to his teaching such a task is impossible to me by nature even with the help of ordinary grace. Besides I know very well that in the future, either through frailty or laziness, I will probably not be any more attentive to the present moment than I have been in the past. I am completely discouraged. Please help me for the love of Jesus."

Well have you said "for the love of Jesus." For it is in his love that you will find help. In love all things are shared and so if you love Jesus, everything of his is yours. As God he is the creator and dispenser of time; as man he consciously mastered time; as God and man he is the rightful judge of men and their use of time. Bind yourself to Jesus, therefore, in faith and love, so that belonging to him you may share all he has and enter the fellowship of those who love him. This is the communion of the blessed and these will be your friends: our Lady, St. Mary, who was full of grace at every moment; the angels, who are unable to waste time; and all the blessed in heaven and on earth, who through the grace of Jesus employ every moment in love.[12] See, here is your strength. Understand what I am saying and be heartened. But remember, I warn you of one thing above all. No one can claim true fellowship with Jesus, his Mother, the angels, and the saints, unless he does all in his power with the help of grace to be mindful of time. For he must do his share however slight to strengthen the fellowship as it strengthens him.

And so do not neglect this contemplative work. Try also to appreciate its wonderful effects in your own spirit. When it is genuine it is simply a spontaneous desire springing suddenly toward God like spark from fire.[13] It is amazing how many loving desires arise from the spirit of a person who is accustomed to this work. And yet, perhaps only one of these will be completely free from attachment to some created thing. Or again, no sooner has a man turned toward God in love when through human frailty he finds himself distracted by the remembrance of some created thing or some daily care. But no matter. No harm is done; for such a person quickly returns to deep recollection.

And now we come to the difference between the contemplative work and its counterfeits such as daydreaming, fantasizing, or subtle reasoning. These originate in a conceited, curious, or romantic mind whereas the blind stirring of love springs from a sincere and humble heart. Pride, curiosity, and daydreaming must be sternly checked if the contemplative work is to be authentically conceived in singleness of heart. Some will probably hear about this work and suppose that by their own ingenious efforts they can achieve it. They are likely to strain their mind and imagination unnaturally only to produce a false work which is neither human nor divine. Truly, such a person is dangerously deceived. And I fear that unless God intervenes with a miracle inspiring him to abandon these practices and humbly seek reliable counsel he will most certainly fall into mental aberrations or some great spiritual evil of the devil's devising. Then he risks losing both body and soul eternally. For the love of God, therefore, be careful in this work and never strain your mind or imagination, for truly you will not succeed this way. Leave these faculties at peace.[14]

Do not suppose that because I have spoken of darkness and of a cloud I have in mind the clouds you see in an overcast sky or the darkness of your house when your candle fails. If I had, you could with a little imagination picture the summer skies breaking through the clouds or a clear light brightening the dark winter. But this isn't what I mean at all so forget this sort of nonsense. When I speak of darkness, I mean the absence of knowledge.[15] If you are unable to understand something or if you have forgotten it, are you not in the dark as regards this thing? You cannot see it with your mind's eye. Well, in the same way, I have not said "cloud," but *cloud of unknowing*. For it is a darkness of unknowing that lies between you and your God. . . .

A short explanation of contemplation in the form of a
dialogue.

Now you say, "How shall I proceed to think of God as he is in himself?" To this I can only reply, "I do not know."

With this question you bring me into the very darkness and *cloud of unknowing* that I want you to enter. A man may know completely and ponder thoroughly every created thing and its works, yes, and God's works, too, but not God himself. Thought cannot comprehend God. And so, I prefer to abandon all I can know, choosing rather to love him whom I cannot know. Though we cannot know him we can love him. By love he may be touched and embraced, never by thought. Of course, we do well at times to ponder God's majesty or kindness for the insight these meditations may bring. But in the real contemplative work you must set all this aside and cover it over with a *cloud of forgetting*. Then let your loving desire, gracious and devout, step bravely and joyfully beyond it and reach out to pierce the darkness above. Yes, beat upon that thick *cloud of unknowing* with the dart of your loving desire and do not cease come what may.

How a person should conduct himself during prayer with
regard to all thoughts, especially those arising from
curiosity and natural intelligence.

It is inevitable that ideas will arise in your mind and try to distract you in a thousand ways. They will question you saying, "What are you looking for, what do you want?" To all of them you must reply, "God alone I seek and desire, only him."

If they ask, "Who is this God?", tell them that he is the God who created you, redeemed you, and brought you to this work. Say to your thoughts, "You are powerless to grasp him. Be still." Dispel them by turning to Jesus with loving desire. Don't be surprised if your thoughts seem holy and valuable for prayer. Probably you will find yourself thinking about the wonderful qualities of Jesus, his sweetness, his love, his graciousness, his mercy. But if you pay attention to these ideas they will have gained what they wanted of you, and will go on chattering until they divert you even more to the thought of his passion. Then will come ideas about his great kindness, and if you keep listening they will be delighted. Soon you will be thinking about your sinful life and perhaps in this connection you will recall some place where you have lived in the past, until suddenly, before you know it, your mind is completely scattered.

And yet, they were not bad thoughts. Actually, they were good and holy thoughts, so valuable, in fact, that anyone who expects to advance without having meditated often on his own sinfulness, the Passion of Christ, and the kindness, goodness, and dignity of God, will most certainly go astray and fail in his purpose. But a person who has long pondered these things must eventually leave them behind beneath a *cloud of forgetting* if he hopes to pierce the *cloud of unknowing* that lies between him and his God. So whenever you feel drawn by grace to the contemplative work and are determined to do it, simply raise your heart to God with a gentle stirring of love. Think only of God, the God who created you, redeemed you, and guided you to this work. Allow no other ideas about God to enter your mind. Yet even this is too much. A naked intent toward God, the desire for him alone, is enough.

If you want to gather all your desire into one simple word that the mind can easily retain, choose a short word rather than a long one. A one-syllable word such as "God" or "love" is best. But choose one that is meaningful to you. Then fix it in your mind so that it will remain there come what may. This word will be your defense in conflict and in peace. Use it to beat upon the cloud of darkness above you and to subdue all distractions, consigning them to the *cloud of forgetting* beneath you. Should some thought go on annoying you demanding to know what you are doing, answer with this one word alone. If your mind begins to intellectualize over the meaning and connotations of this little word, remind yourself that its value lies in its simplicity. Do this and I assure you these thoughts will vanish. Why? Because you have refused to develop them with arguing.

37. The Heart: Threshold Between Two Worlds
by Kabir Helminski

Kabir Helminski, author, translator and Sufi shaikh of the Mevlevi dervish tradition, presents a traditional explanation of the heart's knowing. For him, the heart is an inner organ of perception that attends to the qualities of higher being. He writes: "A cheap, mass-produced teddy bear becomes an object of love because it has been qualified by the affection of a child's heart."

ANYONE WHO HAS probed the inner life, who has sat in silence long enough to experience the stillness of the mind behind its apparent noise, is faced with a mystery. Apart from all the outer attractions of life in the world, there exists at the center of human consciousness something quite satisfying in itself, a beauty without features. The mystery is not so much that these two dimensions exist—an outer world and the mystery of the inner world—but that we are suspended between them—as a space in which both worlds meet. It is as if the human being is the meeting point, the threshold between two worlds. Anyone who has explored this inwardness to a certain degree will know that it holds a great power. In fact, to be unaware of this mystery of inwardness is to be incomplete.

According to the great formulator of Sufi psychology, Al-Ghazalli:

> There is nothing closer to you than your self. If you don't know your self, how will you know others? You might say, "I know myself," but you are mistaken. . . . The only thing you know about your self is your physical appearance. The only thing you know about your inside (batin, your unconscious) is that when you are hungry you eat, when you are angry, you fight, and when you are consumed by passion, you make love. In this regard you are equal to any animal. You have to seek the reality within yourself. . . . What are you? Where have you come from and where are you going? What is your role in the world? Why have you been created? Where does your happiness lie? If you would like to know yourself, you should know that you are created by two things. One is your body and your outer appearance (zahir) which you can see with your eyes. The other is your inner forces (batin). This is the part you cannot see, but you can know with your insight. The reality of your existence is in your inwardness (batin, unconscious). Everything is a servant of your inward heart.

In Sufism, "knowing" can be arranged in seven stages. These stages offer a comprehensive view of the various faculties of knowledge within which the heart comprises the sixth level of knowing:

1. Hearing about something, knowing what it is called. "Someone who has learned to play music on a musical instrument is a musician."

2. Knowing through the perception of the senses. "I have seen a musician and heard music."

3. Knowing "about" something. "I have read some books about music and musicians."

4. Knowing through doing or being something. "I studied an instrument and became a musician."

5. Knowing through understanding and being able to apply that understanding. "I have mastered my instrument and taught others to be musicians."

6. Knowing through the subconscious faculties of the heart. "I play more than the notes on the page; I play from my heart."

7. Knowing through Spirit alone. This is much more difficult to describe, but in the moment when all separation dissolves, there is nothing that cannot be known.

The outer world of physical existence is perceived through the physical senses, through a nervous system that has been refined and purified by nature over millions of years. We can only stand in awe of this body's perceptive ability.

On the other hand, the mystery of the inner world is perceived through other even subtler senses. It is these "senses" that allow us to experience qualities like yearning, hope, and intimacy, or to perceive meaning and beauty, and to know our situation in the universe.

When our awareness is turned away from the physical senses and the field of conventional thoughts and emotions, we may find that we can sense an inner world of spiritual qualities, independent of the outer world.

Our modern languages lack precision when it comes to naming or describing that perceptive capacity which can grasp the qualities of this inner world. Perhaps the best word we have is "heart." Used rather loosely, a look at Webster's Dictionary offers these definitions of heart among others: The seat of the emotions and will; the inmost conscious; the vital or most essential part; secret meaning.

In the vocabulary of Sufism, which derives chiefly from the Qur'an and the sayings of Muhammad, the heart is not a vague or accidental term, but a precise term, and one rich with meaning. Some hearts are described as diseased or hardened, while some are "humble before the unseen." One of the axioms of the tradition is expressed in this saying of God: "The heavens and the earth cannot contain Me; only the *heart* of My faithful servant can contain Me."

The Sufi is someone who approaches the Divine Reality through the heart. The heart is an intelligence beyond intellect, a knowing that operates at a subconscious level, the only human faculty expansive enough to embrace the infinite qualities of the universe. Intellect can take us only so far; it can *think* about faith, hope, and love, for instance, but it cannot entirely *experience* these qualities. This is the function of the heart. The heart is the faculty of knowing that can apprehend a qualitative universe.

A UNIVERSE OF QUALITIES

The heart is the perceiver of qualities. If we say for instance that a certain book has a particular number of pages on a certain subject by a particular author, we have described its distinguishing outer characteristics. If we say, however, that the book is inspiring, depressing, boring, fascinating, profound, trivial, or humorous, we are describing qualities. Although qualities seem to be subjective and have their reality in an invisible world, they are more essential, more valuable, because they determine our relationship to a thing. Qualities modify things. But where are qualities experienced if not within ourselves? The significant question is this: Is our inner world completely subjective, that is to say, contained within the individual mind? Or are qualities, somehow, the objective features of another "world," another state of being?

According to the understanding of Sufism, Reality possesses qualities, or attributes. All of material existence manifests these qualities, but the qualities exist *prior* to their manifestation in material forms. Forms manifest the qualities of an invisible dimension, a "higher world." A cosmic creativity is overflowing with qualities, and these qualities eventually manifest as the world of material forms.

The human being, living both in an outer and an inner world, is a conscious instrument of that cosmic creativity. The human heart is a kind of mirror in which divine qualities and significances may appear. Those qualities are as much within the heart as within the outer thing that awakens those qualities in the heart. The divine qualities are primary; the heart is the interior mirror, and the world is the outer mirror that reflects the heart's projections of these divine qualities.

We human beings have a capacity to project qualities onto things. A cheap, mass-produced teddy-bear becomes an object of love because it has been lent qualities by the affection of a child's heart. Things lose or gain importance for us as they are qualified by qualities whose immediate source is the human heart but whose ultimate source are the divine qualities themselves.

This subject may seem abstract and elusive because we are so conditioned to attributing qualities to the things and events of the world. In so doing, we overlook the fact that everything of true significance is happening *within* us. When a parent loves a child, for instance, the parent's capacity for love is projected upon the child. The love itself is a quality that preexists in a greater reality upon which both parent and child depend. We live in a universe of Love. That love is pouring through us and being discovered in all the objects of our love.

So far we have proposed that:

1. We live in a universe that is not only material and quantitative, but qualitative as well, and that the heart is the organ of perception for this qualitative universe. Furthermore,

2. Every quality that the human being recognizes in the world of outer appearances is derived first of all from the inner knowing of its own heart, which contains a complete sampling of the universe of qualities.

The significant conclusion we can draw is that while the mirror of the world can reveal to us what the heart itself contains, the qualities themselves are latent within the heart. All of outer existence is merely a pretext for revealing to us what the heart itself encompasses.

We have proposed that the heart includes a spectrum of subtle faculties for knowing reality immediately and qualitatively. In other words, the heart is intuitive. The heart, however, is obscured, or "veiled" from its intuitive knowing by much of our habitual thoughts and emotions, and particularly in so far as these are derived from the distortions of ego.

How can we know whether we are following the concealed desire of the false self or the guidance of the heart? The ego desires multiplicity and suffers the fragmentation caused by the conflicting attractions of the world. In the condition we find ourselves, our confused discernment continually faces ambiguous situations.

Reason, which is the wise and skillful use of the conscious mind, can be used to clear the mirror of the heart from the distortions of compulsion, defensiveness, and illusion. To some extent this is the work of a true psychotherapy.

But while the effects of past wounds can be mitigated by making psychological patterns more conscious, a true spirituality can awaken the healing qualities contained within the heart: humbleness, gratitude, and love.

However, for these qualities to be authentic and spontaneous, and not merely the outcome of a moral obligation, it is necessary to establish a rapport with Spirit, which is the source of these qualities, deep within the heart. Spirit, here, can be imagined as a nondimensional point contained within the heart.

THE MIDPOINT BETWEEN EGO AND SPIRIT

Now we must make a further clarification in our practical understanding of the heart. For most people, the ego-self is constructed from and identified with the outer world. The ego is our attempt to attain control and security as a separate entity. An extreme example of this is the materialistic person who believes only in tangible existence and seeks satisfaction through the acquisition of things and security through power over the world. If ego is the part of ourselves most identified with outer existence, and if in our most inner point we are one with Spirit, then the heart with all its subtle faculties is the midpoint between the two. Like a transformer, the heart receives the energy of the Spirit and conveys it to the ego-self, which is transformed through this relationship.

But if the heart is dominated by the demands of the ego-self, the heart is, in a sense, not a heart at all. But when the heart orients itself toward Spirit, which exists like a nondimensional point within the heart, it discovers within itself objective and essential qualities such as faith, hope, patience, generosity, humility, and love. To the extent that it is receptive, the heart receives the qualities of Spirit and distributes these to all of our human faculties, from where these qualities can radiate to the rest of creation.

A person of "heart" is someone primarily concerned with the cultivation of qualities and meaning. Such a person can trust in the qualitative universe, the beneficent and meaningful order that lies behind outer appearances. Such a person, therefore, lives in a different reality from the materialist. Everything that happens, happens within this boundless Affection. Even the self's preoccupations, our petty thoughts and emotions, are seen within this context.

The heart is the center of the individual psyche. It is suspended in a dynamic tension between the two poles of ego and Spirit. It is through the mediation of the heart that the completion of the human psyche is attained.

The heart always has an object of love; it is always attracted to some sign of beauty. Rumi said, "If your thought is a rose, you are the rose garden. If your thought is a thorn, you are kindling for the bath stove."[1] Suspended between the attractions of the physical world and the ego, on the one hand, and spirit and its qualities on the other, the heart is pulled from different sides. But behind all these various attractions lies one great Attractor. Rumi addressed this issue in a conversation recorded and presented in *Fihi ma fihi*[2] (Herein is what is herein):

> All desires, affections, loves, and fondnesses people have for all sorts of things, such as fathers, mothers, friends, the heavens and the earth, gardens, pavilions, works, knowledge, food, and drink—one should realize that every desire is a desire for food, and such things are all "veils." When one passes beyond this world and sees that King without these "veils," then one will realize that all those things were "veils" and "coverings" and that what they were seeking was in reality one thing. All problems will then be solved. All the heart's questions and difficulties will be answered, and everything will become clear. God's reply is not such that He must answer each and every problem individually. With one answer all problems are solved.[3]

There are countless attractions in the world of multiplicity. Whatever we give our attention to, its qualities will become our qualities. If we give the heart to multiplicity, the heart will be fragmented and dispersed. If we give the heart to spiritual unity, the heart will be unified. Ultimately the heart's desire is unity in which it finds peace.

Truly, in the remembrance of God hearts find rest.[4]

OUTER AND INNER

The heart allows us to sense a meaningful order behind appearances. We may, then, begin to wonder if there is a reason for our being embodied. Were we brought into the world only in order to escape it? The perspective of Sufism is always one of unifying all levels of existence, from the material to the spiritual.

In this life, no pleasure is entirely physical or spiritual, outer or inner. The most outer, material pleasures would mean nothing if there were not some qualities of personal relationship, anticipation, and other associations. Likewise for a living human being, the most spiritual pleasure is nevertheless experienced through the agency of the human nervous system. We experience the spiritual qualities as states of relaxation, of heart expansion, of coming alive.

The word for heart in Arabic is "qalb" and literally means that which fluctuates; the heart expands and contracts, and even in its purified condition passes through many states.

Ibn 'Arabi says:

> God made the heart the locus of longing to bring actualization of His reality near to the human being, since there is fluctuation in the heart. If this longing were in the rational faculty, the person might seem to be in a constant state. But since it is in the heart, fluctuation comes upon him always. For the heart is between the two fingers of the Compassionate, so its situation is not to remain in a single state. (II 532.30)

The heart experiences constant expansion and contraction, but if the heart is awake, it begins to grasp the Divine through the intoxication of expansion and the aridity of contraction. The heart is always occupied with some object of longing through which it is coming to know the qualities of spiritual life.

PURITY OF HEART

The subtle faculties of the heart are our deepest knowing. That knowing is frequently veiled, or confused by more superficial levels of the mind: by opinions, by desires, by social conditioning, and especially by our fears. The mirror of the heart may be obscured by the veils of conditioned thought, by the soot of emotions, by the corrosion of negative attitudes. In fact we easily confuse the ego's emotions with the feelings of the heart. Typically, in the name of following our hearts, we actually follow the desires and fears of the ego. It may also be that certain people glorify and celebrate their personal emotions and mistake these for the heart, but a highly emotional person—reacting from the limited perspective of the small self—is not necessarily a person of heart. One can be quite emotional and yet be out of touch with one's own heart.

The heart may be sensitive or numb, awake or asleep, healthy or sick, whole or broken, open or closed. In other words, its perceptive ability will depend on its capacity and condition.

Purity of the heart refers to the heart's overall soundness and health. The heart, if it is truly a heart, is in contact with Spirit. Traditional teachers agree that one of the consequences of preoccupation with "the world and the worldly" is the death of the heart. If the heart assumes the qualities of whatever attracts it, its attraction to the dense matter of the world results at best in a limited reflection of the divine reality. At worst, the heart's involvement with the purely physical aspects of existence results in the familiar compulsions of ego: sex, wealth, and power.

Sufi wisdom offers cures for an ailing heart.

The first and most important of these is the *zhikr,* the remembrance of God. Zhikr is a state of conscious presence and invocation of God. The purpose of this remembrance is to bring "light" into the heart in order that the heart may function as a perceptive organ.

Another is contemplating the meanings of the revealed books of the sacred traditions, and the words of the saints, since these perform an action upon the heart, removing its illusions, healing its ills, restoring its strength. The same function can be served by inspired art, literature, and music, which also performs an action upon us.

Another cure for the heart is keeping one's stomach empty. An excess of food hardens the heart. Fasting is the opposite of the subtle and not so subtle addictions with which we numb ourselves to the experience of heart. When through fasting we expose the heart's pain to ourselves, we become more emotionally vulnerable and honest. Only then can the heart be healed.

Keeping a night vigil and prayer before sunrise have been mainstays of the Sufis. In these early morning hours the activity of the world has been reduced to its minimum, the psychic atmosphere has become still, and we are more able to reach the depths of concentration upon our own unconscious.

Finally, keeping company with "heart" people can restore faith and health to the heart. "The best among you are those who when seen remind you of God."[5]

It is only a matter of degree to move from the ailing heart to the purified heart. This eventual purification could be understood to proceed through four primary activities or stages:

Liberating oneself from psychological distortions and complexes that prevent forming a healthy, integrated individuality.

Freeing oneself from the slavery to the attractions of the world, all of which are secondary reflections of the qualities within the heart, itself.

Transcending the subtlest veil, or illusion, which is the self and its selfishness.

Centering oneself and all one's attention in the reality of divine Love, which has the power to unify our fragmented being and reconnect us with the unified field of all levels of existence.

The first three stages—minimizing our psychological distortions, overcoming the slavery of our attractions, and seeing beyond the veil of selfishness—prepare us for making our contact with the divine reality of Love. Without the power of Love, we can only follow our egos and the desires of the world. Without the centering power of Love recognized by the heart, we suffer fragmentation, dispersion in the multiplicity. To work on transforming the ego from within the ego is a tedious and discouraging process. But if we can bring the ego, the intellect, and the emotions into the boundlessness of the heart, this places them in a truer context. To view them apart from the heart is to view them in a partial or distorted context. Much of our human foolishness is the result of our mind and feelings being divorced from our hearts, divorced from our love.

An essential practice is to bring the thinking-mind down into the heart, to submerge it in the heart space, and thus to bring reason and heart into unity. Then, in that state, we may discover a deep receptivity to infinite spiritual Presence. When we can center ourselves and our attention on the presence of the Divine Reality, we not only become unified within ourselves, we recognize our unity with all of Life. This is the unifying function of the heart.

THE SUBTLE ORGANS OF KNOWLEDGE

The Sufi schools sometimes delineate the subtle intelligence of the heart into various modes of knowing. What are called in some schools the *latifas* (literally, the subtleties, *al-lataif*) are faculties that allow us to know spiritual realities beyond what the senses or intellect can offer.

The latifas are developed by carrying the light-energy of *zhikr* (the spiritual practices of remembrance) to precise locations in the chest and head in order to energize and activate the faculties. It is, of course, impossible to exactly define these faculties, themselves, although they can be verified by personal experience. The first five stages of knowing are really refinements of one another: Qalb contains Ruh, Ruh has the inner dimension of Sirr, and so on. When enough spiritual refinement is realized, it is used to transform the self (nafs). Whether we understand these to be a literal anatomy of the subtle nervous system or metaphors for our spiritual capacities, the seven *latifas* and their functions are:

1. *Qalb* (Heart).[6] Through this faculty we begin opening to an inner spaciousness. At this stage we purify our emotional life, and we come in touch with a sense of essential, objective hope.

2. *Ruh* (Spirit). With the awakening to Ruh, we discover that the heart contains a point of contact with the infinite dimension of Spirit, the source of all qualities. If we can allow Spirit to rule our hearts, instead of ego, a new life flows in. At this stage we begin to purify ourselves of mental distractions and projections. We dissolve self-images and our narcissistic fictions. We learn to keep our thought processes in alignment with the divine reality.

3. *Sirr* (Secret). With the awakening of Sirr we begin to discern the Real from the illusory. We strengthen our faith and trust in the divine reality through a more conscious relationship with it. We begin to see the divine reality more clearly in the multiplicity of forms.

4. *Khafi* (Hidden). With the discovery of Khafi we recognize that everything we long for is infinitely close. Infinite possibilities are contained within a dimensionless point accessible to us within our own heart.

5. *Sirr al Asraar* (Secret of the Secrets). With the attainment of the Secret of Secrets we know ourselves as a reflection of the Divine. We are elevated to Unity. The Sufi never claims identity with God; rather he (or she) understands his servanthood to be subsumed in God.

6. *Nafs* (Soul/Self). Nafs is also the word for the untransformed ego, but here it refers to a new relationship to our selfhood. At this stage we bring all of the first five qualities and capacities "down" into our individuality. We embody Spirit more fully and begin to radiate the divine qualities.

7. *Haqq* (Truth). At this stage we are further expanded, realizing our identity with all levels of Being, knowing the truth of the Quranic statement: "Wheresoever you look is the Face of God." This latifa could be understood as the final perceptual organ of unity and wholeness, the unitive "sense."

CONCLUSION

The heart can be understood as an aggregation of qualitative, subconscious faculties, which function in a unified way. Once activated, these faculties support and illuminate each other, much as eye-hand coordination is superior to either touch or sight alone. While these functions seem to be separate, they serve a unifying purpose, which is to know the nondual reality beyond multiplicity. They are the subtle nervous system's means of realizing unity.

The fathoming of the human heart and the spiritual qualities it contains is the work of all life, art, spirituality. It is possible to know the heart without the veils of our fears, preoccupations, desires, and strategies. The purification of the heart is a comprehensive education that has physical, intellectual, psychological, and moral dimensions.

In its purified state, the human heart is the hologram of the seen and unseen worlds; it is the part that reflects the whole. The heart is the point at which the individual human being is closest to the Divine. Sufi tradition expresses it this way: The heart is the throne of the All-Merciful Spirit: when the heart is pure, it is guided directly by the Divine Intelligence.

The heart is the center of our motivation and our knowing, possessing a depth and strength of will that the personality lacks. When we say that the heart has an integrative power, we are not talking in abstract, metaphorical, or merely intellectual terms. The realization and purification of the heart both opens a doorway to the Infinite, and also results in a restructuring of neural pathways, a refinement and reorganization of our entire nervous system, which allows the fullest expression of our human possibilities.

38. Epilogue: The Old Man and the Tree
by Mark Robert Waldman

My heart center activated when I read this piece—a sudden total focus on the hole in my chest—and the familiar dart of burning. I remember thinking that the inner perceptions of body, heart, and a quiet mind are what remain at the end of life, when all that we have ever loved accumulates to help us.

ONCE THERE WAS a very old man who lived in the middle of an ancient forest. For many years he lived alone, for his wife had died and his children had grown and moved to the town at the edge of the woods.

"Now it is my time to go," he said to the birds who came to perch by his window. "I must prepare." And so the old man picked up his axe and hobbled into the deepest part of the forest. Soon he found what he was seeking: a stately elderberry tree he had sown from seed when he was just a little boy. "Your strength will be my vessel to hold this frail body of mine," he spoke unto the tree. And then he took his axe and felled it, carving himself a handsome box in which to lie. Slowly he carried the hollowed tree to a clearing next to his cottage.

For the next three days he fasted, and set the house in order. He laid out his finest garments and took a long hot bath with herbs and oil. Carefully he dressed, and as he closed the door tears swelled up within him. "Goodbye, dear house," he whispered. "You have served my family well."

He walked to the clearing and laid himself down inside the tree. "Now I am ready," he said to the heavens, and began to sing a song.

Suddenly a great wind arose, roaring through the branches, nearly overturning the old man and his coffin. Terrified, he watched as an enormous winged creature descended from the sky, part woman and part bird, standing more than twenty feet tall with wings that were as broad as her height. She leaned towards the shivering man and touched his heart with her beak. "Ah, you are so very warm!" Her voice was radiant.

"What kind of demon are you?" cried out the man, who had nowhere left to hide.

"I am a messenger from the Angel of Death," sung the birdlike woman, "but you are not quite ready to eat, for your heart is empty and sad."

"I am just a poor old man who is lonely and ready to die. My life is done and empty, for my wife and children have gone, and all my work is complete."

"Yes," spoke the strangely beautiful creature. "I see you've put your house in order, but I shall not take you with an empty heart. You shall turn to dust and never see my world."

"But I have lived an honest life," pleaded the man. "I've done no harm to others and have given charitably to those in need. I have cared for my wife and children and provided them with all they needed for a good and happy life."

"All this is true," spoke the wise and knowing beast, "but you have not felt the joys of life."

When the man heard these words he burst into tears, knowing that the angel was right. "Oh, how I wish I could feel such joy," sobbed the man in a torrent of self-pity. And the great winged woman again leaned forward and drove her beak deep into the heart of the man. The old man tried to scream, but instead of sound a thousand sparrows flew out of his mouth and blotted out the sun. Spinning in a sea of wings, the old man felt a burning fire rush through his blood and veins, and when it reached his brain he thought he'd lose all consciousness. He felt a great explosion which blinded him from the light.

"Alas, I am surely doomed," thought the trembling man, but when the smoke receded he found himself beside his dying wife. "Oh!" gasped the man, as he gazed upon her delicate body. "How much I loved you, but I could not shed a tear." And then his heart opened up, bursting with love, and the soul of his wife slipped into his own. "Now my heart is warm and full," thought the man. "Certainly the messenger will take me now." But instead he felt a tearing in his being and felt the terrible blackness overhead. This time he could not stand it and he fainted straight away.

When he awoke, he found himself a young and handsome man. "Where am I now?" wondered the old man in a young man's body. But the meadow was so magnificent that he could not resist the flowers. Filling his hands with poppies and lilacs, he ran across the field and into the country church. There he saw his bride-to-be, dressed in fine white silk and satin. All time stood still as once again he savored that wonderful moment in life. He remembered the birth of his children, emerging from the womb into the arms of mother and father, and his heart was filled with pride.

"Certainly now I must be full, for I have witnessed the miracle of birth, the rapture of marriage, and the mystery of death. I have smelt the flowers and have been touched by the secrets of nature. Now I am ready to go." But again the cold black darkness engulfed the little man.

He awoke once more, a young boy, walking with his father to plant the seeds of an elderberry tree. Once again he knelt and felt the loamy soil in his hands as he buried all the seeds. He took his father's hand and listened once again to those forgotten words: "You have given birth to this tree as I have given birth to you, and when you come to play this tree will hold you in its limbs. One day, the time will come when it shall embrace and carry you to a land unknown by you or me." In that moment he knew his father's love.

Suddenly, the old man found himself back inside the coffin, embraced by the tree he had grown and cared for. For every year the tree had lived he could remember the fullness of his own. Now he truly knew his life, of its sorrows and its joys, of its richness and its mysteries. He lay there humbled, grateful in his newfound wisdom.

"Thank you, oh creature of tomorrow," spoke the gentle man, "for granting me illumination." And at that very moment the great winged woman opened her beak and swallowed up the man.

All throughout the forest the animals rejoiced.

Notes

4. Walsh, "Hidden Wisdom"

1. Zimmer, H. *Philosophies of India.* Princeton: Princeton University Press, 1969.
2. Walsh, R. Can Western philosophers understand Asian philosophies? *Crosscurrents* 34 (1989): 281–99, 1989.
3. Nyanaponika Thera. *Abhidharma Studies.* Kandi, Sri Lanka: Buddhist Publication Society, 1976, p. 7.
4. Radhakrishnan. *Indian Philosophy.* Vol. I. 1929. Reprint. Bombay: Blackie & Sons, 1940, p. 43.
5. Vimilo, B. *Awakening to the Truth.* Visaka Puja, Thailand: Buddhist Assoc., 1974, p. 73.
6. Huxley, A. *The Perennial Philosophy.* New York: Harper & Row, 1945, p. vii.
7. Schumacher, E. F. *A Guide for the Perplexed.* New York: Harper & Row, 1977, pp. 61, 42, 43.

5. Vaughan and Walsh, "Technology of Transcendence"

1. Freud, S. *A General Introduction to Psychoanalysis.* Garden City, N.Y.: Garden City Publishers, 1917, p. 252.
2. Prabhavananda, S., and Isherwood, C. (Trans.). *The Song of God: Bhagavad Gita.* Hollywood: Vedanta Press, 1944, p. 85.
3. Ram Dass. *Association for Transpersonal Psychology Newsletter,* 1975, p. 9.
4. Plato. *The Republic.* Trans. F. Cornford. Oxford: Oxford University Press, 1945, p. 516.
5. Ramana Maharshi. *Who Am I?* (Trans. T. Venkataran.) 8th ed. India, 1955.
6. Gampopa. *The Jewel Ornament of Liberation.* Trans. H. Guenther, Boston: Shambhala, 1971, p. 271.
7. Schumacher, E. F. *Small Is Beautiful: Economics as If People Mattered.* New York: Harper & Row, 1973, p. 67.
8. James, W. *Talks to Teachers on Psychology and to Students on Some of Life's Ideals.* 1899. New York: Dover, 1962, p. 51.
9. James, W. *Principles of Psychology.* 1910. New York: Dover, 1950, p. 424.
10. Ram Dass. *Journey of Awakening.* New York: Doubleday, 1978.
11. Walsh, R. *Meditation Research: Paths Beyond Ego.* Edited by Roger Walsh and Frances Vaughan. Los Angeles: Jeremy P. Tarcher, 1993, p. 60–66.

12. Schindler, C., and Lapid, G. *The Great Turning: Personal Peace, Global Victory.* Santa Fe: Bear and Company, 1989.

13. Hardy, T. *Collected Poems of Thomas Hardy.* New York: Macmillan, 1926, p. 154.

14. Wilber, K. *A Sociable God.* New York: McGraw-Hill, 1983.

15. Alexander, F. "Buddhist training as an artifical catatonia (the biological meaning of psychic occurrences)." *Psychoanalytic Review 18* (1931): 129–45.

16. Wilber, K. *The Atman Project.* Wheaton, IL: Quest, 1980, p. 155.

6. Hastings, "The Tradition of Oracles and Channels"

1. Vandenberg, P. *The Mystery of the Oracles.* New York: Macmillan, 1982, p. 20f.

2. *Ibid.*

3. Parke, H. W., & Wormell, D. E. W. *The Delphic Oracle* (two vols.). Oxford: Basil Blackwell, 1956.

4. Tart, C. *States of Consciousness.* New York: Dutton, 1975.

5. Glass, J. (Pseud. of Alice E. Corrall). *They Foresaw the Future: The Story of Fulfilled Prophecy.* New York: G. P. Putnam's Sons, 1969.

6. Vandenberg, P. *The Mystery of the Oracles,* p. 20f.

7. Herodotus. *The Histories of Herodotus* (Harry Carter, Trans.). New York: Heritage Press, 1958, p. 17.

8. Glass, J. *They Foresaw the Future.*

9. Govinda, Anagarika. *The Way of the White Clouds.* London: Rider, 1966, p. 185.

8. Jung, "Foreword to the *I Ching*"

1. Jung, C. F. "Synchronicity: An Acausal Connecting Principle," *The Structure and Dynamics of the Psyche* (Coll. Works of C. G. Jung, vol. 8).

2. Rhine, J. B. *The Reach of the Mind* (New York and London, 1928).

3. They are *shen,* that is "spirit-like." "Heaven produced the 'spirit-like things' " (Legge, p. 41).

4. For example, the *invidi* ("the envious") are a constantly recurring image in the old Latin books on alchemy, especially in the *Turba philosophorum* (11th or 12th century).

5. From the Latin *concipere,* "to take together," e.g., in a vessel: *concipere* derives from *capere,* "to take," "to grasp."

6. This is the classical etymology. The derivation of *religio* from *religare,* "bind to," originated with the Church Fathers.

7. I made this experiment before I actually wrote the foreword.

8. The Chinese interpret only the changing lines in the hexagram obtained by use of the oracle. I have found all the lines of the hexagram to be relevant in most cases.

9. Walsh, "Shamanism"

1. Merton, T. *The Way of Chuang Tzu.* New York: New Directions, 1969.

2. Rasmussen, K. *Intellectual Culture of the Iglulik Eskimos.* Copenhagen: Gyldendalske Boghandel, Nordisk Forlag, 1929.

3. Campbell, J. *The Inner Reaches of Outer Space: Metaphor as Myth and as Religion*. New York: Alfred van der Marck Editions, 1986.

4. Blacker, C. *The Catalpa Bow: A Study of Shamanistic Practices in Japan*. Boston: Allen & Unwin (1986).

5. Vaughan, F. *The Inward Arc: Healing and Wholeness in Psychotherapy and Spirituality*. Boston: New Science Library/Shambhala, 1986.

6. Bandura, A. *Social Foundations of Thought and Action*. Englewood Cliffs, NJ: Prentice-Hall, 1986.

7. Brown, D., and Engler, J. The stages of mindfulness meditation: A validation study. Part II. Discussion. In K. Wilber, J. Engler, and D. Brown (eds.). *Transformations of Consciousness: Conventional and Contemplative Perspectives on Development*. Boston: New Science Library/Shambhala, 1986, p. 214.

8. Blacker, C. *The Catalpa Bow*.

9. *Ibid.*, p. 23.

10. *Ibid.*, p. 88.

11. *Ibid.*, p. 91.

12. *Ibid.*, p. 92.

13. Rasmussen, K. *Intellectual Culture of the Iglulik Eskimos*. Copenhagen: Glydendalske Boghandel, Nordisk Forlag, 1929, p. 114.

14. *Ibid.*, pp. 118–119.

15. Walsh, R. Initial meditative experiences: Part I. *Journal of Transpersonal Psychology* 9, 1977, pp. 151–192. Quote on p. 161.

16. Freud, S. *A General Introduction to Psychoanalysis*. Garden City, NY: Garden City Publishers, 1917, p. 252.

17. Ramana Maharshi. *Who Am I?* 8th ed. (T. Venkataran, Trans.). India, 1955.

18. Rasmussen, K. *Across Arctic America*. New York: G. P. Putnam, 1927, pp. 82–84.

19. Ostermann, H. *The Alaskan Eskimos, as described in the posthumous notes of Dr. Knud Rasmussen* (Report of the Fifth Thule Expedition, 1921–24, Vol. X, No. 3). Copenhagen: Nordisk Forlag, 1952, p. 99.

20. Yalom. I., *Existential Psychotherapy*. New York: Basic Books, 1980, p. 398.

10. Elkin, "Aboriginal Men of High Degree"

1. Elkin, A. P. "Primitive Medicine Men." *The Medical Journal of Australia* (November 30, 1935): 750–57.

2. Mr. Dunlop added, "from fear of death." I doubt this. He was dying under what he regarded as a sentence of death from the dream world and was not afraid.

3. This was the situation as I saw it during fieldwork in 1930. But migration from the tribal territories south and southwest of the Aranda had been going on for decades. See A. P. Elkin, "R. H. Mathews: His Contribution to Aboriginal Studies," *Oceania* 46, no. 3 (1976): 214, 218–20.

4. East of the Pidjina (the name for the Pidjandja-djara used in 1930 and earlier by the few white men who had anything to do with them), the Jankundja-djara (eastern

Musgraves to the Everard Ranges) and the Andakarinya were in this same arc of tribes. A. P. Elkin, "Kinship in South Australia," *Oceania* 10, no. 2:202, 204.

5. Rose, F. G. G. *The Wind of Change in Central Australia.* Berlin: Akademie-Verlag, 1965, pp. 86, 135. Professor Rose thought another man was also a doctor.

6. Brokensha, Peter. *The Pitjantjatjara and their Crafts,* pp. 11, 17, 19, 35. Also, Hamilton, Annette. *Socio-Cultural Factors in Health among the Pitjantjatjara,* pp. 1–18, n.d.

7. Lockwood, Douglas. *I, the Aboriginal,* Adelaide, Australia: Rigby, pp. 231–35.

8. *Ibid.,* pp. 226–28.

9. Waipuldanya attended in 1957 a conference in Noumea on hygiene among native peoples. He was impressed by one lecturer who "told us in great detail how native medical assistants could help in promoting health and hygiene among their own people." The lecturer also gave sound advice on getting the cooperation of tribal witch doctors. Lockwood, *I, the Aboriginal,* pp. 218–19.

10. Pulsford, R. L., and Cawte, J. *Health in a Developing Country.* Brisbane, Australia: Jacaranda, 1972.

13. Ullman, "Dreaming Consciousness"

1. Snyder, R. "Toward an evolutionary theory of dreaming." *American Journal of Psychiatry,* 123, 1996, pp. 121–136.
Tolaas, J. "REM sleep and the concept of vigilance." *Biological Psychiatry, 13,* 1978, pp. 135–148.
Ullman, M. "Dreaming, altered states of consciousness and the problem of vigilance." *Journal of Nervous and Mental Disorders,* 133, 1961, pp. 529–535.

2. Rycroft, C. *The Innocence of Dreams.* New York: Pantheon, 1979.

3. Chomsky, N. "On the nature of language." In S. R. Harnad, H. D. Steckliss, and J. Lancaster, eds., *Origin and Evolution of Language and Speech.* New York: New York Academy of Sciences, 1976, pp. 46–57.

4. Burrow, T. *Preconscious Foundations of Human Experience.* New York: Basic Books, 1964.

14. Fromm, "Psychoanalysis and the Art of Knowing"

1. We have no word to express this transformation. We could say "reversion of repressedness," or, more concretely, "awakening"; I propose the term "de-repression."

2. Cf. S. Ferenczi, *Collected Papers,* ed. by Clara Thompson (Basic Books, Inc.), and the excellent study of Ferenczi's ideas in Izette de Forest's *The Leaven of Love* (New York: Harper, 1954).

3. Cf. my paper on "The Limitations and Dangers of Psychology," published in *Religion and Culture,* ed. by W. Leibrecht (New York: Harper, 1959).

15. Dallett, "Active Imagination in Practice"

1. Hannah, B. "Some remarks on active imagination." *Spring* 1953: 38–58, p. 38.

2. Franz, M.-L. von. "On active imagination." In *Methods of Treatment in Analytical Psychology,* ed. I.F. Baker, pp. 88–89. Fellbach: Verlag Adolf Bonz, 1980, p. 88.

3. Jung, C.G. "Comentary on 'The secret of the golden flower.' " In *CollectedWorks,* vol. 13, pp. 1–56. Princeton: Princeton University Press, 1967, 1929, p. 16.

4. Jung, C.G. "The aims of psychotherapy." In *CollectedWorks,* vol. 16, pp. 36–52. New York: Pantheon, 1954, 1931, p. 46.

20. Goleman, "The Mechanics of Attention"

1. Erdelyi, Matthew Hugh. "A New Look at the New Look: Perceptual Defense and Vigilance," *Psychological Review 81* (1974), 19.

2. Norman, Donald A. "Toward a Theory of Memory and Attention," *Psychological Review* 75 (1968), 522–536.

21. Novak, "The Practice of Attention"

1. Benoit, H. *The Supreme Doctrine.* New York: Viking Press, 1959, p. 40.

2. Green, Arthur. *Your Word Is Fire.* New York: Schocken Books, 1977, pp. 15–16.

3. A concept for which we are indebted to Arthur I. Deikman in "Deautomatization and the Mystic Experience," *Psychiatry* 29 (1966): 324–338.

22. Csikszentmihalyi, "The Flow Experience"
References

Abrahams, G. *The Chess Mind.* London: Penguin, 1960.

Attneave, R. *Applications of Information Theory to Psychology.* New York: Henry Holt, 1959.

Beach, F. A. "Current concepts of play in animals." *American Naturalist,* 1945, 79, 523–541.

Bekoff, M. "The development of social interaction, play, and metacommunication in mammals: An ethological perspective." *Quarterly Review* of Biology, 1972, 47 (4), 412–434.

Berger, P., & Luckmann, T. *The Social Construction of Reality.* Garden City, New York: Doubleday, 1967.

Berlyne, D. E. *Conflict, Arousal and Curiosity.* New York: McGraw-Hill, 1960.

Bhagavad Gita, Juan Mascaro (Trans.), Harmondsworth: Penguin, 1962.

Brown, N. O. *Life against Death.* Middleton, Conn.: Wesleyan University Press, 1959.

Callois, R. *Les Jeaux et les Hommes.* Paris: Gallimard, 1958.

Csikszentmihalyi, M., & Bennett, S. H. "An exploratory model of play." *American Anthropologist,* 1971, 73 (1), 45–58.

de Charms, R. *Personal Causation.* New York: Academic Press, 1968.

Deren, M. *Divine Horseman.* London: Thames and Hudson, 1953.

Dillon, J. T. Approaches to the study of problem-finding behavior. Unpublished manuscript, The University of Chicago, 1972.

Dostoevski, F. M. *Letters*. New York: Horizon, 1961.

Eibi-Eibesbeldt, I. *Ethology:The Biology of Behavior*. New York: Holt, Rinehart and Winston, 1970.

Eliade, M. *Yoga: Immortality and Freedom*. Princeton: Princeton University Press, 1969.

Erikson, E. H. *Childhood and Society*. New York: Norton, 1950.

Fagen, R. "Selective and evolutionary aspects of animal play." *The American Naturalist*, 1974, 108, 850–858.

Freud, S. *The Ego and the Id*. London: Allen and Unwin, 1927.

Getzels, J. W., & Csikszentmihalyi, M. Creative problem-finding: A longitudinal study with artists. Unpublished manuscript, University of Chicago, 1974.

Ghiselin, B. (ed.). *The Creative Process*. New York: Mentor, 1952.

Herrigel, E. *Zen in the Art of Archery*. New York: Pantheon, 1953.

Huizinga, J. *Homo Ludens*. Boston: Beacon Press, 1950.

Jewell, P. A., & Loizos, C. "Play, exploration and territoriality in mammals." *Symposia of the Zoological Society*, London, 1966, 18.

Kenyon, G. S. "Six scales for assessing attitude toward physical activity." In W. P. Morgan (Ed.). *Contemporary Readings in Sport Psychology*. Springfield, Illinois:Thomas, 1970.

Laski, M. *Ecstasy: A Study of Some Secular and Religious Experiences*. Bloomington, Ind.: Indiana University Press, 1962.

Mackay, D. H. *Information, Mechanism and Meaning*. Cambridge: MIT Press, 1969.

Maslow, A. *Toward a Psychology of Being*. Princeton, New Jersey:Van Nostrand, 1962.

Maslow, A. "Humanistic science and transcendent experiences." *Journal of Humanistic Psychology*, 1965, 5 (2), 219–227.

Maslow, A. *The Farther Reaches of Human Nature*. New York:Viking, 1971.

Mead, G. H. *Mind, Self, and Society*. Chicago:The University of Chicago Press, 1934.

Moltman, J. *Theology of Play*. New York: Harper and Row, 1972.

Montmasson, J. M. *Invention and the Unconscious*. New York: Harcourt, Brace, 1939.

Murphy, M. *Gold and the Kingdom*. New York:Viking, 1972.

Naranjo, C., & Ornstein, R. E. *On the Psychology of Meditation*. New York:Viking, 1971.

Piaget, J. *Play, Dreams and Imitation in Childhood*. New York: Norton, 1951.

Piaget, J. *The Moral Judgment of the Child*. New York:The Free Press, 1965.

Rahner, H. *Man at Play*. New York: Herder and Herder, 1967.

Roberts, J. M., Arth, M. S., & Bush, R. "Games in culture." *American Anthropologist*, 1959, 61, 597–605.

Roberts, J. M., & Sutton-Smith, B. "Child training and game involvement." *Ethnology*, 1962, 1 (2), 166–185.

Roberts, J. M., & Sutton-Smith, B. "Cross-cultural correlates of games of chance." *Behavior Science Notes*, 1966, 3, 131–144.

Sartre, J. P. *Being and Nothingness*. New York: Philosophical Library, 1956.

Schiller, C. F. *Essays Aesthetical and Philosophical*. London: Bell, 1884.

Steiner, G. "Fields of force." *The New Yorker*, Oct. 28, 1972, 42–117.

Sutton-Smith, B. "Play, games, and controls." In J. P. Scott & S. F. Scott, (Eds.), *Social Control and Social Change*. Chicago: The University of Chicago Press, 1971.

Turner, V. *The Ritual Process*. Chicago: Aldine, 1969.

Unsworth, W. *North Face*. London: Hutchinson, 1969.

Worsley, P. *The Trumpet Shall Sound*. New York: Schocken, 1968.

23. Cornell, "The Focusing Technique"
References

Cornell, Ann Weiser. *The Focusing Student's Manual*. Third Edition. 1994. Focusing Resources, 2625 Alcatraz Ave. #202, Berkeley, CA 94705.

Gendlin, Beebe, Cassens, Klein, and Oberlander. "Focusing Ability in Psychotherapy, Personality and Creativity." *Research in Psychotherapy, Vol. III,* ed. J. Shlien. Washington, DC: American Psychological Association, 1968.

Gendlin, Eugene. *Focusing*. New York: Bantam Books, 1981.

Gendlin, Eugene. *Let Your Body Interpret Your Dreams*. Wilmette, IL: Chiron Publications, 1986.

25. Deikman, "Intuition"

1. Morris, W., ed. *American Heritage Dictionary of the English Language*. Boston: Houghton Mifflin, 1969, p. 1086.

2. Jowett, B., Trans. *The Dialogues of Plato, Great Books of the Western World,* vol. 7, ed. R. Hutchins. Chicago: Encyclopaedia Britannica, 1952, p. 180.

3. Richards, I. *The Republic of Plato*. New York: W. W. Norton, 1942, p. 192.

4. Waters, F. *The Book of the Hopi*. New York: Ballantine Books, 1963.

5. Wolf, A. "The Life and Writings of Spinoza," in *The Encyclopaedia Britannica,* vol. 21. Chicago: Encyclopaedia Britannica, 1951, pp. 235–236.

6. [In] Russell, B. *A History of Western Philosophy*. New York: Simon and Schuster, 1945, p. 708, Bertrand Russell points out that "intuition" is a poor translation of *Anschauung,* which means "looking at" or "view." Space and time, according to Kant, are a priori in the sense of being part of the apparatus of perception; they did not imply to him the existence of another mode or channel of knowledge.

7. Von Mises, R. "Mathematical Postulates and Human Understanding," in *The World of Mathematics,* vol. 3, ed. J. R. Newman. New York: Simon & Schuster, 1956, p. 1743.

8. Barrett, W., & Aiken, H. *Philosophy in the Twentieth Century: An Anthology,* vol. 3. New York: Random House, 1962, pp. 303, 305.

9. Freud, S. "New Introductory Lectures," p. 159, in *Standard Edition of the Complete Psychological Works of Sigmund Freud,* vol. 22, ed. J. Strachey (London: Hogarth Press, 1964).

10. Hartmann, H. *Essays on Ego Psychology*. New York: International Universities Press, 1952.

11. Kris, E. *Psychoanalytic Explorations in Art.* New York: International Universities Press, 1952.

12. Campbell, J. ed. *The Portable Jung.* New York: Viking Press, 1971, p. 114.

13. *Ibid.,* p. 20.

14. Although one would expect that Jung was familiar with the mystical definition of intuition, it is hard to find any clear statement about it in his writing.

15. Bruner, J. *On Knowing: Essays for the Left Hand.* Cambridge: Harvard University Press, 1963, p. 102.

16. *Ibid.,* p. 20.

17. Westcott, M. R. *Toward a Contemporary Psychology of Intuition.* New York: Holt, Rinehart & Winston, 1968, p. 22.

18. Recently, there has been more recognition of intuition as a mode of knowing; see Vaughan.

19. Le Shan, L. *The Medium, The Mystic and the Physicist.* New York: Viking Press, 1974.

20. Capra, F. *The Tao of Physics.* Berkeley, CA: Shambhala, 1975.

21. Zukav, G. *The Dancing Wu Li Masters: An Overview of the New Physics.* New York: William Morrow, 1979.

22. Greene, M., ed. *Toward a Unity of Knowledge,* Psychological Issues 6(2). New York: International Universities Press, 1969, p. 45.

23. Greene, M. *Toward a Unity of Knowledge,* p. 60.

24. Polanyi, M. *Personal Knowledge.* Chicago: University of Chicago Press, 1958, p. 131.

26. Vaughan, "Mental, Emotional, and Body-Based Intuition"

1. Gerard, R. Workshop notes. Professional training in psychosynthesis: Intuitive awareness. Berkeley, October 1972.

2. Dreyfuss, A., & Feinstein, D. "My Body Is Me: Body-based Approaches to Personal Enrichment," *Humanistic Perspectives: Current Trends in Psychology,* ed. B. McWaters. Monterey, CA: Brooks Cole, 1977, p. 43.

3. "Female Intuition Measured at Last?" *New Society.* London, 1977.

4. Wescott, M. R. *Toward a Contemporary Psychology of Intuition.* New York: Holt, Rinehart and Winston, 1968, pp. 49–51.

5. Hadamard, J. *An Essay on the Psychology of Invention in the Mathematical Field.* Princeton: Princeton University Press, 1945, p. 142, Appendix.

6. Holton, G. "Where Is Reality? The Answers of Einstein," *Science and Synthesis.* New York, Heidelberg, Berlin: Springer-Verlage, 1971, p. 69.

7. Schilpp, P. (ed.). *Albert Einstein: Philosopher-Scientist.* The Library of Living Philosophers, Inc. Evanston, IL, 1949, p. 131.

8. "The Structure of Creativity in Physics," *Vistas in Physical Reality,* eds. E. Laszlo and E. Sellon. New York: Sellon Press, 1976, p. 154.

9. Mihalasky, J. "Extrasensory Perception in Management," *Advanced Management Journal,* July 1976.

10. "Planning on the Left Side and Managing on the Right," *Harvard Business Review,* July–August 1976, pp. 49–58.

11. Goleman, D. "Split-brain Psychology: Fad of the Year," *Psychology Today,* October 1977, p. 89.

12. Dean, D., et al. *Executive ESP.* Englewood Cliffs, NJ: Prentice Hall, 1974.

13. "Dialogue: Your Most Exciting Moment in Research?" *LBL Newsmagazine,* Fall, 1976, p. 2.

14. Assagioli, R. *Psychosynthesis.* New York: Hobbs Dohrman, 1965, p. 220.

15. Bugental, J. F. T. *The Search for Existential Identity.* San Francisco: Jossey Bass, 1976, p. 296.

16. Maslow, A. H. *The Farther Reaches of Human Nature.* New York: Viking, 1971.

17. Wilber, K. *The Spectrum of Consciousness.* Wheaton, IL: Theosophical Publishing House, 1977, p. 46.

18. Yogananda, P. *The Autobiography of a Yogi.* Los Angeles: Self-Realization Fellowship, 1969, p. 31.

19. *Sri Aurobindo, or The Adventure of Consciousness.* Pondicherry, India: Sri Aurobindo Society, 1970, p. 192.

30. Tart, "Mindfulness Practice for the Whole Spectrum of Life"

References

Buddha, G., 1989. "The Kalama sutra." *Inquiring Mind, 1,* No. 1, 4.

Nicoll, M., 1984. *Psychological Commentaries on the Teaching of Gurdjieff and Ouspensky.* Boston: Shambhala Publications.

Ouspensky, P. D., 1949. *In Search of the Miraculous.* New York: Harcourt, Brace & World.

Ouspensky, P. D., 1981. *The Psychology of Man's Possible Evolution.* New York: Random House.

Speeth, K., 1976. *The Gurdjieff Work.* Berkeley: And/Or Press.

Tart, C., 1972. "States of consciousness and state-specific sciences." *Science, 176,* 1203–1210.

Tart, C., 1975. *States of Consciousness.* New York: E. P. Dutton.

Tart, C., 1986. *Waking Up: Overcoming the Obstacles to Human Potential.* Boston: New Science Library.

Tart, C., 1994. *Living the Mindful Life.* Boston: Shambhala Publications.

33. Palmer, "The Intuitive Body"

1. O Sensei is the familiar name for Morihei Ueshiba, the founder of the martial art known as aikido.

35. Chödrön, "A Practice of Compassion"

1. Lojong means "mind training." The lojong teachings are organized around seven points that contain pithy slogans, reminding us about how to awaken our hearts. These teachings belong to the Mahayana school of Buddhism, which emphasizes compassionate communication and relationship with others.

2. *Bodhichitta*. Here taken to mean the place within ourselves where compassion awakens. The teachings under discussion concern how to awaken compassion.

3. The slogan "Drive all blames into one" means diving into what it feels like when we blame others, to investigate the "shaky tenderness" or emotional vulnerability that underlies a need to blame.

36. Johnston, "The Cloud of Unknowing"

All cross-references to the writings of St. John of the Cross are taken from *The Collected Works of St. John of the Cross* translated by Kiernan Kavanaugh, O.C.D., and Otilio Rodriguez, O.C.D. Washington, D.C.: ICS Publications, Institute of Carmelite Studies. The key to the references is as follows: A = *The Ascent of Mt. Carmel*; N = *The Dark Night*; C = *The Spiritual Canticle*; F = *The Living Flame of Love*.

1. C29, 2; F1, 3; F3, 39
2. A2, 9, 4; N2, 11, 1
3. A2, 24, 4
4. A2, 15, 4; A3, 15, 1; F3, 46
5. Atom: the smallest medieval measure of time = 15/94 of a second.
6. A2, 8, 5; A2, 24, 4
7. A2, 8, 4
8. F1, 13
9. F1, 14
10. C38, 5
11. F1, 21
12. C36, 4; F3, 79; Sayings: 25
13. C25, 5; F1, 4; F1, 8; F1, 33
14. A2, 12, 8; N1, 10, 5, 6
15. A2, 9, 4

37. Helminski, "The Heart: Threshold Between Two Worlds"

1. Rumi, *Mathnawi*.
2. Published by Threshold Books as: *Signs of the Unseen*. Translated by Wheeler Thackston, Jr.
3. Rumi, *Signs of the Unseen*.
4. Qur'an.
5. A saying of Muhammad.
6. While the Qalb is identified as a latifa with its particular location, it also in some sense contains the totality of all the following organs of knowledge.

Permissions

1. From *The Doors of Perception,* by Aldous Huxley (New York: Harper & Brothers, 1954). Reprinted by permission of the Estate of Aldous Huxley.

2. From an interview of Owen Barfield by Gary Lachman originally published in *Lapis.* Reprinted by permission of *Lapis.*

3. From "The Transfiguration of the Westen Mind," by Richard Tarnas, a paper presented to the conference on "Philosophy and the Human Future," Cambridge University, England, © 1989 by Richard Tarnas. Used by permission of the author. August 8, 1989.

4. From *Paths Beyond Ego,* by Roger Walsh and Frances Vaughan. © 1993 by Roger Walsh, Ph.D., and Frances Vaughan, Ph.D. Reprinted by permission of the Putnam Publishing Group/Jeremy P. Tarcher, Inc.

5. From *Paths Beyond Ego,* by Roger Walsh and Frances Vaughan. © 1993 by Roger Walsh, Ph.D., and Frances Vaughan, Ph.D. Reprinted by permission of the Putnam Publishing Group/Jeremy P. Tarcher, Inc.

6. From *With the Tongues of Men and Angels: A Study of Channeling,* by Arthur Hastings. © 1991. Reprinted by permission of the Institute of Noetic Sciences.

7. From *The Tao of Psychology,* by Jean Shinoda Bolen (pages 14–22). © 1979 by Jean Shinoda Bolen. Reprinted by permission of HarperCollins Publishers, Inc.

8. From the foreword by Carl Jung to *The I Ching or Book of Changes.* The Richard Wilhelm translation rendered into English by Cary F. Baynes, Bollingen Series XIX. © 1950, © 1967, © renewed 1977 by Princeton University Press. Pp. xxii–xxxii, used with permission.

9. From *The Spirit of Shamanism,* by Roger Walsh. © 1990 by Roger Walsh. Reprinted by permission of the Putnam Publishing Group/Jeremy P. Tarcher, Inc.

10. From *Aboriginal Men of High Degree,* by A. P. Elkin. © 1978 by A. P. Elkin. Reprinted by permission of University of Queensland Press, St. Lucia, and A. P. Elkin Inner Traditions International.

23. An essay written especially for this volume by Ann Weiser Cornell, Ph.D. © 1994 by Ann Weiser Cornell, Ph.D. Used by permission of the author.

24. An essay written especially for this volume by Betty Edwards. © 1995 by Betty Edwards. Used by permission of the author.

25. From *The Observing Self,* by Arthur J. Deikman. © 1982 by Arthur J. Deikman. Reprinted by permission of Beacon Press.

26. From *Awakening Intuition,* by Frances E. Vaughan. © 1979 by Frances E. Vaughan. Used by permission of Doubleday, a division of Bantam Doubleday Dell Publishing Group, Inc., and by permission of Frances E. Vaughan.

27. From *The Intuitive Edge,* by Philip Goldberg. © 1983 by Philip Goldberg. Reprinted by permission of the Putnam Publishing Group/Jeremy P. Tarcher, Inc.

28. From *A Path with Heart,* by Jack Kornfield. © 1993 by Jack Kornfield. Used by permission of Bantam Books, a division of Bantam Doubleday Dell Publishing Group, Inc.

29. From *A Path with Heart,* by Jack Kornfield. © 1993 by Jack Kornfield. Used by permission of Bantam Books, a division of Bantam Doubleday Dell Publishing Group, Inc.

30. An essay written especially for this volume by Charles Tart. © 1994 by Charles Tart. Used by permission of the author.

31. From *The Experience of Insight,* by Joseph Goldstein. © 1976 by Joseph Goldstein. Reprinted by arrangement with Shambhala Publications, Inc., 300 Massachusetts Avenue, Boston, Mass. 02115.

32. From *Hara: The Vital Centre of Man,* by Karfield Graf Von Dürckheim. © 1956 by Karfield Graf Von Dürckheim. Reprinted by permission of Allen & Unwin, an imprint of HarperCollins Publishers, Limited.

33. From *The Intuitive Body: Aikido as a Clairsentient Practice,* by Wendy Palmer. © 1994 by Wendy Palmer. Reprinted by permission of North Atlantic Books, P.O. Box 12327, Berkeley, CA 94710.

34. From *It's Easier Than You Think: The Buddhist Way to Happiness,* by Sylvia Boorstein. © 1995 by Sylvia Boorstein. Reprinted by permission of HarperCollins Publishers, Inc.

35. From *Start Where You Are: A Guide to Compassionate Living,* by Pema Chödrön. © 1976 by Pema Chödrön. Reprinted by arrangement with Shambhala Publications, Inc., 300 Massachusetts Avenue, Boston, Mass. 02115.

36. From *The Cloud of Unknowing and The Book of Privy Counselling,* by William Johnston.

Contributors

Bruno Bettelheim, M.D., was born in Vienna in 1903. He received his doctorate at the University of Vienna, and came to America in 1939, after a year in the concentration camps of Dachau and Buchenwald. He was Distinguished Professor of Education and Professor of both psychology and psychiatry at the University of Chicago. Dr. Bettelheim is the author of many celebrated books.

Jean Shinoda Bolen, M.D., is a psychiatrist and Jungian analyst. A fellow of the American Psychiatric Association, Dr. Bolen also teaches and leads seminars in the San Francisco Bay area and throughout the country. She has also written *Goddesses in Everywoman: A New Psychology of Women.*

Sylvia Boorstein teaches mindfulness meditation and leads retreats across the United States. She is a cofounding teacher (with Jack Kornfield) at the Spirit Rock Meditation Center in Woodacre, California, and a senior teacher at the Insight Meditation Society in Barre, Massachusetts. Boorstein is also a practicing psychotherapist. *It's Easier Than You Think* is her first book.

Mihaly Csikszentmihalyi is former chairman of the Department of Psychology at the University of Chicago and author of *Flow: The Psychology of Optimal Experience and Beyond Boredom and Anxiety* and coauthor of *The Creative Vision*; *Optimal Experience: Studies in Flow Consciousness*; and *Television and the Quality of Life.*

Pema Chödrön is an American Buddhist nun and one of the foremost students of Chögyam Trungpa, the renowned meditation master. She is the Director of Gampo Abbey, Nova Scotia, the first Tibetan monastery in North America established for Westerners.

Ann Weiser Cornell, Ph.D. (linguistics), learned Focusing from Eugene Gendlin, author of *Focusing* (Bantam, 1981) in 1972, and today is internationally recognized as one of the leading innovators and theoreticians of Focusing. She has taught Focusing in twelve countries on five continents. Her book, *The Power of Focusing: A Practical Guide to Emotional Self-Healing* (1996) is available from New Harbinger Publications.

Janet Dallett, Ph.D., practices Jungian analysis in Los Angeles, California. A member of the Society of Jungian Analysts of Southern California, she is a former director of training of the C. G. Jung Institute of Los Angeles and has taught in its analyst training program. A graduate of Kalamazoo College, she received her Ph.D. in psychology from UCLA and the diploma in analytical psychology from the C. G. Jung Institute of Los Angeles. She edited *The Dream: The Vision of the Night,* by Max Zeller, and has published several papers, including "Theories of Dream Function" and "Looking for Jung: The Man in the Myth."

Arthur Deikman, M.D., is clinical professor of psychiatry at the University of California at San Francisco. He is the author of *The Observing Self: Mysticism and Psychotherapy* and *The Wrong Way Home: Uncovering Patterns of Cult Behavior.*

Betty Edwards is an author and originator of a technique popularly known as drawing from the right side of the brain. She conducts workshops utilizing the technique throughout the United States and has been personally responsible for introducing thousands of people to this important tool for accessing nonlinear thinking.

A. P. Elkin, former head of the anthropology department at the University of Sydney, authored eight books and numerous articles in Australia, the United States, France, and England, including *The Australian Aborigines.*

Erich Fromm, Ph.D., was born in 1900 in Frankfurt, Germany. He studied sociology at the universities of Heidelberg, Frankfurt, and Munich, receiving a Ph.D. degree from Heidelberg in 1922. He is the author of many articles and a number of best-selling books, including *The Art of Loving, The Sane Society,* and *You Shall Be as Gods.*

Philip Goldberg lectures widely in the areas of human development and consciousness. He holds degrees in psychology and education.

Joseph Goldstein has been leading insight and lovingkindness meditation retreats worldwide since 1974. He is a cofounder of the Insight Meditation Society in Barre, Massachusetts, where he is one of the resident guiding teachers. Joseph first became interested in Buddhism as a Peace Corps volunteer in Thailand. He has studied and practiced insight meditation since 1967. He is also the author of *The Experience of Insight: A Simple and Direct Guide to Buddhist Meditation* and coauthor of *Seeking the Heart of Wisdom: The Path of Insight Meditation.*

Daniel Goleman, Ph.D., covers the behavioral and brain sciences for the *New York Times,* and his articles appear throughout the world in syndication. He has taught at Harvard University (where he received his Ph.D.) and was formerly senior editor at *Psychology*

Today. His books include *Emotional Intelligence*; *Vital Lies, Simple Truths*; *The Meditative Mind*; and, as coauthor, *The Creative Spirit.*

Arthur Hastings is a professor of psychology and founding faculty member of the Institute of Transpersonal Psychology, Palo Alto, California. He has authored *With the Tongues of Men and Angels: A Study of Channeling,* regarded as the standard reference on the subject. He has also written numerous articles on altered states, parapsychology, and transpersonal psychology.

Richard Heinberg is the editor and publisher of the monthly *MuseLetter* and a contributing editor of *Intuition.*

Kabir Helminski is the North American representative of the Mevlevi Order of Sufism, the director of the Threshold Society, and the author of several books, including *Living Presence.*

Aldous Huxley was a polymath and influential social critic who popularized the ideal of the perennial philosophy. His many books include *The Perennial Philosophy*; *Island*; *Brave New World*; *Eyeless in Gaza*; and *Antic Hay.*

Carl Jung is probably best known as one of the founders of psychoanalysis. Jung's overriding interest was the mystery of consciousness and personality and the spiritual dilemma of the modern individual. His many books include *The Collected Works* (twenty volumes); *Modern Man in Search of a Soul*; *Man and His Symbols*; and his popular autobiography, *Memories, Dreams, Reflections.*

Jack Kornfield, Ph.D., was trained as a Buddhist monk in Thailand, Burma, and India and has taught meditation worldwide since 1974. He is one of the key teachers to introduce Theravada Buddhist practice to the West. For many years, his work has been focused on integrating and bringing alive the great Eastern spiritual teachings in an accessible way for Western students and Western society. Jack also holds a Ph.D. in clinical psychology. He is a husband, father, psychotherapist, and founding teacher of the Insight Meditation Society in Barre, Massachusetts, and the Spirit Rock Center in Woodacre, California. His books include *Seeking the Heart of Wisdom, A Still Forest Pool,* and *Stories of the Spirit, Stories of the Heart.*

J. Krishnamurti was born in southern India and educated in England. He devoted his life to speaking and counseling. Author of many books, including *Truth and Actuality, The Wholeness of Life, Krishnamurti's Journal,* and *The Network of Thought,* he is treasured by many as a writer of exceptional clarity and understanding.

Gary Lachman is an American writer living in London. He is a regular contributor to *Gnosis: A Journal of the Western Inner Tradition* and *Lapis: The Meaning of Contemporary Life* and has written for the San Francisco *Chronicle,* the *Guardian,* the *L.A.Weekly,* the *Literary Review, ReVision, Common Boundary, Quest, Abraxas,* and the Journal for Anthroposophy. He is the author of two volumes in the Pauper's Press Colin Wilson series. As Gary Valentine, he has been a composer and performer with the rock groups Blondie, Iggy Pop, and The Know, and has composed for film and television. Recently he has reunited with Blondie after twenty years and is active on the music and performance scene in London.

Abraham H. Maslow, Ph.D., was one of the twentieth century's most influential psychologists and has been described as a founding father of both humanistic and transpersonal psychologies. His books include *Toward a Psychology of Being* and *The Farther Reaches of Human Nature.*

Wendy Palmer is a fourth-degree black belt in aikido. She cofounded and teaches at the Tamalpais Aikido Dojo in Mill Valley, California, and currently directs the Prison Integrated Health Project, a women's program at the Federal Correctional Institute in Dublin, California.

Philip Novak, Ph.D., is a professor and chairman of the Department of Philosophy and Religion at Dominican College of San Rafael, California, where he has taught for seventeen years, and he has also been a visiting professor at the University of California, Berkeley. He is the author of *The World's Wisdom, The Vision of Nietzsche,* and numerous articles and reviews in both scholarly and popular journals. Professor Novak has been a student of meditation for over twenty years.

Janet Lynn Roseman specializes in celebrity interviews. She is the author of *The Way of the Woman Writer* (Harrington Park Press, 1995).

Hyemeyohsts Storm is the internationally renowned author of the best-selling classic *Seven Arrows.* He is a Northern Cheyenne Indian and German mixed blood raised on the Northern Cheyenne and Crow Reservations in Montana. He was the first writer to introduce the modern world to the sacred medicine wheels—the sophisticated Earth philosophy of many Native American peoples.

Richard Tarnas, Ph.D., is an intellectual historian and, as of fall 1993, professor of philosophy and psychology at the California Institute of Integral Studies. A graduate of Harvard University and Saybrook Institute, he was formerly director of programs and education at Esalen Institute.

Charles T. Tart, Ph.D., holds the Bigelow Chair of Consciousness Studies at the University of Nevada at Las Vegas; Institute of Transpersonal Psychology; University of California, Davis; and Institute of Noetic Sciences. He is one of the foremost researchers on states of consciousness and transpersonal theory; his books include *Waking Up* and *Transpersonal Psychologies*.

Montague Ullman, M.D., is a New Yorker who attended Townsend Harris Hall, the City College of New York, and New York University School of Medicine, where he received his medical degree in 1938. He has written numerous papers on the neuro-physiological, clinical, and social aspects of dreams and is the author and coauthor of several books, including *Dream Telepathy* (1988) and *Working With Dreams* (1979), and is co-editor of *The Handbook of States of Consciousness* (1986) and *The Variety of Dream Experience* (1988).

Frances Vaughan, Ph.D., is a psychotherapist in private practice in Mill Valley, California, and is past president of the Association for Transpersonal Psychology.

Karlfried Graf Von Dürckheim is well known as an expert both on psychotherapy and meditation. Before his long stay in Japan he was professor of psychology and philosophy in the University of Kiel.

Mark Robert Waldman is a therapist and ministerial counselor in Woodland Hills, California; the Los Angeles Regional Coordinator for the Spiritual Emergence Network; founding editor of the *Transpersonal Review*; and an internationally published author on transpersonal studies. He is the editor of *The Art of Staying Together* and the author of *Love Games: Practical Exercises for Developing Consciousness, Communication and Intimacy*.

Roger Walsh, M.D., Ph.D., attended Queensland and Stanford Universities and is currently professor of psychiatry, philosophy, and anthropology at the University of California at Irvine. He has published more than one hundred scientific papers and ten books, and his writings have received some twenty national and international awards.

Helen Palmer's books on the Enneagram system are international best-sellers and are available in fourteen languages.

For over 25 years, she has focused on integrating the principles of contemporary Western psychology with the theory and practices of world spiritual traditions. She has pursued these cultural variations in search of the common principles that bind them. That work has produced a unique perspective on personality type as the interface between ordinary and higher consciousness.

Her office will furnish information about the current international teaching schedule, video and audio tape materials, the Enneagram Professional Training Program, and a network of graduates who teach in your area of the country.

Helen Palmer Workshops
1442A Walnut Street, Suite 377, Berkeley, CA 94709
Phone (510) 843-7621 Fax (510) 540-7626

OTHER BOOKS AND PUBLICATIONS BY THE EDITOR

The Enneagram:
Understanding Yourself and the Others in Your Life

The Enneagram in Love and Work

The Pocket Enneagram

The Enneagram Advantage:
Putting the Nine Types to Work in the Office

Audio Tapes from Sounds True Recordings

Intuition Training

Helen Palmer's Enneagram Workshop:
Attention, Awareness, and Neurotic Trends

The Enneagram

Video Tapes
The Stanford University Panels
Nine Points of View on Addiction and Recovery
Men On Relationship
Women On Relationship